CLYMER ®

YAMAHA

XS1100 FOURS · 1978-1981

The world's finest publisher of mechanical how-to manuals

PRIMEDIA
Intertec

P.O. Box 12901, Overland Park, Kansas 66282-2901

Copyright ©1982 PRIMEDIA Intertec

FIRST EDITION
First Printing February, 1980

SECOND EDITION
First Printing January, 1982
Second Printing July, 1990
Third Printing March, 1992
Fourth Printing October, 1993
Fifth Printing July, 1995
Sixth Printing August, 1997
Seventh Printing October, 1998

Printed in U.S.A.

CLYMER and colophon are registered trademarks of PRIMEDIA Intertec.

ISBN: 0-89287-309-4

MEMBER

 MOTORCYCLE
INDUSTRY
COUNCIL, INC.

COVER: *Photographed by Mike Brown, Visual Imagery, Los Angeles, California. Assisted by Dennis Gilmore. Motorcycle courtesy of Bill Krause Sportcycles, Inglewood, California.*

CONTENTS

QUICK REFERENCE DATA

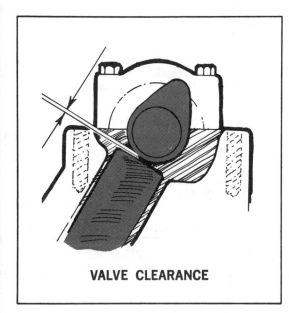

VALVE CLEARANCE

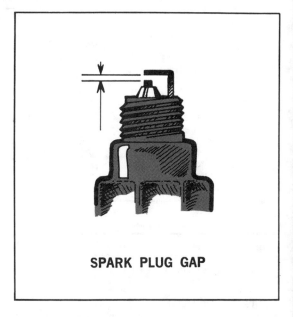

SPARK PLUG GAP

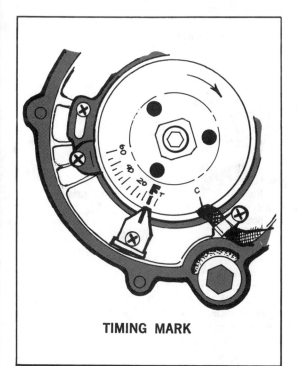

TIMING MARK

FREE PLAY ADJUSTMENTS

Clutch lever	0.08-0.12 in. (2-3mm)
Front brake lever	0.02-0.03 in. (5-8mm)
Rear brake pedal	½-⅝ in. (13-15mm)

TUNE-UP SPECIFICATIONS

Cylinder head nuts	
Upper	25 ft.-lb. (35 N•m)
Lower	14 ft.-lb. (20 N•m)
Valve clearance (cold)	
Intake (1978-1979)	0.006-0.008 in.
	(0.16-0.20mm)
Intake (since 1980)	0.004-0.006 in.
	(0.11-0.15mm)
Exhaust (All years)	0.008-0.010 in.
	(0.21-0.25mm)
Spark plug	
Type	NGK BP-6ES,
	Champion N-8Y
Gap	0.028-0.31 in.
	(0.7-0.8mm)
Idle speed	
Models E and F	950-1,050 rpm
All other models	1,050-1,150 rpm
Compression pressure	
Cold at sea level	142 ± 14 psi
	(10 ± 1.0 kg/cm^2)

FLUIDS

Item	Type	Quantity
Engine oil		
Above 40°F (5°C)	SAE 20W-40	3.2 U.S. qt. (3.0 liter; 2.66 Imp. qt.)
Below	SAE 10W-30	
Fork oil	SAE 10W fork oil	
Models E and F		7.17 U.S. oz. (2.12cc; 5.97 Imp. oz.)
Model SF		7.61 U.S. oz. (225cc; 6.34 Imp. oz.)
Brake fluid	DOT-3	Upper level line
Middle gear case and		
final drive case	Hypoid gear oil	10.0 U.S. oz. (300cc; 10.56 Imp. oz.)
All weather	SAE 80W 90/GL4	
Above 40°F (5°C)	SAE 90/GL4	
Below 40°F (5°C)	SAE 80/GL4	
Fuel	Regular	
Models E and F		5.3 U.S. gal. (20 liters; 4.4 Imp. gal.)
Model SF		3.97 U.S. gal. (15 liters; 3.3 Imp. gal.)

TIRES

Load	Pressure (All Models)
Up to 198 lb. (90 kg)	
Front	26 psi (1.8 kg/cm^2)
Rear	28 psi (2.0 kg/cm^2)
198-337 lb. (90-153 kg)	
Front	28 psi (2.0 kg/cm^2)
Rear	36 psi (2.5 kg/cm^2)
Maximum Load Limit*	
Front — 420 lb. (190 kg)	36 psi (2.6 kg/cm^2)
Rear — 670 lb. (304 kg)	40 psi (2.8 kg/cm^2)

*Maximum load includes the total weight of motorcycle with accessories, rider(s), and luggage.

ELECTRICAL SYSTEM

Fuse	
Main	30 amp
Headlight	10 amp
Tail/brakelight	20 amp
Ignition	10 amp
Battery	12 volt, 20 amp hour
Replacement bulbs	
Headlight	
Except special models	50/60 watt
Special model	55/60 watt
Tail/brakelight	8/27 watt
Directional light	27 watt
Instrument light	3.4 watt
Meter light	3.4 watt
License light	3.8 watt

ENGINE TORQUE SPECIFICATIONS

Item	Foot-Pounds (Ft.-lb.)	Newton Meters (N•m)
Cylinder head nuts		
Upper	25	34
Lower	14	19
Camshaft cap nuts	7.2	10
Oil filter bolt	23	31
Alternator rotor bolt	47	65
Clutch center bolt	51	70

FRAME TORQUE SPECIFICATIONS

Item	Foot-pounds	Newton Meters
Steering stem		
Top bolt	61.5	85
Pinch bolt	14.5	20
Top fork bridge	14.5	20
Lower fork bridge		
Except special model	12.5	17
Special model	14.5	20
Handle bar holder	13	18
Front axle nut	77	107
Front axle holder nuts		
Except special model	14.5	20
Front axle pinch bolt	14.5	20
Rear axle nut		
Except special model	108	147
Special model	76	105
Rear axle pinch bolt		
Models E and F	4.5	6
Model SF	14.5	20
Rear swing arm pivot		
Bolt	47	64
Locknut	72	100
Engine mounting bolts		
Front and rear		
through bolts	72	100
Mounting bracket		
bolts	48	67
Final drive flange nuts	30	42
Brake rotor to wheel		
bolts — front and rear	15	20
Front caliper assembly		
Except special model		
Upper bolt	32	45
Lower bolt	13	18
Special model		
Mounting bolt	18	24
Brake hose union		
bolts (all)	18	24
Rear master cylinder		
to frame	16	23

NOTE: If you own a 1980 or 1981 model, first check the Supplement at the back of the book for any new service information.

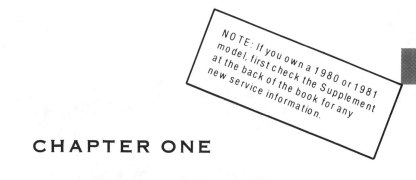

CHAPTER ONE

GENERAL INFORMATION

This detailed, comprehensive manual covers the Yamaha XS1100. The expert text gives complete information on maintenance, tune-up, repair, and overhaul. Hundreds of photos and drawings guide you through every step. The book includes all you need to know to keep your Yamaha running right.

A shop manual is a reference. You want to be able to find information fast. As in all Clymer books, this one is designed with you in mind. All chapters are thumb tabbed. Important items are extensively indexed at the rear of this book. Finally, all most frequently used specifications and capacities are summarized on the blue Quick Reference pages at the front of the book.

Keep the book handy in your tool box. It will help you to better understand your Yamaha, lower repair and maintenance costs, and generally improve your satisfaction with your bike.

Refer to **Figure 1** for locations of major controls and components.

MANUAL ORGANIZATION

All dimensions and capacities are expressed in English units familiar to U.S. mechanics as well as in metric units.

This chapter provides general information and specifications. See **Table 1** at the end of this chapter. It also discusses equipment and tools useful both for preventive maintenance and troubleshooting.

Chapter Two provides methods and suggestions for quick and accurate diagnosis and repair of problems. Troubleshooting procedures discuss typical symptoms and logical methods to pinpoint the trouble.

Chapter Three explains all periodic lubrication and routine maintenance necessary to keep your bike running well. Chapter Three also includes recommended tune-up procedures, eliminating the need to constantly consult chapters on the various assemblies.

Subsequent chapters describe specific systems such as the engine, transmission, and electrical system. Each chapter provides disassembly, repair, and assembly procedures in simple step-by-step form. If a repair is impractical for a home mechanic, it is so indicated. It is usually faster and less expensive to take such repairs to a dealer or competent repair shop. Specifications concerning a particular system are included at the end of the appropriate chapter.

Some of the procedures in this manual specify special tools. In all cases, the tool is illustrated either in actual use or alone. A well-

1. Seat
2. Fuse panel and accessory fuse
3. Fuel shutoff valve
   (right-hand side)
4. Front brake lever
5. Speedometer, tachometer,
   indicator lights
6. Headlight
7. Footpegs, front and rear
8. Kickstarter shaft and lever
9. Rear brake pedal
10. Clutch
11. Alternator

12. Spark plugs
13. Front reflex reflector (amber)
14. Front turn signal
15. Clutch lever
16. Light, horn, and turn switch
17. Start button and engine stop switch
18. Throttle grip
19. Fuel tank
20. Fuel shutoff valve (left-hand side)
21. Battery
22. Rear turn signal
23. Tail/brake light and rear
    reflex reflector (red)

24. Speedometer drive
25. Front fork air cap (air/oil forks)
26. Ignition timing plate
27. Choke lever
28. Gear shift lever
29. Starter motor
30. Centerstand
31. Kickstand
32. Helmet lock
33. Shock absorber adjustment (upper
    location, on models with air/oil
    front forks only)

Table 1   GENERAL SPECIFICATIONS (1978-1979)

Engine type	Air cooled, 4-stroke, DOHC, 4 cylinder
Bore and stroke	2.815 x 2.701 in. (71.5 x 68.6mm)
Displacement	67.25 cu. in. (1,102cc)
Compression ratio	9.2 to 1
Carburetion	4 Mikuni, constant velocity, 30mm
Models E and F	BS34-11 2H7-00
Model SF	BS34-11 3H3-00
Ignition	Battery, fully transistorized
Lubrication	Wet sump, filter, oil pump
Clutch	Wet, multi plate (7)
Transmission	5-speed, constant mesh
Transmission ratios	
1st	2.235
2nd	1.625
3rd	1.285
4th	1.032
5th	0.882
Starting	Electric (emergency manual kick)
Wheelbase	60.8 in. (1,545mm)
Steering head angle	29.5°
Trail	5.12 in. (130mm)
Ground clearance	
Models E and F	5.9 in. (150mm)
Model SF	6.9 in. (175mm)
Seat height	
Models E and F	31.9 in. (810mm)
Model SF	31.7 in. (805mm)
Overall height	
Models E and F	46.3 in. (1,175mm)
Model SF	48.4 in. (1,230mm)
Overall width	
Models E and F	36.2 in. (920mm)
Model SF	33.7 in. (855mm)
Overall length	
Models E and F	89.0 in. (2,260mm)
Model SF	89.6 in. (2,275mm)
Front suspension	Telescopic fork, 6.9 in. (175mm) travel
Rear suspension	Swing arm, adjustable shock absorbers, 4.3 in. (108mm) travel
Front tire	
Models E and F	3.25 H-19 4PR
Model SF	3.50 H-19 4PR (tubeless)
Rear tire	
Models E and F	4.50 H-17 4PR
Model SF	130/90H-16 (tubeless)
Fuel capacity	
Models E and F	5.3 U.S. gal. (20 liter; 4.4 Imp. gal.)
Model SF	3.97 U.S. gal. (15 liter; 3.3 Imp. gal.)
Oil capacity	
Oil change	3.2 U.S. qt. (3.0 liter; 2.7 Imp. qt.)
Oil and filter change	3.7 U.S. qt. (3.5 liter; 3.1 Imp. qt.)
Weight (net)	
Models E and F	562 lb. (262 kg)
Model SF	556 lb. (252 kg)

equipped mechanic may find that he can substitute similar tools already on hand or fabricate his own.

The terms NOTE, CAUTION, and WARNING have specific meanings in this manual. A NOTE provides additional information to make a step or procedure easier or clearer. Disregarding a NOTE could cause inconvenience, but would not cause damage or personal injury.

A CAUTION emphasizes areas where equipment damage could result. Disregarding a CAUTION could cause permanent mechanical damage; however, personal injury is unlikely.

A WARNING emphasizes areas where personal injury or even death could result from negligence. Mechanical damage may also occur. WARNINGS *are to be taken seriously*. In some cases, serious injury or death has resulted from disregarding similar warnings.

Throughout this manual, keep in mind two conventions. "Front" refers to the front of the bike. The front of any component, such as the engine, is the end which faces toward the front of the bike. The "left" and "right" sides refer to a person sitting on the bike facing forward. For example, the shift lever is on the left side. These rules are simple, but even experienced mechanics occasionally become disoriented.

SERVICE HINTS

Most of the service procedures covered are straightforward and can be performed by anyone reasonably handy with tools. It is suggested, however, that you consider your own capabilities carefully before attempting any operation involving major disassembly of the engine.

Some operations, for example, require the use of a press. It would be wiser to have these performed by a shop equipped for such work than to try to do the job yourself with makeshift equipment. Other procedures require precise measurements. Unless you have the skills and equipment required, it would be better to have a qualified repair shop make the measurements for you.

Repairs go much faster and easier if your machine is clean before you begin work. There are special cleaners, like Gunk Cycle Degreaser,

for washing the engine and related parts. Just brush or spray on the cleaning solution, let it stand, then rinse it away with a garden hose. Clean all oily or greasy parts with cleaning solvent as you remove them.

WARNING
Never use gasoline as a cleaning agent. It presents an extreme fire hazard. Be sure to work in a well-ventilated area when using cleaning solvent. Keep a fire extinguisher, rated for gasoline fires, handy in any case.

Special tools are required for some repair procedures. These may be purchased at a dealer, rented from a tool rental dealer, or fabricated by a mechanic or machinist, often at a considerable savings.

Much of the labor charge for repairs made by dealers is for removal and disassembly of other parts to reach the defective unit. It is frequently possible to perform preliminary operations yourself and then take the defective unit to the dealer for repair at considerable savings.

Once you have decided to tackle the job yourself, read the entire section in this manual which pertains to it, making sure you have identified the proper one. Study the illustrations and text until you have a good idea of what is involved in completing the job satisfactorily. If special tools are required, make arrangements to get them before you start. It is frustrating and time-consuming to get partly into a job and then be unable to complete it.

Simple wiring checks can be easily made at home; but knowledge of electronics is almost a necessity for performing tests with complicated electronic testing gear.

During disassembly of parts, keep a few general cautions in mind. Force is rarely needed to get things apart. If parts are a tight fit, like a bearing in a case, there is usually a tool designed to separate them. Never use a screwdriver to pry apart parts with machined surfaces such as crankcase halves and cam cover. You will mar the surfaces and end up with leaks.

Make diagrams wherever similar-appearing parts are found. For instance, case cover screws are often not the same length. You may think

1

you can remember where everything came from — but mistakes are costly. There is also the possibility you may be sidetracked and not return to work for days, or even weeks, in which interval, carefully laid out parts may have become disturbed.

Tag all similar internal parts for location and mark all mating parts for position. Record number and thickness of any shims as they are removed. Small parts, such as bolts, can be identified by placing them in plastic sandwich bags. Seal and label the bags with masking tape.

Wiring should be tagged with masking tape and marked as each wire is removed. Again, do not rely on memory alone.

Disconnect battery ground (negative) cable before working near electrical connections and before disconnecting wires. Never run the engine with the battery disconnected; the alternator could be seriously damaged.

Protect finished surfaces from physical damage or corrosion. Keep gasoline and brake fluid off painted surfaces.

Frozen or very tight bolts and screws can often by loosened by soaking with penetrating oil, like WD-40 or Liquid Wrench, then sharply striking the bolt head a few times with a hammer and punch (or screwdriver for screws). Avoid heat unless absolutely necessary, since it may melt, warp, or remove the temper from many parts.

Avoid flames or sparks when working near a charging battery or flammable liquids such as brake fluid or gasoline.

No parts, except those assembled with a press fit, require unusual force during assembly. If a part is hard to remove or install, find out why before proceeding.

Cover all openings after removing parts to keep dirt, small tools, etc., from falling in.

When assembling two parts, start all fasteners, then tighten evenly.

Clutch plates, wiring connections, and brake pads and discs should be kept clean and free of grease and oil.

When assembling parts, be sure all shims and washers are replaced exactly as they came out.

Whenever a rotating part butts against a stationary part, look for a shim or washer. Use new gaskets if there is any doubt about the condition of old ones. Generally, you should apply gasket cement to one mating surface only so the parts may be easily disassembled in the future. A thin coat of oil on gaskets helps them seal effectively.

Heavy grease can be used to hold small parts in place if they tend to fall out during assembly. However, keep grease and oil away from electrical components or brake pads and discs.

High spots may be sanded off a piston with sandpaper, but emery cloth and oil do a much more professional job.

Carburetors are best cleaned by disassembling them and soaking the parts in a commercial carburetor cleaner. Never soak gaskets and rubber parts in these cleaners. Never use wire to clean out jets and air passages; they are easily damaged. Use compressed air to blow out the carburetor only if the float has been removed first.

A baby bottle makes a good measuring device for adding oil to forks and transmissions. Get one that is graduated in ounces and cubic centimeters.

Take your time and do the job right. Do not forget that a newly rebuilt motorcycle engine must be broken-in the same as a new one. Keep rpm's within the limits given in your owner's manual when back on the road.

TORQUE SPECIFICATIONS

Torque values throughout this manual are given in foot-pounds (ft.-lb.) and Newton meters (N•m). Newton meters are being adopted in place of meter kilograms (mkg) in accordance with the *International Modernized Metric System*. Tool manufacturers are beginning to introduce torque wrenches calibrated in Newton meters and Sears has introduced a Craftsman line calibrated in both of these values.

Existing torque wrenches, calibrated in meter kilograms, can be used by performing a simple conversion. All you have to do is move the decimal point one place to the right, e.g. 4.7 mkg = 47 N•m. This conversion is sufficient for use in this manual even though the exact mathematical conversion is 3.5 mkg = 34.3 N•m.

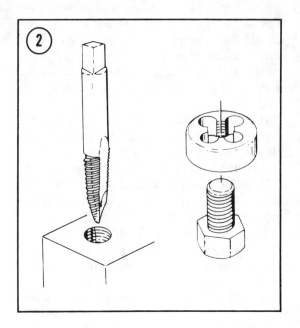

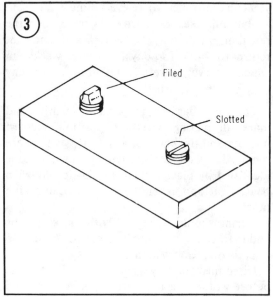

Filed

Slotted

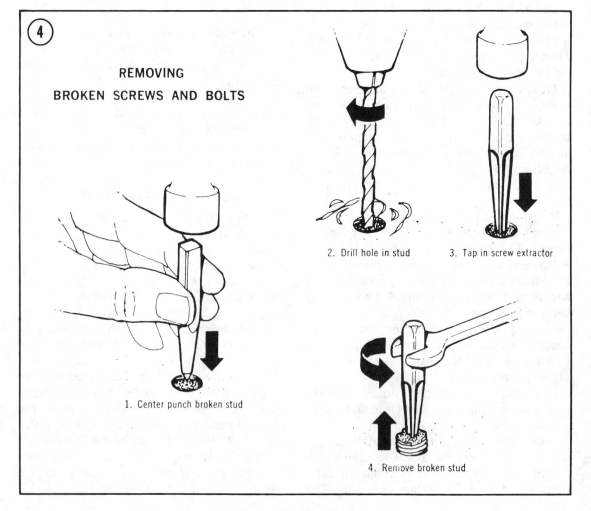

REMOVING
BROKEN SCREWS AND BOLTS

1. Center punch broken stud

2. Drill hole in stud

3. Tap in screw extractor

4. Remove broken stud

SAFETY FIRST

Professional motorcycle mechanics can work for years and never sustain a serious injury. If you observe a few rules of common sense and safety, you can enjoy many hours servicing your own machine. You could hurt yourself or damage the bike if you ignore these rules.

1. Never use gasoline as a cleaning solvent.
2. Never smoke or use a torch in the vicinity of flammable liquids such as cleaning solvent in open containers.
3. Never smoke or use a torch in an area where batteries are being charged. Highly explosive hydrogen gas is formed during the charging process.
4. If welding or brazing is required on the machine, remove the fuel tank to a safe distance, at least 50 feet away. Welding on gas tanks requires special safety procedures and must be performed by someone skilled in the process.
5. Use the proper sized wrenches to avoid damage to nuts and injury to yourself.
6. When loosening a tight or stuck nut, be guided by what would happen if the wrench should slip. Protect yourself accordingly.
7. Keep your work area clean and uncluttered.
8. Wear safety goggles during all operations involving drilling, grinding, or use of a cold chisel.
9. Never use worn tools.
10. Keep a fire extinguisher handy and be sure it is rated for gasoline and electrical fires.

MECHANIC'S TIPS

Removing Frozen Nuts and Screws

When a fastener rusts and cannot be removed, several methods may be used to loosen it. First, apply penetrating oil such as Liquid Wrench or WD-40 (available at any hardware or auto supply store). Apply it liberally. Rap the fastener several times with a small hammer; do not hit it hard enough to cause damage.

For frozen screws, apply penetrating oil as described, then insert a screwdriver in the slot and rap the top of the scewdriver with a hammer. This loosens the rust so the screw can be removed in the normal way. If the screw head is too chewed up to use a screwdriver, grip the head with Vise-Grip pliers and twist screw out.

Remedying Stripped Threads

Occasionally, threads are stripped through carelessness or impact damage. Often the threads can be cleaned up by running a tap (for internal threads on nuts) or die (for external threads on bolts) through threads. See **Figure 2**.

Removing Broken Screws or Bolts

When the head breaks off a screw or bolt, several methods are available for removing the remaining portion.

If a large portion of the remainder projects out, try gripping it with Vise Grips. If the projecting portion is too small, try filing it to fit a wrench or cut a slot in it to fit a screwdriver. See **Figure 3**.

If the head breaks off flush, try using a screw extractor. To do this, centerpunch the exact center of the remaining portion of the screw or bolt. Drill a small hole in the screw and tap the extractor into the hole. Back the screw out with a wrench on the extractor. See **Figure 4**.

PARTS REPLACEMENT

Yamaha makes frequent changes during a model year — some minor, some relatively major. When you order parts from the dealer or other parts distributor, always order by engine and frame number. Write the numbers down and carry them with you. Compare new parts to old before purchasing them. If they are not alike, have the parts manager explain the difference to you.

EXPENDABLE SUPPLIES

Certain expendable supplies are also required. These include grease, oil, gasket cement, wiping rags, cleaning solvent, and distilled water. Ask your dealer for the special locking compounds, silicone lubricants, and lube products which make motorcycle maintenance simpler and easier. Solvent is available at most service stations and distilled water for the battery is available at most supermarkets.

TOOLS

To properly service your motorcycle, you will need an assortment of ordinary tools. As a minimum, these include:

- a. Combination wrench
- b. Socket wrenches
- c. Plastic mallet
- d. Small hammer
- e. Snap ring pliers
- f. Phillips screwdrivers
- g. Slot screwdrivers
- h. Impact driver
- i. Pliers
- j. Feeler gauges
- k. Spark plug gauge
- l. Spark plug wrench
- m. Drift
- n. Torque wrench
- o. Allen wrenches

An original equipment tool kit, like the one shown in **Figure 5** is available through most Yamaha dealers and is suitable for most minor servicing.

Engine tune-up and troubleshooting procedures require a few more tools, described in the following sections.

Hydrometer

This instrument measures state of charge of the battery, and tells much about battery conditions. Such an instrument is available at any auto parts stores and through most larger mail order outlets. A satisfactory one costs less than $3. See **Figure 6**.

Multimeter or VOM

This instrument (**Figure 7**) is invaluable for electrical system troubleshooting and service. A few of its functions may be duplicated by locally fabricated substitutes, but for the serious hobbyist, it is a must. Its uses are described in

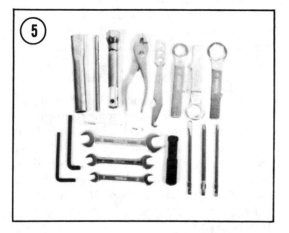

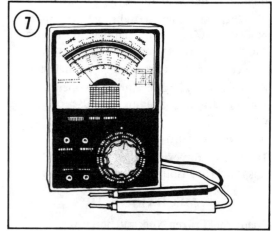

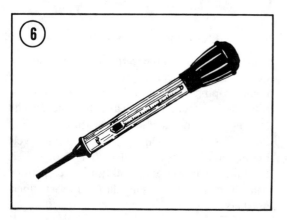

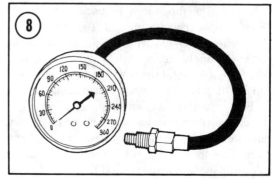

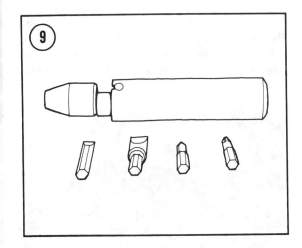

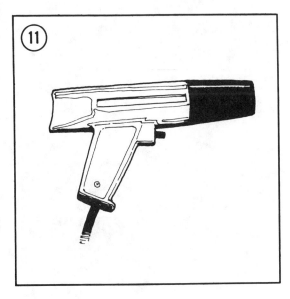

the applicable sections of this book. Prices start at around $20 at electronics hobbyist stores and mail order outlets.

Compression Gauge

An engine with low compression cannot be properly tuned and will not develop full power. A compression gauge measures engine compression. The one shown in **Figure 8** has a flexible stem, which enables it to reach cylinders where there is little clearance between the cylinder head and frame. Less expensive ones start around $5 and are available at auto accessory stores or by mail order from large catalog order firms.

Impact Driver

This tool makes removal of engine components easy, and eliminates damage to bolt heads. Good ones run about $15 at larger hardware stores. See **Figure 9**.

Ignition Gauge

This tool has round wire gauges for measuring spark plug gap. See **Figure 10**.

Strobe Timing Light

This instrument is necessary for tuning. By flashing a light at the precise instant the cylinder fires, the position of the flywheel at that instant can be seen. Marks on the ignition governor plate and the stationary scale on the crankcase must align.

Suitable lights range from inexpensive neon bulb types ($2-3) to powerful xenon strobe lights ($20-40). See **Figure 11**. Neon timing lights are difficult to see and must be used in dimly lit areas. Xenon strobe timing lights can be used outside in bright sunlight. Both types work on this motorcycle; use according to the manufacturer's instructions.

Other Special Tools

A few other special tools may be required for major service. These are described in the appropriate chapters and are available from Yamaha dealers.

SERIAL NUMBERS

You must know the model serial number for registration purposes and when ordering special parts.

The frame serial number is stamped on the right side of the steering head, (**Figure 12**) and on the VIN plate on the steering head. The engine number is stamped on the top right-hand side of the crankcase (**Figure 13**).

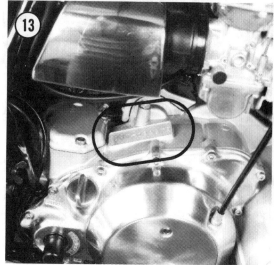

CHAPTER TWO

TROUBLESHOOTING

Diagnosing mechanical problems is relatively simple if you use orderly procedures and keep a few basic principles in mind.

The troubleshooting procedures in this chapter analyze typical symptoms, and show logical methods of isolating causes. These are not the only methods. There may be several ways to solve a problem, but only a systematic, methodical approach can guarantee success.

Never assume anything. Do not overlook the obvious. If you are riding along and the bike suddenly quits, check the easiest, most accessible problem spots first. Is there gasoline in the tank? Is the shut-off valve in the ON or RESERVE position? Has a spark plug wire fallen off? Check ignition switch. Sometimes the weight of keys on a key ring may turn the ignition off suddenly.

If nothing obvious turns up in a cursory check, look a little further. Learning to recognize and describe symptoms will make repairs easier for you or a mechanic at the shop. Describe problems accurately and fully. Saying that "it won't run" isn't the same as saying "it quit on the highway at high speed and wouldn't start," or that "it sat in my garage for three months and then wouldn't start."

Gather as many symptoms together as possible to aid in diagnosis. Note whether the engine lost power gradually or all at once, what color smoke (if any) came from the exhaust, and so on. Remember that the more complicated a machine is, the easier it is to troubleshoot because symptoms point to specific problems.

After the symptoms are defined, areas which could cause the problems are tested and analyzed. Guessing at the cause of a problem may provide the solution, but it can easily lead to frustration, wasted time, and a series of expensive, unnecessary part replacements.

You do not need fancy equipment or complicated test gear to determine whether repairs can be attempted at home. A few simple checks could save a large repair bill and time lost while the bike sits in a dealer's service department. On the other hand, be realistic and do not attempt repairs beyond your abilities. Service departments tend to charge heavily for putting together a disassembled engine that may have been abused. Some won't even take on such a job — so use common sense, don't get in over your head.

OPERATING REQUIREMENTS

An engine needs three basics to run properly: correct gas/air mixture, compression, and a spark at the right time. If one or more are missing, the engine won't run. The electrical system is the weakest link of the three basics. More problems result from electrical breakdowns than from any other source. Keep that in mind before you begin tampering with carburetor adjustments and the like.

If a bike has been sitting for any length of time and refuses to start, check the battery for a charged condition first, and then look to the gasoline delivery system. This includes the tank, fuel shut-off valves, lines, and the carburetors. Rust may have formed in the tank, obstructing fuel flow. Gasoline deposits may have gummed up carburetor jets and air passages. Gasoline tends to lose its potency after standing for long periods. Condensation may contaminate it with water. Drain old gas and try starting with a fresh tankful.

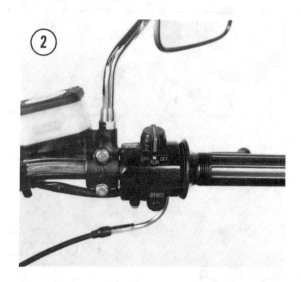

TROUBLESHOOTING INSTRUMENTS

Chapter One lists many of the instruments needed and detailed instructions on their use.

EMERGENCY TROUBLESHOOTING

When the bike is difficult to start or won't start at all, it does not help to grind away at the starter or kick the tires. Check for obvious problems even before getting out your tools.

Go down the following list step-by-step. Do each one; you may be embarrassed to find your kill switch off, but that is better than wearing out your leg or wearing your battery down with the starter. If the bike still will not start, refer to the appropriate troubleshooting procedures which follow in this chapter.

1. Is there fuel in the tank? Remove the filler cap and rock the bike; listen for fuel sloshing around.

WARNING
Do not use an open flame to check in the tank. A serious explosion is certain to result.

2. Are both fuel shut-off valves on? Turn both to RESERVE (**Figure 1**) to be sure that you get the last remaining gas. Make sure that the vacuum lines are attached and are tight. Without engine vacuum, the shut-off valves will not operate.

3. Is the kill switch in RUN position (**Figure 2**)?

4. Are spark plug wires on tight? See **Figure 3**.

5. Is the choke lever in the right position? It should be pulled out for a cold engine (**Figure 4**) and pushed in for a warm engine.

6. Is the battery dead? Check it with a hydrometer.

7. Has the main fuse (**Figure 5**) blown? Replace it with a good one.

8. Is the transmission in neutral or the clutch lever pulled in? The bike will not start in gear without pulling in the clutch.

STARTER

Starter system troubles are relatively easy to isolate. The following are common symptoms and cures.

1. *Engine cranks very slowly or not at all* — If the headlight is very dim or not lighting at all, most likely the battery or its connecting wires are at fault. Check the battery condition using the procedures described in Chapter Seven. Check the wiring for breaks, shorts, and dirty connections.

If the battery and connecting wires check good, the trouble may be in the starter, starter solenoid, or wiring. To isolate the trouble, short the 2 large starter solenoid terminals together (not to ground); if the starter cranks normally, check the starter solenoid wiring as described under symptoms 2 and 3. If the starter still fails to crank properly, remove the starter and test it. Refer to Chapter Seven.

2. *Starter only operates when clutch lever is pulled in, even in neutral* — If the neutral light does not come on in neutral, but engine starts when clutch lever is pulled in, the neutral switch is defective or the connecting wire is open.

3. *Starter operates while transmission is in gear without pulling in the clutch lever* — The neutral switch or connecting wire is shorted to ground.

4. *Starter will not operate while transmission is in gear with the clutch lever pulled in* — The clutch lever switch or connecting wire is shorted to ground.

5. *Loud grinding noises when starter runs* — This may mean the teeth are not meshing properly, or it may mean the starter drive mechanism is damaged. In the first case, remove the starter and examine the gear teeth. In the latter case, remove the starter and replace the starter drive mechanism.

6. *Starter engages, but will not disengage when ignition switch is released* — This trouble is usually caused by a sticking starter solenoid.

CHARGING SYSTEM

Troubleshooting an alternator system is somewhat different from troubleshooting a generator. For example, *never* short any terminals to ground on the alternator or the voltage regulator/rectifier. The following symptoms are typical of alternator charging system troubles.

1. *Battery requires frequent charging* — The charging system is not functioning or is undercharging the battery. Test the alternator and voltage regulator/rectifier as described in Chapter Seven.

2. *Battery requires frequent additions of water, or lamps require frequent replacement* — The alternator is probably overcharging the battery. Check voltage regulator/rectifier as described in Chapter Seven.

ENGINE

These procedures assume that the starter cranks the engine over normally. If not, refer to *Starter* section in this chapter.

Poor Performance

1. *Engine misses erratically at all speeds* — Intermittent trouble like this can be difficult to find. The fault could be in the ignition system, exhaust system (exhaust restriction), or fuel system. Follow troubleshooting procedures for these systems carefully to isolate the trouble.

2. *Engine misses at idle only* — Trouble could exist anywhere in ignition system. Refer to *Ignition System* in Chapter Seven. Trouble could exist in the carburetor idle circuits.

3. *Engine misses at high speed only* — Trouble could exist in the fuel system or ignition system. Check the fuel lines, etc., as described under *Fuel System Troubleshooting*. Also check spark plugs and wires. Refer to *Ignition System* in Chapter Seven.

4. *Poor performance at all speeds, lack of acceleration* — Trouble usually exists in ignition or fuel system. Check each with the appropriate troubleshooting procedure.

5. *Excessive fuel consumption* — This can be caused by a wide variety of seemingly unrelated factors. Check for clutch slippage, brake drag, and defective wheel bearings. Check ignition and fuel system as described later.

ENGINE NOISES

1. *Valve clatter* — This is a light to heavy tapping sound from under cam cover. It is usually caused by excessive valve clearance. Adjust clearance as described under *Valve Clearance Adjustment* in Chapter Three. If noise persists, disassemble the cam and valve mechanism as described under *Camshaft and Valve Assemblies* in Chapter Four. Look for broken springs, worn cams and bearings.

2. *Knocking or pinging during acceleration* — Caused by using a lower octane fuel than recommended. May also be caused by poor fuel available at some "discount" gasoline stations. Pinging can also be caused by spark plugs of the wrong heat range. Refer to *Correct Spark Plug Heat Range* in Chapter Three.

3. *Slapping or rattling noises at low speed or during acceleration* — May be caused by piston slap, i.e., excessive piston-cylinder wall clearance.

4. *Knocking or rapping while decelerating* — Usually caused by excessive rod bearing clearance.

5. *Persistent knocking and vibration* — Usual-

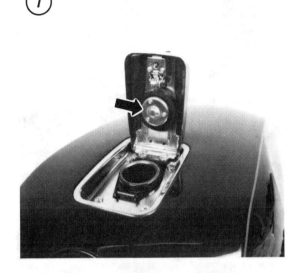

ly caused by excessive main bearing clearance.

6. *Rapid on-off squeal* — Compression leak around cylinder head gasket or spark plugs.

EXCESSIVE VIBRATION

This can be difficult to find without disassembling the engine. Usually this is caused by loose engine mounting hardware or worn engine or transmission bearings.

LUBRICATION TROUBLES

1. *Excessive oil consumption* — May be caused by worn rings and bores. Overhaul is necessary to correct this; see Chapter Four. May also be caused by worn seals. Also check for exterior leaks.

2. *Oil pressure lamp does not light when ignition switch is on* — The oil pressure sending unit is located on the top of the upper crankcase, just below the carburetor (**Figure 6**). Check that the wire is connected to the sender and makes good contact. Pull off wire and ground it. If the lamp lights, replace the sender. If the lamp does not light, replace the lamp.

3. *Oil pressure lamp lights or flickers when engine is running* — This indicates low or complete loss of oil pressure. Stop the engine immediately; coast to a stop with the clutch

disengaged or transmission out of gear. This may simply be caused by a low oil level, or an overheating engine. Check the oil level. Check for a shorted oil pressure sender with an ohmmeter or other continuity tester. Listen for unusual noises indicating bad bearings, etc. Do not restart engine until you know why the light went on and have corrected the problem.

FUEL SYSTEM

Fuel system troubles must be isolated to the carburetor, fuel tank, fuel shut-off valve, or fuel lines. These procedures assume that the ignition system has been checked and properly adjusted.

1. *Engine will not start* — First, determine that the fuel is being delivered to the carburetor. Turn the fuel shut-off valves to the ON position, remove the flexible fuel lines to the carburetor. Place the loose end onto a small container, turn the shut-off valves to the PRIME position. Fuel should run out of the tube. If it does not, remove the shut-off valves and check for restrictions within them or the fuel tank. Make sure the vent hole in the fuel fill cap is not plugged (**Figure 7**). Refer to Chapters Three and Six.

2. *Rough idle or engine miss with frequent stalling* — Check carburetor adjustment. See Chapter Three.

3. *Stumbling when accelerating from idle* — Check idle speed adjustment. See Chapter Three.

4. *Engine misses at high speed or lacks power* — This indicates possible fuel starvation. Clean main jets and float needle valves.

5. *Black exhaust smoke* — Black exhaust smoke means a badly overrich mixture. Check that manual choke disengages. Check idle speed. Check for leaky floats or worn float needle valves. Also check that jets are proper size.

CLUTCH

All clutch troubles except adjustments require partial engine disassembly to identify and cure the problem. Refer to Chapter Five for procedures.

1. *Slippage* — This is most noticeable when accelerating in a high gear at relatively low speed. To check slippage, shift to second gear and release the clutch as if riding off. If the clutch is good, the engine will slow and stall. If the clutch slips, continued engine speed will give it away. Slippage results from insufficient clutch lever free play, worn discs or pressure plate, or weak springs.

2. *Drag or failure to release* — This trouble usually causes difficult shifting and gear clash, especially when downshifting. The cause may be excessive clutch lever free play, warped or bent pressure plate or clutch disc, or broken or loose linings.

3. *Chatter or grabbing* — A number of things can cause this trouble. Check tightness of engine mounting bolts. Also check lever free play.

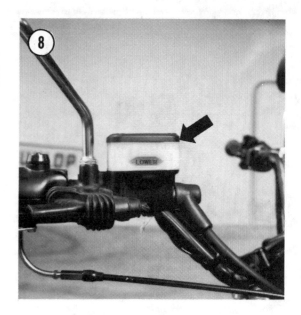

TRANSMISSION

Transmission problems are usually indicated by one or more of the following symptoms:

    a. Difficulty shifting gears
    b. Gear clash when downshifting
    c. Slipping out of gear
    d. Excessive noise in neutral
    e. Excessive noise in gear

Transmission symptoms are sometimes hard to distinguish from clutch symptoms. Be sure that the clutch is not causing the trouble before working on the transmission. Refer to Chapter Five.

BRAKES

1. *Brake lever or pedal goes all the way to its stop* — There are numerous causes for this including excessively worn pads, air in the hydraulic system, leaky brake lines, leaky calipers, or leaky or worn master cylinder. Make the brake fluid level up to the upper level line (**Figure 8**) on both reservoirs. Check for leaks and thin brake pads. Bleed the brakes. If this does not cure the trouble, rebuild the calipers and/or master cylinder.

2. *Spongy lever* — Normally caused by an air in the system; bleed the brakes as described in Chapter Ten.

3. *Dragging brakes* — Check for swollen rubber parts due to improper brake fluid or contamination, and obstructed master cylinder bypass port. Clean or replace defective parts.

4. *Hard lever or pedal* — Check brake pads for contamination. Also check for restricted brake line and hose and brake pedal needing lubrication.

5. *High speed fade* — Check for glazed or contaminated brake pads. Ensure that recommended brake fluid is installed. Drain entire system and refill if in doubt. Refer to Chapter Three.

6. *Pulsating lever or pedal* — Check for excessive brake disc runout. Undetected accident damage is also a frequent cause of this.

FRONT SUSPENSION AND STEERING

1. *Too stiff or too soft* — Make sure forks have not been leaking and oil is correct. If in doubt, drain and refill as described under *Front Fork Oil Change*. On Model SF, make sure the air pressure is correct.

2. *Leakage around seals* — There should be a light film of oil on fork tubes. However, large amounts of oil on tubes means the seals are leaking. Replace seals as described under *Front Fork Disassembly/Assembly* in Chapter Eight.

3. *Fork action is rough* — Check for bent tube.

4. *Steering wobbles* — Check for correct steering head bearing tightness as described under *Steering Head Adjustment* in Chapter Eight.

ELECTRICAL PROBLEMS

Bulbs which continuously burn out may be caused by excessive vibration, loose connections that permit sudden current surges, poor battery connections, installation of the wrong type bulb, or a faulty voltage regulator/rectifier.

A dead battery or one which discharges quickly may be caused by a faulty alternator or rectifier. Check for loose or corroded terminals. Shorted battery cells or broken terminals will keep a battery from charging. Low water levels will decrease a battery's capacity. A battery left uncharged after installation will sulphate, rendering it useless.

A majority of light and horn or other electrical accessory problems are caused by loose or corroded ground connections. Check those first, and then substitute known good units for easier troubleshooting.

2

NOTE: If you own a 1980 or 1981 model, first check the Supplement at the back of the book for any new service information.

CHAPTER THREE

PERIODIC MAINTENANCE, LUBRICATION AND TUNE-UP

Regular maintenance is the best guarantee for a safe, troublefree, good performing, long lasting motorcycle. An afternoon spent now — cleaning, inspecting, and adjusting — can prevent costly mechanical problems in the future and unexpected breakdowns on the road.

The procedures presented in this chapter can be easily carried out by anyone with average mechanical skills. The operations are presented step-by-step. If they are followed, it is difficult to go wrong.

ROUTINE CHECKS

The following simple checks should be performed at each stop at a service station for gas.

Engine Oil Level

Refer to *Checking Engine Oil Level* under *Periodic Lubrication* in this chapter.

General Inspection

1. Quickly examine the engine for signs of oil or fuel leakage.

2. Check the tires for imbedded stones. Pry them out with your ignition key.

3. Make sure all lights work.

> NOTE: *At least check the brakelight. It can burn out anytime. Motorists cannot*

stop as quickly as you and need all the warning you can give.

Tire Pressure

Tire pressure must be checked with the tires cold. Correct tire pressure depends a lot on the load you are carrying. See **Table 1**.

Battery

Remove the seat and the left-hand side cover and check the battery electrolyte level. The level must be between the upper and lower marks on the case **(Figure 1)**. For complete details see *Battery, Checking Electrolyte Level* in this chapter.

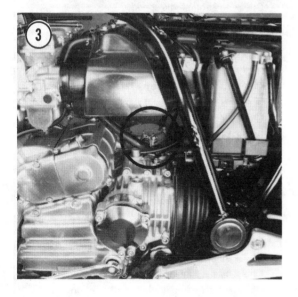

Check the level more frequently in hot weather.

Exhaust System

Check for leakage at all fittings. Do not forget the bolt (**Figure 2**) on the crossover pipe. Tighten all bolts and nuts; replace any gaskets as necessary.

Crankcase Breather Hose

Inspect the hose for cracks and deterioration and make sure that the hose clamps are tight (**Figure 3**).

Final Checks

Inspect the entire motorcycle for loose fasteners, oil and fuel leaks, cracks in the frame and wheels, worn insulation on electrical wires, or anything else which might create unsafe riding conditions.

SERVICE INTERVALS

The services and intervals shown in **Table 2** are recommended by the factory. Strict adherence to these recommendations will go a long way toward insuring long service from your Yamaha XS1100.

For convenience of maintaining your motorcycle, most of the services shown in the table are described in this chapter. However, some procedures which require more than minor disassembly or adjustment are covered elsewhere in the appropriate chapter.

Table 1   TIRE PRESSURES

Load	Pressure (All Models)
Up to 198 lb. (90 kg)	
Front	26 psi (1.8 kg/cm²)
Rear	28 psi (2.0 kg/cm²)
198-337 lb. (90-153 kg)	
Front	28 psi (2.0 kg/cm²)
Rear	36 psi (2.5 kg/cm²)
Maximum Load Limit*	
Front — 420 lb. (190 kg) 36 psi (2.6 kg/cm²)	
Rear — 670 lb. (304 kg) 40 psi (2.8 kg/cm²)	
*Maximum load includes the total weight of motorcycle with accessories, rider(s), and luggage.	

Table 2 SERVICE INTERVALS

Every month	• Check tire pressure.
Every 2,500 miles (4,000km) **or 6 months**	• Change engine oil. • Lubricate all control cables with oil. • Adjust free play of front brake hand lever and rear brake lever. • Examine disc brake pads for wear. • Lubricate rear brake pedal arm and shift lever shaft. • Lubricate side and centerstand pivots. • Inspect front steering assembly for looseness. • Check wheel bearings for smooth operation. • Check battery condition. • Check ignition timing. • Inspect exhaust system for leaks. • Synchronize carburetors. • Check and adjust idle speed. • Check clutch lever free play. • Clean fuel shutoff valves and filters. • Lubricate speedometer gear housing.
Every 4,000 miles (6,400km)	• Complete engine tune-up.
Every 5,000 miles (8,000km) **or 12 months**	• Clean air filter element. • Inspect spark plugs; regap if necessary. • Adjust cam chain tensioner. • Check and adjust valve clearance. • Inspect all fuel lines for chafed, cracked, or swollen ends. • Inspect throttle operation. • Inspect crankcase ventilation hose for cracks, deterioration, or loose hose clamps. • Check engine mounts for side play. • Check all suspension components. • Change middle and final gear lubrication. • Replace oil filter.
Every 8,000 miles (12,000km)	• Dismantle carburetors and clean. • Replace spark plugs. • Change oil in front forks. • Inspect and repack steering head bearings. • Inspect and repack rear swing arm bushings. • Inspect and repack wheel bearings. • Lubricate drive shaft joint.
Every 2 years	• Change brake fluid. • Replace master cylinder and caliper cylinder internal seals.
Every 4 years	• Replace all brake hoses.

TIRES

Pressure

Tire pressure should be checked and adjusted to accommodate rider and luggage weight. A simple, accurate gauge (**Figure 4**) can be purchased for a few dollars and should be carried in your motorcycle tool kit. The appropriate tire pressures are shown in **Table 1**.

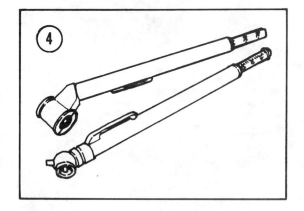

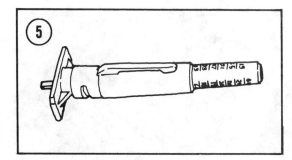

Inspection

Check tread for excessive wear, deep cuts, imbedded objects such as stones, nails, etc. If you find a nail in a tire, mark its location with a light crayon before pulling it out. This will help locate the hole in the inner tube. Refer to *Tire Changing* in Chapter Eight.

Check local traffic regulations concerning minimum tread depth. Measure with a tread depth gauge (**Figure 5**) or small ruler. Yamaha recommends replacement when the tread depth is 0.03 in. (0.8mm) or less. Tread wear indicators appear across the tire when tread reaches minimum safe depth. Replace the tire at this point.

Table 3   AXLE NUT TORQUE SPECIFICATIONS

Item	Ft.-lb.	Newton Meters
Front axle nut		
Except special model	77.4	107
Special model	76	103
Front axle holding nuts		
Except special model	14.5	20
Front axle pinch bolt		
Special model	15	20
Rear axle nut		
All models	108	147
Rear axle pinch bolt		
All models	4	5

Table 4   RECOMMENDED COMBINATION — FRONT FORK AIR PRESSURE TO REAR SHOCK ABSORBER SETTING

Load	Front Fork Air Pressure	Rear Shock Absorber Lower Spring Seat	Damping Adjuster
Rider	5.7-14 psi (0.4-1.0 kg/cm²)	A-E	1
Rider plus passenger	5.7-14 psi (0.4-1.0 kg/cm²)	A-E	2
Rider plus passenger and/or luggage	14-21 psi (1.0-1.5 kg/cm²)	C-E	3
Maximum vehicle load limit*	21 psi (1.5 kg/cm²)	E	4

*Maximum load limit — front 420 lb. (190 kg), rear 670 lb. (304 kg). This includes total weight of motorcycle with rider(s), accessories, and luggage.

WHEELS

Check the aluminum wheels for cracks, bends, or warpage. These wheels cannot be serviced, except for balancing, and if found to be damaged they must be replaced. Refer to Chapter Eight for complete wheel inspection and balancing procedures.

The stock Yamaha wheel is not designed to be used with tubeless tires. Always use a tube type tire.

Check both axle nuts for tightness. Refer to **Table 3** for the correct torque values.

FRONT FORKS AND REAR SHOCKS

Air/Oil Front Fork Models

The air pressure in the front forks must be adjusted for various load conditions (see **Table 4**). An easy way to accomplish this is with the S & W Mini-Pump (**Figure 6**). Attach it to the air fitting (**Figure 7**) on the top of each fork and inflate to the desired pressure.

> CAUTION
> *Never exceed the maximum allowable air pressure of 36 psi (2.5 kg/cm²) as the oil seal will be damaged. The pressure difference between the two forks should be 1.4 psi (0.1kg/cm²) or less.*

The rear shock absorbers must be adjusted to correspond to front fork air pressure and vehicle load (see **Table 4**). Turn the upper damping adjuster (**Figure 8**) with your finger or screwdriver to the correct setting.

> NOTE: *Always turn the adjuster until it **clicks into a position**. If it is set between any click position it will be set at the maximum (No. 4) position. Always set both shocks to the same position.*

The lower spring seat (**Figure 9**) must also be adjusted in accordance to the specifications in **Table 4**. Rotate the cam ring at the base of the spring — *clockwise to increase* preload and *counterclockwise to decrease it*.

> NOTE: *Use the spanner wrench furnished in the XS1100 tool kit for this adjustment. Set both shocks to the same position.*

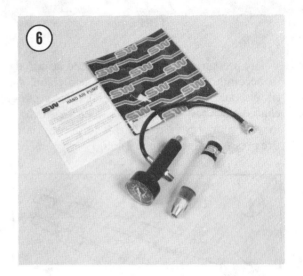

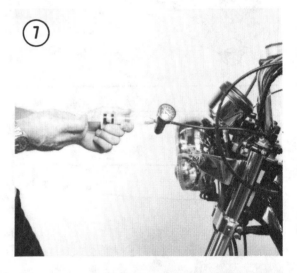

BATTERY

Checking Electrolyte Level

The battery is the heart of the electrical system. It should be checked and serviced as indicated. The majority of electrical system troubles can be attributed to neglect of this vital component.

The electrolyte level may be checked with the battery installed. However it is necessary to remove the seat. The electrolyte level should be maintained between the two marks on the battery case (**Figure 1**). If the electrolyte level is low, it's a good idea to remove the battery so that it can be thoroughly serviced and checked.

1. Loosen the 2 nuts (**Figure 10**) securing the seat to the frame. Slide the seat forward to release the seat from the studs and remove the seat.

2. Remove the left-hand side panel (**Figure 11**).

3. Remove the clamp securing the battery in place (A, **Figure 12**).

4. Remove the vent tube (B, **Figure 12**).

5. Disconnect both the negative (black) and positive (red) electrical cables.

6. Slide the battery out of the frame.

> CAUTION
> *Be careful not to spill battery electrolyte on painted or polished surfaces. The liquid is highly corrosive and will damage the finish. If it is spilled, wash it off immediately with soapy water and thoroughly rinse with clean water.*

7. Remove the filler plug (**Figure 13**) and slowly add distilled water. Each cell will be filled automatically and will not allow any cell to be filled above the UPPER LEVEL line. Stop filling when the excess water starts to flow out the vent tube outlet. Never add electrolyte (acid) to correct the level.

> CAUTION
> *Use only distilled water as ordinary tap water contains minerals that are harmful to the battery.*

8. Securely tighten the filler plug.

9. After the level has been corrected and the battery allowed to stand for a few minutes, check the specific gravity of the electrolyte in each cell with a hydrometer (**Figure 14**). Follow the manufacturer's instructions for reading the instrument.

Testing

Hydrometer testing is the best way to check battery condition. Use a hydrometer with numbered graduations from 1.100 to 1.300 rather than one with color-coded bands. To use the hydrometer, squeeze the rubber ball, insert the tip into the cell and release the ball. Draw enough electrolyte to float the weighted float inside the hydrometer. Note the number in line with surface of the electrolyte; this is the specific gravity for this cell. Return the electrolyte to the cell from which it came.

The specific gravity of the electrolyte in each battery cell is an excellent indication of that cell's condition. A fully charged cell will read 1.275-1.280, while a cell in good condition may read from 1.250-1.280. A cell in fair condition reads from 1.225-1.250 and anything below 1.225 is practically dead.

Specific gravity varies with temperature. For each 10° that electrolyte temperature exceeds 80°F, add 0.004 to reading indicated on hydrometer. Subtract 0.004 for each 10° below 80°F.

If the cells test in the poor range, the battery requires recharging. The hydrometer is useful for checking the progress of the charging operation. **Table 5** shows approximate state of charge.

Charging

> CAUTION
> *Always remove the battery from the motorcycle before connecting charging equipment.*

> WARNING
> *During charging, highly explosive hydrogen gas is released from the battery. The battery should be charged only in a well-ventilated area, and open flames and cigarettes should be kept away. Never check the charge of the battery by arcing across the terminals; the resulting spark can ignite the hydrogen gas.*

1. Connect the positive (+) charger lead to the positive battery terminal and the negative (−) charger lead to the negative battery terminal.

2. Remove all vent caps from the battery, set the charger at 12 volts, and switch it on. If the output of the charger is variable, it is best to select a low setting — 1½ to 2 amps.

Table 3   STATE OF CHARGE

Specific Gravity	State of Charge
1.110 - 1.130	Discharged
1.140 - 1.160	Almost discharged
1.170 - 1.190	One-quarter charged
1.200 - 1.220	One-half charged
1.230 - 1.250	Three-quarters charged
1.260 - 1.280	Fully charged

3. After battery has been charged for about 8 hours, turn off the charger, disconnect the leads and check the specific gravity. It should be within the limits specified in **Table 4**. If it is, and remains stable after one hour, the battery is charged.

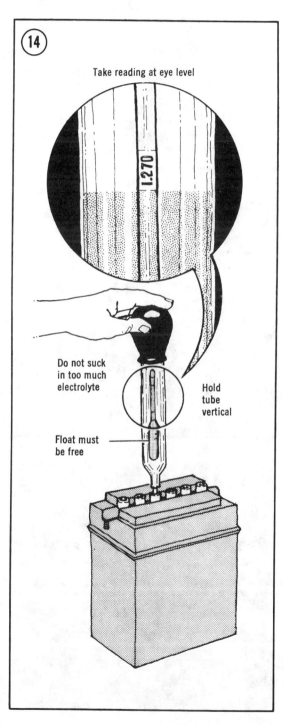

Take reading at eye level

1.270

Do not suck
in too much
electrolyte

Hold
tube
vertical

Float must
be free

4. Clean the battery terminals, case, and tray and reinstall them in the motorcycle, reversing the removal steps. Coat the terminals with Vaseline or silicone spray to retard decomposition of the terminal material. Install the breather tube without any kinks or sharp bends. It must be clear in order to dissipate the gas normally given off by the battery.

New Battery Installation

When replacing the old battery with a new one, be sure to charge it completely (specific gravity 1.260-1.280) before installing it in the bike.

Failure to do so, or using the battery with a low electrolyte level, will permanently damage the battery.

If the battery vent tube was completely removed, be sure to reinstall it as shown in **Figure 15**.

PERIODIC LUBRICATION

Checking Engine Oil Level

Engine oil level is checked by viewing the oil level window located on the lower right-hand side of the crankcase cover.

1. Place the bike on the centerstand on a level surface.

2. Start the engine and allow it to run for a couple of minutes.

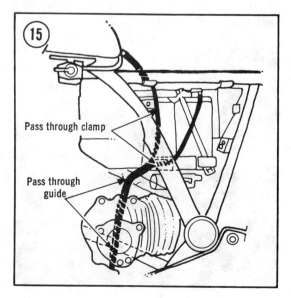

Pass through clamp

Pass through
guide

3. Shut off engine and allow the oil to settle.

4. Check the oil level through the oil level window (**Figure 16**).

5. The oil level should be between the maximum and minimum marks to the left of the window. If necessary, add the recommended weight of oil (**Figure 17**) to correct the level; do not overfill. Add oil through the filler hole.

Changing Engine Oil and Filter

The factory-recommended oil change interval is 2,500 miles (4,000 km). The filter should be changed every other oil change. This assumes that the motorcycle is operated in moderate climates. In extremely cold climates, oil should be changed every 30 days. The time interval is more important than the mileage interval because acids formed by gasoline and water vapor from combustion will contaminate the oil even if the motorcycle is not run for several months. If motorcycle is operated under dusty conditions, the oil will get dirty more quickly and should be changed more frequently than recommended.

Use only a detergent oil with an API rating of SE or better. The quality rating is stamped on top of the can (**Figure 18**). Try always to use same brand of oil. Use of oil additives is not recommended. Refer to **Figure 17** for the correct weight of oil to use under different temperatures.

To drain the oil and change the filter, you will need the following:

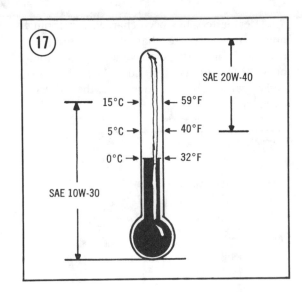

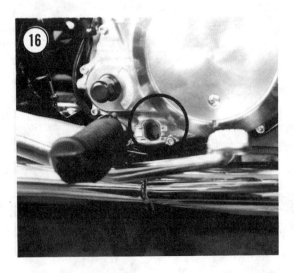

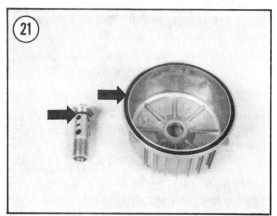

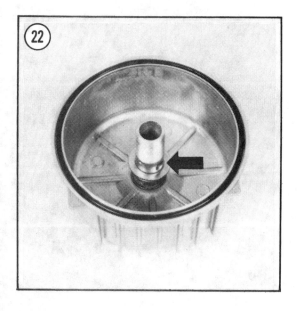

a. Drain pan
b. Funnel
c. Can opener or pour spout
d. 19mm wrench (drain plug), 12mm wrench (filter bolt)
e. 4 quarts of oil
f. Oil filter

There are a number of ways to discard the old oil safely. The easiest way is to pour it from the drain pan into a gallon plastic bleach or milk bottle. Tighten the cap and place it carefully in the trash.

NOTE: *Some service stations and oil retailers will accept your used oil for recycling, some may even give you money for it.*

1. Place the motorcycle on the centerstand.

2. Start the engine and run it unti it is at normal operating temperature, then turn it off.

3. Place a drain pan under the crankcase and remove the drain plug (A, **Figure 19**). Remove the oil fill cap (**Figure 20**); this will speed up the flow of oil.

4. Let it drain for at least 15-20 minutes during which time, hit the starter a couple of times to help drain any remaining oil.

CAUTION
Make sure the ignition switch is in the OFF *position.*

NOTE: *Before removing filter cover, thoroughly clean off all road dirt and oil around it.*

5. To remove the oil filter, unscrew the bolt securing the filter cover (B, **Figure 19**) to the crankcase.

6. Remove the cover and the filter, discard the old filter and clean out the cover and the bolt with cleaning solvent and dry thoroughly. Remove all solvent residue.

7. Inspect the O-ring on the cover and the bolt (**Figure 21**). Replace it if deteriorated or damaged. Make sure it is properly positioned within the cover, prior to installation.

8. Insert the bolt into the cover and install the spring and washer (**Figure 22**). Insert the filter and reinstall into the crankcase.

Table 6 MIDDLE AND FINAL GEAR OIL SPECIFICATIONS

Item	Type	Quantity
Middle gear case	Hypoid gear oil	12.0 U.S. oz. (375cc; 10.56 Imp. oz.)
Final gear case	Hypoid gear oil	10.0 U.S. oz. (300cc; 8.45 Imp. oz.)
Temperature		
All weather	SAE 80W-90/GL4	
Above 40°F (5°C)	SAE 90/GL4	
Below 40°F (5°C)	SAE 80/GL4	

9. Tighten the filter cover bolt to 20-25 ft.-lb. (29-32 N•m). Install the drain plug and tighten to 31 ft.-lb. (43 N•m).

10. Fill the crankcase with the correct weight (**Figure 17**) and quantity of oil.

> NOTE: *The capacity with a filter change is approximately 3.7 U.S. qt. (3.5 liters; 3.0 Imp. qt.). Without a filter change it is 3.2 U.S. qt. (3.0 liters; 2.7 Imp. qt.).*

11. Screw in the fill cap and start the engine; let it idle at moderate speed and check for leaks.

12. Turn off the engine and check for correct oil level.

13. Start the engine; the oil light should go off within 1-2 seconds. If it says on, shut off the engine immediately and locate the problem. Do not run the engine with the light on.

Checking Middle Gear Oil Level

Check the middle gear oil with the level gauge furnished in the owner's tool kit. The engine and gear case should be cool. If the bike has been run, allow it to cool down (10-15 minutes), then check the oil level.

1. Place the bike on the centerstand on a level surface.

2. Wipe the area around the filler cap clean, and unscrew the cap. Do not allow any dirt or foreign matter to enter the gear case opening.

3. Insert the end of the gauge marked MIDDLE into the hole until it rests on the filler opening (**Figure 23**).

4. Remove the gauge. The correct oil level is between the two lines on the end of the gauge (**Figure 24**).

5. Add oil to maintain correct level. Refer to **Table 6**, for recommended type and weight oil.

6. Install the filler cap and tighten it securely.

Changing Middle Gear Oil

The factory-recommended oil change interval is every 5,000 miles (8,000km).

To drain the oil you will need the following:

a. Drain pan
b. Funnel
c. 19mm wrench
d. One pint of gear oil (refer to **Table 6**)

Discard old oil in the same manner as outline under *Changing Engine Oil* in this chapter.

1. Start the engine and let it run for a couple of minutes.

2. Shut it off and place bike on centerstand.

3. Place drain pan under the crankcase below the drain plug.

4. Wipe the area around the drain plug clean of all road dirt and remove drain plug (**Figure 25**). Loosen the filler cap as this will speed up the draining process.

3

5. Allow the oil to drain for at least 10-15 minutes.

6. Install the drain plug and tighten it to 31 ft.-lb. (43 N•m).

7. Remove filler cap and refill the case with 12.0 U.S. oz. (375cc; 10.56 Imp. oz.) of the recommended type and weight oil. See **Table 6**.

Checking Final Drive Oil Level

Final drive gear oil is checked using the level gauge furnished in the owner's tool kit. The gear case should be cool. If the bike has been run, allow it to cool down, then check the oil level. When checking or changing the final drive gear oil, do not allow any dirt or foreign matter to enter the gear case opening.

1. Place the bike on the centerstand on a level surface.

2. Wipe the area around the filler cap clean and unscrew the cap.

3. Insert the end of the level gauge marked REAR into the hole until it rests on the filler opening (**Figure 26**). Remove the gauge.

4. The correct oil level is between the two marks on the end of the gauge (**Figure 27**).

5. Add oil to maintain the correct level. Refer to **Table 6** for the recommended type and weight oil. Install the filler cap and tighten it securely.

Changing Final Drive Gear Oil

The factory-recommended oil change interval is every 5,000 miles (8,000km).

To drain the oil you will need:

  a. Drain pan

  b. Funnel

  c. 19mm wrench

  d. One pint of gear oil (refer to **Table 6**)

Discard old oil in the same manner as outlined under *Changing Engine Oil* in this chapter.

1. Place the bike on the centerstand.

2. Place a drain pan under the final drive gear housing drain plug.

3. Wipe the area around the drain plug clean of all road dirt and remove drain plug (**Figure 28**). Loosen the filler cap as this will speed up the flow of oil.

4. Allow the oil to drain for at least 10-15 minutes.

CAUTION

Do not allow any of the oil to come in contact with any of the brake components or drip onto the rear tire.

5. Install the drain plug and tighten it to 17 ft.-lb. (23 N•m).

6. Remove the filler cap and refill the case with 10 U.S. oz. (300cc; 8.45 Imp. oz.) of the recommended type and weight oil. See **Table 6**.

Front Fork Oil Change

The factory-recommended fork oil change interval is every 10,000 miles (16,000km).

1. Remove the front wheel as described under *Front Wheel Removal/Installation* in Chapter Eight.

2. Remove the 4 rubber caps (A, **Figure 29**) and 4 Allen bolts (B, **Figure 29**) securing the handlebar assembly and lay it back over the fuel tank.

CAUTION

Cover the fuel tank with a heavy cloth or plastic tarp to protect it from accidental spilling of brake fluid. Wash any brake fluid off of any painted or plated surface immediately, as it will destroy the finish. Use soapy water and rinse thoroughly.

3. On regular forks, remove the rubber cap (C, **Figure 29**) and cap bolt (D, **Figure 29**) from the top of each fork.

4. On air/oil forks, remove the air valve caps (**Figure 30**), depress the valve stem (**Figure 31**) and bleed out the air from each fork tube. Remove the cap bolt from each fork.

5. Place a drip pan under the fork and remove the drain screw (**Figure 32**). Allow the oil to drain for at least 5 minutes.

CAUTION
Do not allow the fork oil to come in contact with any of the brake components.

6. After most of the oil has drained out, carefully move the outer fork tube up and down pumping out any remaining oil.

7. Install the drain screw; make sure the screw gasket is in good condition prior to installation. Replace if necessary.

8. Repeat Steps 5-6 for the other fork.

9. Refill each tube with SAE 10 fork oil. Refer to **Table 7** for specific capacity.

10. Slowly pump the outer fork tubes to distribute the oil.

11. Inspect the condition of the O-ring (**Figure 33**) on the fork cap. Replace if necessary.

12. Install the cap bolt and on regular forks install the rubber caps. Tighten the cap bolt to 16.5 ft.-lb. (23 N•m).

13. On air/oil forks, inflate each fork with the recommended amount of air pressure, refer to **Table 4**.

14. Install all components that were removed.

15. Road test the bike and check for oil and/or air leaks.

Swing Arm Bearings

Repack the rear swing arm bearings every 10,000 miles (16,000km), with a lithium-base, waterproof wheel bearing grease.

Refer to *Swing Arm, Removal/Installation* in Chapter Nine for complete details.

Control Cables

Every 2,500 miles (4,000km) the control cables should be lubricted. Also they should be

Table 7   FRONT FORK OIL CAPACITY

Model	Type	Quantity — Each Fork
Models E and F	SAE 10 motor oil	7.17 U.S. oz. (212cc: 5.97 Imp. oz.)
Model SF	SAE 10 fork oil	7.61 U.S. oz. (225cc: 6.34 Imp. oz.)

inspected at this time for fraying, and the cable sheath should be checked for chafing. The cables are relatively inexpensive and should be replaced when found to be faulty.

The control cables can be lubricated either with oil or with any of the popular cable lubricants and a cable lubricator. The first method requires more time and the complete lubrication of the entire cable is less certain.

Oil method

1. Disconnect the cable from the clutch lever (**Figure 34**) and the throttle grip assembly.

> NOTE: *On the throttle cable it is necessary to remove the 2 screws (Figure 35) that clamp the housing together to gain access to the cable end.*

2. Make a cone of stiff paper and tape it to the end of the cable sheath (**Figure 36**).

3. Hold the cable upright and pour a small amount of light oil (SAE 10W/30) into the cone. Work the cable in and out of the sheath for several minutes to help the oil work it's way down to the end of the cable.

4. Remove the cone, reconnect the cable and adjust the cable(s) as described in this chapter.

> NOTE: *While the throttle housing is separated, apply a light coat of grease to the metal surfaces of the grip assembly.*

Lubricator method

1. Disconnect the cables as previously described.

2. Attach the lubricator following the manufacturer's instructions.

3. Insert the nozzle of the lubricant can in the lubricator, press the button on the can and hold it down until the lubricant begins to flow out of the other end of the cable.

> NOTE: *Remove the opposite end of the clutch cable so the lubricant will not run into the clutch adjustment housing. Refer to **Clutch Mechanism Adjustment** in this chapter for details.*

4. Remove the lubricator, reconnect the cable(s) and adjust as described in this chapter.

Rear Brake Lever
(Except Special Models)

Every 2,500 miles (4,000km), remove the protective cap (**Figure 37**) and lubricate the shaft using the grease fitting (**Figure 38**). Use molybdenum disulfide grease (**Figure 39**) and apply with a small hand held grease gun (**Figure 40**).

> NOTE: *Be sure to reinstall the protective cap to prevent the entry of dirt and moisture.*

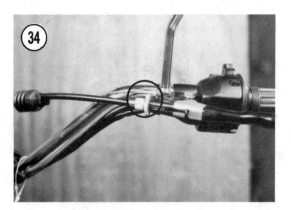

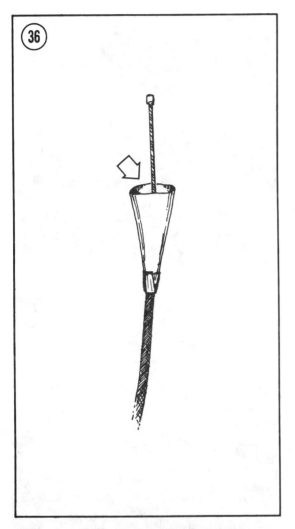

3

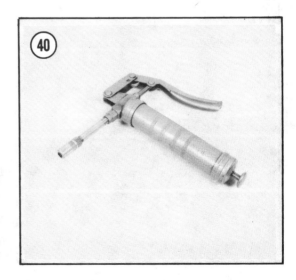

Drive Shaft Joint

Lubricate the drive shaft joint every 2,500 miles (4,000km), using the grease fitting located just forward of the final drive unit (**Figure 41**). Use molybdenum disulfide grease (type NLG 1-2M or equivalent, see **Figure 42**). Apply with a small handheld grease gun and fill with approximately 1 U.S. oz. (30cc).

Miscellaneous Lubrication Points

Lubricate the clutch lever (**Figure 43**), front brake lever (**Figure 44**), center and side stand pivot points (**Figure 45**), and footpeg pivot points (**Figure 46**). Use SAE 10W/30 motor oil.

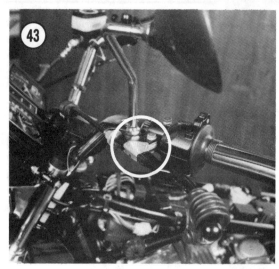

3

PERIODIC MAINTENANCE

Disc Brakes — Front and Rear

The hydraulic fluid level in the disc brake master cylinders should be checked every month or 1,000 miles and the brake pads should be checked for wear. Bleeding the hydraulic system, servicing the master cylinder, caliper, and disc and replacing brake pads are covered in Chapter Ten.

Disc Brake Fluid Level

1. Clean the outside of the reservoir cap thoroughly with a dry rag and remove the screws securing the cap. Remove the cap, gasket, and diaphragm (**Figure 47**).

2. The fluid level in the reservoir should be up to the upper level line. See **Figure 48** for the front brake and **Figure 49** for the rear brake. If it is necessary, correct the level by adding fresh brake fluid.

> WARNING
> *Use brake fluid clearly marked DOT 3 only and specified for disc brakes. Others may vaporize and cause brake failure.*

> CAUTION
> *Be careful not to spill brake fluid on painted or plated surfaces as it will destroy the surface. Wash immediately with soapy water and thoroughly rinse it off.*

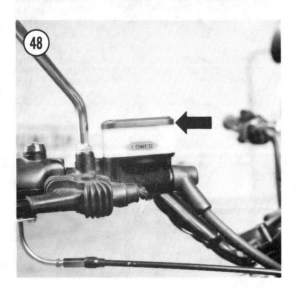

3. Reinstall the washer, diaphragm, and cap; make sure that the cap is screwed on tightly.

Disc Brake Lines

Check brake lines between the master cylinders and the brake calipers. If there is any leakage, tighten the connections and bleed the brakes as described under *Bleeding the System* in Chapter Ten. If this does not stop the leak, or if a line is obviously damaged, cracked, or chafed, replace the line and bleed the brake.

Brake lines should be replaced every four years or earlier if cracked or damaged.

Disc Brake Pad Wear

To check the amount of wear, open the indicator cap on both the front (**Figure 50**) and rear caliper assembly (**Figure 51**). If the pads are worn to the red line (**Figure 52**) they must be replaced. Inspect the pads for scoring, oil or grease on the pads, or uneven wear.

> NOTE: *Always replace both pads at the same time.*

If any of these conditions exist, replace the pads as described under *Brake Pad Replacement* in Chapter Ten.

Disc Brake Fluid Change

Every time you remove the reservoir cap a small amount of dirt and moisture enters the brake fluid. The same thing happens if a leak occurs, or any part of the hydraulic system is loosened or disconnected. Dirt can clog the system and cause unnecessary wear. Water in the fluid vaporizes at high temperatures, impairing the hydraulic action and reducing brake performance.

To maintain peak performance, change the brake fluid every 10,000 miles (16,000km) or two years.

1. Remove dust cap from the caliper bleeder valve. Connect a small clear hose to the valve and place the free end into a container. Refer to **Figure 53** for the front wheel and **Figure 54** for the rear wheel.

2. Open the bleeder valve with a wrench about ½ turn.

3. Squeeze the brake lever several times to force out as much brake fluid as possible. Close the bleeder valve.

> WARNING
> *Do not reuse brake fluid which has been drained from a brake system. Contaminated fluid can cause brake failure.*

4. Fill the reservoir with new brake fluid, install the cap and bleed the system as described under *Bleeding the System* in Chapter Ten.

> WARNING
> *Use brake fluid clearly marked DOT 3
> only. Others may vaporize and cause
> brake failure.*

Front Brake Lever Adjustment

The front brake lever should be adjusted every 2,500 miles (4,000km).

The clearance between the pads and discs are automatically adjusted as the pads wear. The free play of the hand grip should be maintained to avoid brake drag.

Loosen the locknut (A, **Figure 55**) and turn the adjusting screw (B, **Figure 55**) in or out. The proper amount of free play is 0.2-0.3 in. (5-8mm) measured at the end of the lever. After adjustment is completed, tighten the locknut.

Rear Brake Height and Free Play Adjustment

The rear brake should be adjusted every 2,500 miles (4,000km).

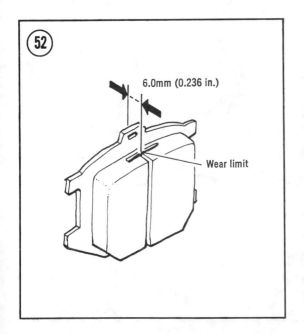

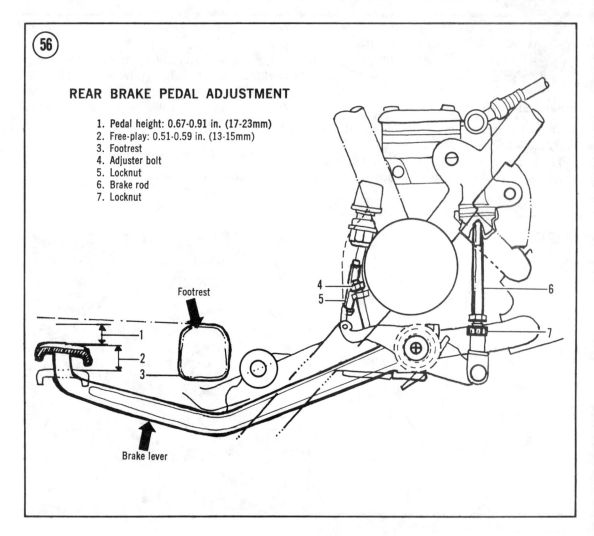

REAR BRAKE PEDAL ADJUSTMENT

1. Pedal height: 0.67-0.91 in. (17-23mm)
2. Free-play: 0.51-0.59 in. (13-15mm)
3. Footrest
4. Adjuster bolt
5. Locknut
6. Brake rod
7. Locknut

Footrest

4
5

6

1
2
3

7

Brake lever

Refer to **Figure 56** for this procedure.

1. Place the motorcycle on the centerstand.

2. Check to be sure that the brake pedal is in the "at-rest" position.

3. Loosen pedal height adjuster locknut (5).

4. Turn adjuster bolt (4) so that the top of pedal is approximately 0.67-0.91 in. (17-23mm) below the footrest.

5. Tighten the adjuster locknut (5).

6. Loosen the brake rod adjuster locknut (7).

7. Screw the brake rod (6) down and away from the master cylinder until there is noticeable free play.

8. Turn the brake rod (6) upward until it lightly touches the master cylinder. Back it off 1⅓ turns for the correct free play, approximately 0.50-0.59 in. (13-15mm).

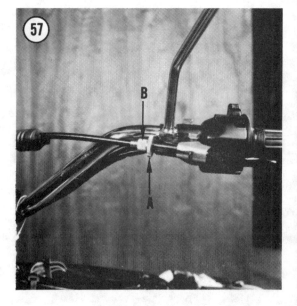

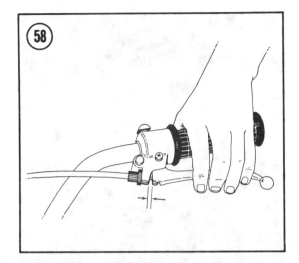

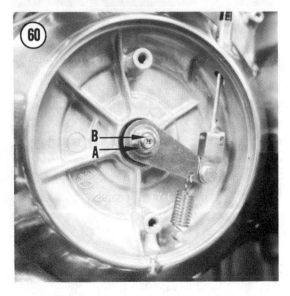

CAUTION
The punch mark on the brake rod (6) is not to show above the top surface of the adjuster locknut (7) after final tightening. If this happens, check for excessive brake pad wear and/or low brake fluid level in the master cylinder.

Clutch Adjustment

The clutch should be adjusted every 2,500 miles (4,000km).

There are two different clutch adjustment procedures. Both must be properly maintained for proper clutch operation. The cable adjustments take up slack, caused by cable stretching, thus maintaining sufficient free play. The mechanism adjuster, located within the clutch assembly maintains the correct amount of clutch throw, necessary for proper disengagement.

Cable Adjustment

Loosen the locknut (A, **Figure 57**) at the hand grip and rotate the adjuster (B, **Figure 57**) until there is 0.08-0.12 in. (2-3mm) of slack between the cable end of the lever and the amount (**Figure 58**). Tighten the locknut.

NOTE: *If proper amount of free play cannot be achieved by this adjustment and the mechanism adjustment, the cable has stretched to the point that it needs replacing. Refer to Clutch Cable Removal/Installation in Chapter Five for the complete procedure.*

Mechanism Adjustment

1. Remove the 2 screws (**Figure 59**) securing the mechanism cover and remove it.
2. Loosen the locknut (A, **Figure 60**) and turn the adjusting screw (B, **Figure 60**) in (clockwise) until it positively but lightly touches the clutch pressure plate.

NOTE: *The screw has an O-ring on it so there will be some resistance on it at all times while turning the screw. Be sure screw positively but lightly touches the clutch pressure plate.*

3. Back the screw out (counterclockwise) ¼ turn. Tighten the locknut, make sure the screw does not turn while tightening the locknut.

CAUTION
Do not squeeze the clutch lever until the clutch mechanism adjustment is completed. If squeezed, the steel balls in the adjuster housing will be dislocated. The clutch will not disengage if the balls are out of position. If this does happen, refer to **Clutch Mechanism** *in Chapter Five.*

After completing this adjustment, recheck the free play adjustment at the hand grip, readjust if necessary.

Road test the bike to make sure the clutch fully disengages when the lever is pulled in; if it does not, the bike will creep in gear when stopped. Also, make sure the clutch fully engages; if it does not, the clutch will slip, particularly when accelerating in high gear.

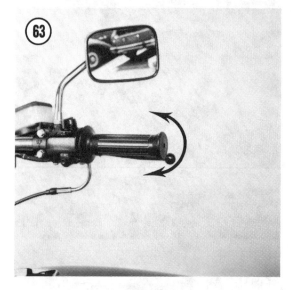

Air Cleaner

A clogged air cleaner can decrease the efficiency and life of the engine. Never run the bike without the air cleaner installed; even minute particles of dust can cause severe internal wear.

Air Cleaner
Removal/Installation

Remove the 4 wing nuts (**Figure 61**) securing the filter case. Remove case and pull element out of it (**Figure 62**). Remove most of the dirt and dust by tapping it, then apply compressed air to the outside surface of the element.

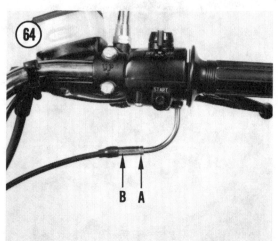

Inspect the element; make sure it is in good condition. Replace if necessary.

Insert the element into the case and install the case onto the air box.

Throttle Operation/Adjustment

The throttle grip should have 10-15° rotational play (**Figure 63**). Make sure there is free play in the cable so the carburetors will be able to close completely when the throttle is turned off. If adjustment is necessary, loosen the cable locknut (A, **Figure 64**) and turn the Adjuster (B, **Figure 64**) in or out to achieve the proper play. Tighten the locknut (A).

Check the throttle cable from grip to carburetors. Make sure they are not kinked or chafed. Replace them if necessary.

Make sure that the throttle grip rotates smoothly from fully closed to fully open. Check at center, full left, and full right position of the steering.

Fuel Shutoff Valve/Filter

Refer to Chapter Six for complete details on removal, cleaning, and installation of the fuel shutoff valves.

Wheel Bearings

The wheel bearings should be cleaned and repacked every 8,000 miles (12,000km). Refer to Chapters Eight and Nine for complete service procedures.

Cam Chain Tensioner Adjustment

The cam chain should be adjusted every 3,000 miles (4,800km) or when it becomes noisy.

1. Remove the spark plugs (this will make it easier to turn the engine over by hand).

2. Remove the screws securing the ignition cover (**Figure 65**).

3. Slowly rotate the crankshaft *clockwise* several times with a wrench on the nut at the left-hand end of the crankshaft (**Figure 66**). Stop the rotation when the "C" mark on the timing plate aligns with the stationary pointer (**Figure 67**).

4. Loosen the cam chain tensioner locknut (**Figure 68**) and loosen the stopper bolt. The tensioner will automatically adjust to the correct tension.

5. Tighten the stopper bolt to 4.3 ft.-lb. (6 N•m) and the locknut to 6.5 ft.-lb. (9 N•m).

6. Install the ignition cover and spark plugs.

Steering Head Adjustment Check

The steering head is fitted with two tapered bearings and should be checked for looseness at least every 2,500 miles (4,000km).

Jack up the bike so that the front wheel is off the ground.

Hold onto the front fork tubes and gently rock the fork assembly back and forth. If you can feel looseness refer to *Steering Head Adjustment* in Chapter Eight.

TUNE-UP

A complete tune-up should be performed every 4,000 miles (6,400km) of normal riding. More frequent tune-ups may be required if the bike is ridden primarily in stop-and-go traffic. The purpose of the tune-up is to restore the performance lost due to normal wear and deterioration of parts.

The spark plugs should be routinely replaced at every other tune-up or if the electrodes show signs of erosion. In addition, this is a good time to clean the air cleaner element. Have the new parts on hand before you begin.

Because different systems in an engine interact, the procedures should be done in the following order:

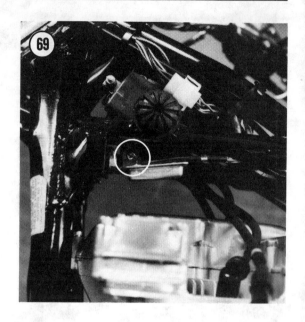

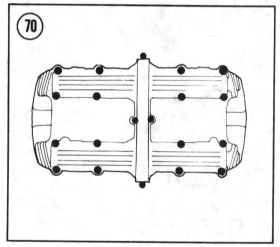

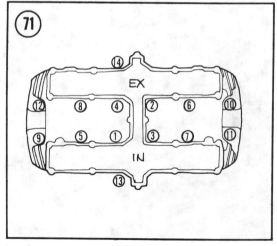

a. Tighten cylinder head nuts

b. Adjust valve clearances

c. Run a compression test

d. Check and adjust ignition timing

e. Synchronize carburetors and set idle speed

3

Cylinder Head Nuts

The engine must be at room temperature for this procedure.

1. Place the bike on the centerstand and remove the seat.

2. Turn the fuel shut-off valves to the ON or RESERVE position and remove the fuel lines to the carburetors. Also remove the vacuum lines to the intake manifolds.

3. Remove the bolt securing the fuel tank at the rear. Disconnect the fuel gauge electrical connector. Slide the tank to the rear and remove it.

4. Remove the ignition ballast resistor (**Figure 69**) from the frame.

5. Remove the 20 Allen bolts (**Figure 70**) securing the cam cover in place. Remove the cam cover and gasket.

6. Tighten the cylinder head nuts in the sequence shown in **Figure 71**. Tighten the upper 12 nuts to 25 ft.-lb. (35 N•m) and the 2 lower nuts, one in the front (**Figure 72**) and one in the rear (**Figure 73**) to 14.5 ft.-lb. (20 N•m).

NOTE: *Figures 72 and 73 are shown with surrounding components removed for clarity only, do not remove them.*

The fuel tank and cam cover should be left off at this time for the following procedures.

Valve Clearance Measurement

Valve clearance measurement must be made with the engine cool, at room temperature.

1. Remove the screws securing the ignition cover.

2. Remove the spark plugs (this makes it easier to turn over the engine by hand).

3. Rotate the cam by turning the crankshaft. Use a wrench on the nut located on the left-hand end of the crankshaft (**Figure 74**). In

order to obtain a correct measurement, the cam lobe must be directly opposite the lifter surface (**Figure 75**).

4. Insert a feeler gauge between the cam and the lifter surface (**Figure 76**). The clearance is measured correctly when there is a slight drag on the feeler gauge when it is inserted and withdrawn.

> NOTE: *The correct valve clearance is 0.21-0.24mm for the exhaust valve and 0.16-0.20mm for the intake valve. For best performance, adjust to the smaller dimension. Measure the valve clearance with a **metric** feeler gauge as it will be easier to calculate pad replacement described later in this section.*

5. To correct the clearance, the pad on top of the valve lifter must be replaced with one of the correct thickness. These pads are available in 25 different thicknesses from No. 200 (2.00mm) to No. 320 (3.20mm) in increments of 0.005mm. These pads are available from Yamaha dealers. The thickness is marked on the pad face that contacts the lifter body, not the cam.

6. Measure all valves and record the clearance. They must be measured very accurately.

Valve Clearance Adjustment

A special tool, Yamaha No. 90890-01245 Valve Adjusting Tool, **Figure 77** is necesary for this procedure. It is attached to the cylinder head, next to the valve being adjusted, with one

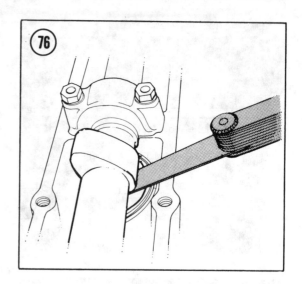

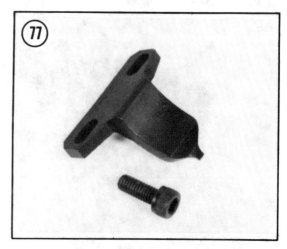

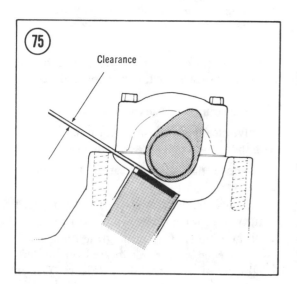

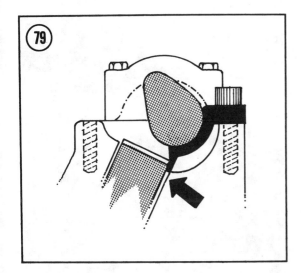

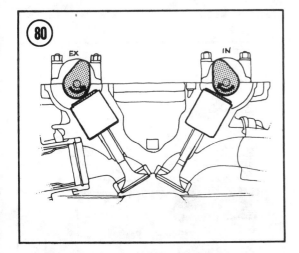

of the Allen bolts used to secure the cam cover (**Figure 78**). This tool holds the valve lifter down so the adjusting pad can be removed and replaced.

There is no set order to follow but it is suggested that you start with the No. 1 cylinder and do all exhaust valves, then return to No. 1 cylinder and do all intake valves.

3

1. The top of the valve lifter has a slot. This slot must be turned opposite the blade of the valve adjusting tool prior to installing the tool.

2. Turn the cam by rotating the crankshaft until the cam lobe fully depresses the valve lifter (valve in the completely open position).

3. Install the adjusting tool, using one of the cylinder head cover Allen bolts, as shown in **Figure 78**. Make sure the tool blade touches only the lifter body (**Figure 79**), not the pad.

CAUTION
Do not allow the cam lobe to come in contact with the valve adjusting tool as it may fracture the cylinder head. To avoid cam contact with the tool, rotate the cams as follows: intake — clockwise and exhaust — counterclockwise, as viewed from the left-hand side looking directly at No. 1 cylinder (Figure 80).

4. Carefully rotate the cam lobe off of the pad so it can be removed. Remove the pad from the lifter with a small screwdriver (**Figure 81**) and needle nose pliers (**Figure 82**), or magnetic tool. Turn the pad over and note the number.

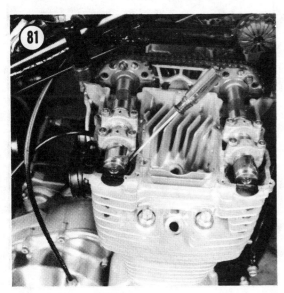

Cold - 130-137-133-155
Hot - 85 - 70-150-140

5. For correct pad selection proceed as follows:

> NOTE: *For calculations use the mid-point of the specified clearance tolerance — e.g., intake valve 0.1-0.22mm = **0.19mm** and exhaust valve 0.21 − 0.25mm = **0.23mm**.*

> NOTE: *The following numbers are for examples only.*

Examples:	**Intake**	**Exhaust**
Actual measured clearance	0.50mm	0.41mm
Subtract specified clearance	− 0.19	− 0.23
Equals excess clearance	= 0.31	= 0.18
Existing pad number	220	245
Add excess clearance	+ 31	+ 18
Equals new pad number	= 251	= 263
(round off to the nearest pad number)	250	265

6. Install the new pad into the lifter with the number facing down. Make sure the pad is positioned correctly into the lifter.

7. Carefully rotate the cam until the lobe comes in contact with the new pad and lifter. Remove the adjusting tool.

8. Rotate the cam a couple of times to make sure the pad has properly seated into the lifter.

9. Recheck valve clearance as described under *Valve Clearance Measurement.* If clearance is incorrect, repeat these steps until proper clearance is obtained.

10. Discard all old pads removed. They are worn and their numbers are no longer accurate.

11. Install the cam cover (make sure the gasket is in good condition; replace if necessary), air scoop, spark plugs, fuel tank, and seat.

Compression Test

Every 4,000 miles (6,400km) check cylinder compression. Record the results and compare them at the next 4,000 mile (6,400km) check. A running record will show trends in deterioration so that corrective action can be taken before complete failure.

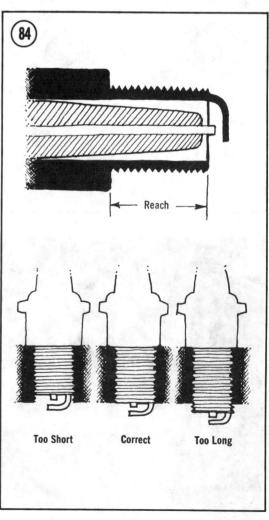

Reach

Too Short   Correct   Too Long

The results, when properly interpreted can indicate general cylinder, piston ring, and valve condition.

1. Warm the engine to normal operating temperature. Ensure that the choke valve and throttle valve are completely open.

2. Remove the spark plugs.

3. Connect the compression tester to one cylinder following manufacturer's instructions (**Figure 83**).

4. Have an assistant crank the engine over until there is no further rise in pressure.

5. Remove the tester and record the reading.

6. Repeat Steps 3-5 for the other cylinders.

When interpreting the results, actual readings are not as important as the difference between the readings. At sea level, the standard compression pressure is 142 psi (10 kg/cm²). Minimum pressure is 128 psi (9 kg/cm²) and maximum 156 psi (11 kg/cm²). Pressure should not vary from cylinder to cylinder by more than 14 psi (1 kg/cm²). Greater differences indicate worn or broken rings, leaky or sticky valves, blown head gasket or a combination of all.

If compression reading does not differ between cylinders by more than 10 psi, the rings and valves are in good condition.

If a low reading (10% or more) is obtained on one of the cylinders, it indicates valve or ring trouble. To determine which, pour about a teaspoon of engine oil through the spark plug hole onto the top of the piston. Turn the engine over once to clear some of the excess oil, then take another compression test and record the reading. If the compression returns to normal, the valves are good but the rings are defective on that cylinder. If compression does not increase, the valves require servicing. A valve could be hanging open but not burned or a piece of carbon could be on a valve seat.

Correct Spark Plug Heat Range

Spark plugs are available in various heat ranges, hotter or colder than plugs originally installed at the factory.

Select plugs of a heat range designed for the loads and temperature conditions under which the bike will run. Use of incorrect heat ranges can cause seized pistons, scored cylinder walls, or damaged piston crowns.

In general, use a hot plug for low speeds, low loads, and low temperatures. Use a cold plug for high speeds, high engine loads, and high temperatures.

In areas where seasonal temperature variations are great, the factory recommends a "two-plug system" — a cold plug for hard summer riding and a hot plug for slower winter operation.

The reach (length) of a plug is also important. A longer than normal plug could interfere with the valves and pistons causing permanent and severe damage. Refer to **Figure 84**.

The standard heat range spark plugs are NGK BP-6ES or Champion N-8Y.

Spark Plug Cleaning/Replacement

1. Grasp the spark plug leads (**Figure 85**) as near to the plug as possible and pull them off the plugs.

2. Blow away any dirt that has accumulated in the spark plug wells.

CAUTION
The dirt could fall into the cylinders when the plugs are removed, causing serious engine damage.

3. Remove spark plugs with a $^{13}/_{16}$ in. spark plug wrench.

NOTE: *If plugs are difficult to remove, apply penetrating oil, like WD-40 or Liquid Wrench, around base of plugs and let it soak in about 10-20 minutes.*

(87) **SPARK PLUG CONDITION**

NORMAL
• Identified by light tan or gray deposits on the firing tip.
• Can be cleaned.

GAP BRIDGED
• Identified by deposit buildup closing gap between electrodes.
• Caused by oil or carbon fouling. If deposits are not excessive, the plug can be cleaned.

OIL FOULED
• Identified by wet black deposits on the insulator shell bore electrodes.
• Caused by excessive oil entering combustion chamber through worn rings and pistons, excessive clearance between valve guides and stems, or worn or loose bearings. Can be cleaned. If engine is not repaired, use a hotter plug.

CARBON FOULED
• Identified by black, dry fluffy carbon deposits on insulator tips, exposed shell surfaces and electrodes.
• Caused by too cold a plug, weak ignition, dirty air cleaner, too rich a fuel mixture, or excessive idling. Can be cleaned.

LEAD FOULED
• Identified by dark gray, black, yellow, or tan deposits or a fused glazed coating on the insulator tip.
• Caused by highly leaded gasoline. Can be cleaned.

WORN
• Identified by severely eroded or worn electrodes.
• Caused by normal wear. Should be replaced.

FUSED SPOT DEPOSIT
• Identified by melted or spotty deposits resembling bubbles or blisters.
• Caused by sudden acceleration. Can be cleaned.

OVERHEATING
• Identified by a white or light gray insulator with small black or gray brown spots and with bluish-burnt appearance of electrodes.
• Caused by engine overheating, wrong type of fuel, loose spark plugs, too hot a plug, or incorrect ignition timing. Replace the plug.

PREIGNITION
• Identified by melted electrodes and possibly blistered insulator. Metallic deposits on insulator indicate engine damage.
• Caused by wrong type of fuel, incorrect ignition timing or advance, too hot a plug, burned valves, or engine overheating. Replace the plug.

4. Inspect spark plugs carefully. Look for plugs with broken center porcelain, excessively eroded electrodes, and excessive carbon or oil fouling. Replace such plugs. If deposits are light, plugs may be cleaned in solvent with a wire brush or cleaned in a special spark plug sandblast cleaner.

5. Gap plugs to 0.028-0.032 in. (0.7-0.8mm) with a wire feeler gauge. See **Figure 86**.

6. Install plugs with a new gasket. First, apply a small drop of oil to threads. Tighten plugs finger-tight, then tighten with a spark plug wrench an additional ½ turn. If you must reuse an old gasket, tighten only an additional ¼ turn.

> NOTE: *Do not overtighten. This will only squash the gasket and destroy its sealing ability.*

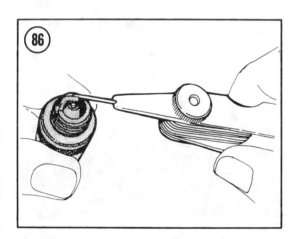

Reading Spark Plugs

Much information about engine and spark plug performance can be determined by careful examination of the spark plugs. This information is only valid after performing the following steps.

1. Ride bike a short distance at full throttle in any gear.

2. Turn off kill switch before closing throttle, and simultaneously, pull in clutch and coast to a stop.

3. Remove spark plugs and examine them. Compare them to **Figure 87**.

If the insulator is white or burned, the plug is too hot and should be replaced with a colder one.

A too-cold plug will have sooty deposits ranging in color from dark brown to black. Replace with a hotter plug and check for too-rich carburetion or evidence or oil blow-by at the piston rings.

If any one plug is found unsatisfactory, discard all four.

Ignition Timing

Timing is set by using a timing light and observing the alignment of the stationary pointer in relationship to the marks on the timing plate.

It is only necessary to check and adjust the timing on the No. 1 cylinder. Once it is adjusted correctly, the other three cylinders will automatically be correct.

> NOTE: *Before starting on this procedure, check all electrical connections related to the ignition system. Make sure all connections are tight and free of corrosion and that all ground connections are tight.*

1. Place the bike on the centerstand.

2. Connect a portable tachometer following the manufacturer's instructions. The bike's tach is not accurate enough in the low rpm range for this adjustment.

3. Connect a timing light to the No. 1 cylinder (left-hand side) following the manufacturer's instructions (**Figure 88**).

4. Start the engine and let it warm up to normal operating temperature. Let the engine idle (1,000 +/- 100 rpm) and aim the timing light toward the timing marks on the timing plate.

5. The stationary pointer should align with the "F" mark on the timing plate (A, **Figure 89**) if not, proceed as follows.

6. Shut off the engine and loosen the 2 pick-up base plate screws (B, **Figure 89**). Slightly rotate the plate in either direction. Tighten the screws. Restart the engine and recheck the timing. Continue this procedure until the timing marks align. Be sure 2 screws are tightened securely.

7. Disconnect and plug the vacuum hose to the vacuum advance mechanism (**Figure 90**). Increase engine speed to 5,200 rpm and check the alignment of the stationary pointer and 36° mark on the timing plate (**Figure 91**) except for special models, or 31° mark (**Figure 92**) for special models. If the idle speed timing is correct but the full advance is incorrect, refer to *Vacuum Advance Mechanism Inspection* in Chapter Seven.

Carburetor Idle Mixture

Idle mixture (**Figure 93**) is preset at the factory and it *is not to be reset*. This pertains to all four carburetors.

Carburetor Synchronization

Prior to synchronizing the carburetors, the ignition timing and valve clearance must be properly adjusted.

This procedure requires a special tool to measure the manifold vacuum for all four cylinders simultaneously.

1. Place the bike on the centerstand. Start the engine and let it reach normal operating temperature. Turn it off.

2. Remove the seat.

3. Remove the rear bolt securing the rear of the fuel tank and slightly elevate it to gain access to the vacuum connections and throttle adjusting screws of the inner two carburetors.

4. Except on special models, turn the fuel shutoff valve to the PRI position.

5. On special models, turn the fuel shutoff valve to the ON position.

6. Remove the vacuum lines from the No. 2 and 3 cylinder manifolds (A, **Figure 94**).

7. Remove the rubber caps (B, **Figure 94**) from the No. 1 and 4 cylinder manifolds.

8. Connect the vacuum lines from the synchronizing tool, following the manufacturer's instructions, to the manifolds.

9. Start the engine and let it warm up a little. Let the engine idle (approximately 1,100 rpm).

10. The carburetors are synchronized if all have the same gauge readings. If not, proceed as follows.

11. The No. 3 carburetor has no synchronizing screw and the other carburetor must be synchronized to it.

> NOTE: *The carburetors are numbered in the same sequence as the cylinders with No. 1 on the left-hand side and continuing with No. 2, 3, and 4 from left to right.*
>
> *The carburetors will be synchronized to each other in pairs. No. 1 and 2 to each other and No. 3 and 4 to each other. Then both set will be synchronized to each other.*

12. First, synchronize No. 1 carburetor to No. 2 by turning screw A, **Figure 95**. Turn the screw until the gauges going to each carburetor have the same reading.

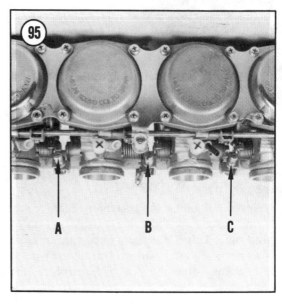

13. Second, synchronize No. 4 carburetor to No. 3 by turning screw C, **Figure 95**. Turn the screw until the gauges going to each carburetor have the same reading.

14. Now match the two sets by turning screw B, **Figure 95**. Turn the screw until the gauges from No. 1 and 2 match the one from No. 3. All gauges should now have the same reading; if not, repeat Steps 12-14 until they all match.

> NOTE: *Figure 95 is shown with the carburetor assembly removed for clarity only. Do not remove it.*

15. Remove the synchronizing tool hoses and install the vacuum lines and rubber caps (**Figure 94**).

Carburetor Idle Speed Adjustment

Before making this adjustment, the air cleaner must be clean, the carburetors must be synchronized and the engine must have adequate compression (see *Compression Test* in this chapter). Otherwise this procedure cannot be done properly.

1. Attach a portable tachometer following the manufacturer's instructions.

> NOTE: *The bike's tach is not accurate enough in the low rpm range for this adjustment.*

2. Start the engine and let it warm up to normal operating temperature.

3. Set the idle speed by turning the idle speed stop screw (**Figure 96**) in to increase or out to decrease idle speed.

> NOTE: *Figure 96 is shown with the carburetor assembly removed for clarity only.*

4. The correct idle speed is 950-1,050 rpm for Model E and 1,050-1,150 rpm for Models F and SF.

STORAGE

Several months of inactivity can cause serious problems and general deterioration of your bike. This is especially important in areas with extremely cold winters. During the winter, you should prepare your bike carefully for "hibernation."

Selecting a Storage Area

Most cyclists store their bikes in their home garage. If you do not have a garage, there are other facilities for rent or lease in most areas. When selecting an area, consider the following points.

1. The storage area must be dry; there should be no dampness or excessive humidity. A heated area is not necessary, but the area should be insulated to minimize extreme temperature variations.

2. Avoid buildings in industrial areas where factories are liable to emit corrosive fumes. Also avoid buildings near large bodies of salt water.

3. Avoid buildings with large window areas. If this is not possible, mask the window to keep direct sunlight off the bike.

4. Select an area where there is a minimum risk of fire, theft, or vandalism. Check with your insurance agent to make sure that your insurance covers the bike where it is stored.

Preparing Bike for Storage

Careful preparation will minimize deterioration and make it easier to restore the bike to service later. Use the following procedure.

1. Wash the bike completely. Make certain to remove any road salt which may have accumulated during the first weeks of winter. Wax all painted and polished surfaces, including any chromated areas.

2. Run the engine for 20-30 minutes to stabilize oil temperature. Drain oil, regardless of mileage since last oil change. Replace the oil filter and fill engine with normal quantity of fresh oil.

3. Remove battery and coat cable terminals with petroleum jelly. If there is evidence of acid spillage in the battery box, neutralize with baking soda, wash clean, and repaint the damaged area. Store the battery in a warm area and recharge it every 2 weeks.

4. Drain all gasoline from fuel tank, interconnecting hoses, and carburetors. Leave fuel petcock in the RESERVE position. As an alternative,

a fuel preservative may be added to the fuel. This preservative is available from many motorcycle shops and marine equipment suppliers.

5. Remove spark plugs and add a small quantity of oil to each cylinder. Turn the engine a few revolutions by hand to distribute the oil and install the spark plugs.

6. One additional safeguard for winter or prolonged storage is the Engine Cylinder Protector that screws into *each spark plug hole* (**Figure 97**). It dispenses a vapor into the cylinder, crankcase, carburetor and muffler which works against rust and acid damage. It is rated to be good for up to two years and is available from the Brookstone Company, 127 Vose Farm Road, Peterborough, New Hampshire 03458. The catalog number is 3304 — Engine Cylinder Protector, and retails for about $3.00 each plus

handling and postage. When this product is used on a multi-cylinder engine like the XS1100, you must install one in each cylinder.

7. Tie or tape a heavy plastic bag over the outlet of the mufflers to prevent the entry of moisture.

8. Check tire pressure. Move the machine to the storage area and store it up on blocks with the wheels off the ground.

After Storage

Before starting the engine after storage, remove the spark plugs, or cylinder protectors, and squirt a small amount of fuel into the cylinder to help remove the oil coating. Install the spark plug but do not connect the spark plug wires. Turn the engine over a few times, then reconnect the spark plug wires and start the engine.

NOTE: If you own a 1980 or 1981 model, first check the Supplement at the back of the book for any new service information.

CHAPTER FOUR

ENGINE

The engine is an air-cooled, four-stroke, in-line four-cylinder with chain driven double overhead camshafts. The counterbalanced crankshaft is supported by five main bearings, one of which is a special side thrust bearing.

> NOTE: *The engine in the XS1100 rotates* **clockwise,** *contrary to Yamaha engines of the past.*

The oil pump supplies oil under pressure throughout the engine and is driven by the driven gear on backside of the clutch housing.

This chapter provides complete service and overhaul procedures for the Yamaha XS1100. **Table 1** provides complete specifications for the engine. Although the clutch and transmission are mounted within the crankcase, they are covered separately in Chapter Five to simplify the presentation of this material.

Prior to removing the engine or any major assembly, clean the entire engine and frame with a good grade commercial degreaser, like Gunk Cycle Degreaser, or equivalent. It is easier to work on a clean engine and you will do a better job.

Make certain you have the necessary tools available, especially any special tools, and purchase any known faulty parts prior to disassembly. Also make sure you have a clean place to work.

It is a good idea to identify and mark parts as they are removed so that errors will be avoided during assembly and installation. Clean all parts thoroughly upon removal, then place them in trays or boxes together with their associated mounting hardware. Make certain all parts related to a particular cylinder, piston, connecting rod, and/or valve assembly are identified for installation in the proper place. Do not rely on memory alone as it may be days or weeks before you complete the job.

Torx bolts are used in several areas of the engine and require a special tool for removal. The size is T-30 and is available in an Allen wrench configuration or one similar to a screwdriver. This tool is shown in the text and they are manufactured by Proto and Apex tool companies. They are available from most large hardware, automotive, or motorcycle supply stores.

Refer to **Table 2** for torque specifications on all engine components.

Table 1   ENGINE SPECIFICATIONS

Item	Specification	Wear Limit
General		
Number of cylinders	4	—
Bore X stroke	2.815 x 2.701 in.	—
	(71.5 x 68.6mm)	
Displacement	67.25 cu. in. (1,102cc)	—
Compression ratio	9.2 to 1	—
Compression pressure		
Warm at sea level	142 ± 18 psi (10 ± 1 kg/cm^2)	—
Maximum difference between		
cylinders	—	14 psi (1 kg/cm^2)
Cylinders		
Bore	2.815 in. (71.5mm)	2.819 in. (71.6mm)
Out-of-round	—	0.004 in. (0.01mm)
Taper	—	0.002 in. (0.05mm)
Cylinder/piston clearance	0.0016-0.0018 in.	0.0039 in. (0.1mm)
	(0.040-0.045mm)	
Pistons		
Diameter	2.8130-2.8134 in.	—
	(71.45-71.46mm)	
Clearance in bore	0.0016-0.0018 in.	—
	(0.040-0.045mm)	
Piston rings		
Number per piston		
Compression	2	—
Oil control	1	—
Ring end gap		
Top/second	0.008-0.016 in.	0.039 in. (1.0mm)
	(0.2-0.4mm)	
Oil control (rails)	0.008-0.035 in.	0.059 in. (1.5mm)
	(0.2-0.9mm)	
Ring side clearance		
Top	0.0016-0.003 in.	—
	(0.04-0.08mm)	
Second	0.0012-0.0028 in.	—
	(0.03-0.07mm)	
Crankshaft		
Main bearing oil clearance	0.0014-0.0023 in.	—
	(0.035-0.059mm)	
Connecting rod oil clearance	0.0017-0.0025 in.	—
	(0.042-0.064mm)	
Main bearing runout	—	0.0016 in. (0.04mm)
Camshaft lobe height		
Intake	1.449 ± 0.002 in.	1.443 in. (36.65mm)
	(36.805 ± 0.05mm)	
Exhaust	1.429 ± 0.002 in.	1.423 in. (36.15mm)
	(36.305 ± 0.05mm)	
	(continued)	

Table 1   ENGINE SPECIFICATIONS (continued)

Item	Specification	Wear Limit
Camshaft-to-cap clearance	0.008-0.0021 in. (0.020-0.054mm)	0.006 in. (0.160mm)
Runout limit	—	0.004 in. (0.1mm)
Valves		
Valve stem clearance (cold)		
Intake	0.0004-0.0016 in. (0.010-0.040mm)	—
Exhaust	0.0010-0.022 in. (0.025-0.55mm)	—
Valve stem runout maximum	—	0.0012 in. (0.03mm)
Valve seat width	0.043 in. (1.1mm)	0.080 in. (2.0mm)
Valve springs		
Free length (inner)		
Intake and exhaust	1.402 in. (35.6mm)	—
Free length (outer)		
Intake and exhaust	1.571 in. (39.9mm)	—
Allowable tilt from vertical		
Intake	—	0.063 in. (1.6mm)
Exhaust	—	0.069 in. (1.75mm)

Table 2   ENGINE TORQUE SPECIFICATIONS

Item	Foot-Pounds (Ft.-lb.)	Newton Meters (N•m)
Cylinder head nuts		
Upper (12)	25	34
Lower (2)	14.5	20
Oil delivery pipe bolts	14.5	20
Camshaft bearing cap nuts	7.2	10
Camshaft sprocket bolts	14.5	20
Camshaft tensioner housing bolts	7.5	10
Tensioner bolt	4.3	6
Tensioner nut	6.5	9
Connecting rod cap nuts	28	39
Crankcase bolts		
6mm	8.7	12
8mm	17.4	24
Alternator rotor bolt	47	65
Secondary gear shaft nut	51	70
Middle gear housing bolts	16	22
Drive shaft coupling	79	110
Engine mounting bolts		
Front and rear through bolts	72	100
Mounting bracket bolts	48	67

4-STROKE OPERATING PRINCIPLES

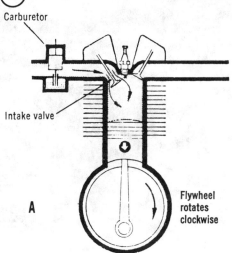

Carburetor

Intake valve

A

Flywheel rotates clockwise

As the piston travels downward, the exhaust valve is closed and the intake valve opens, allowing the new fuel/air mixture from the **carburetor** to be drawn into the cylinder. When the piston reaches the bottom of its travel (BDC), the **intake valve** closes and remains closed for the next revolution-and-a-half of the crankshaft.

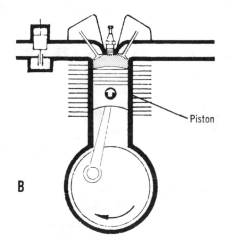

Piston

B

While the crankshaft continues to rotate, the **piston** moves upward, compressing the fuel/air mixture.

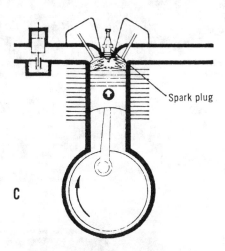

Spark plug

C

As the piston almost reaches the top of its travel, the **spark plug** fires, igniting the compressed fuel/air mixture. The piston continues to top dead center (TDC) and is pushed downward by the expanding gases.

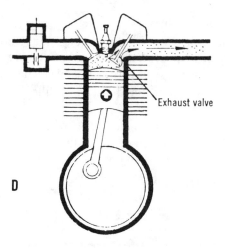

Exhaust valve

D

When the piston almost reaches BDC, the **exhaust valve** opens and remains open until the piston is near TDC. The upward travel of the piston causes the exhaust gases to be pushed out of the cylinder. After the piston has reached TDC, the exhaust valve closes and the cycle starts all over again.

ENGINE PRINCIPLES

Figure 1 explains how the engine works. This will be helpful when troubleshooting or repairing your engine.

SERVICING ENGINE IN FRAME

Many components can be serviced while the engine is mounted in the frame:

- a. Cylinder head and camshafts
- b. Cylinder and pistons
- c. Gearshift mechanism
- d. Clutch
- e. Carburetors
- f. Starter motor and gears
- g. Alternator and electrical systems

It is recommended that prior to engine removal and disassembly the majority of parts be removed from the engine while it is in the frame. By doing so it will reduce the weight of the engine considerably and make engine removal easier and safer.

ENGINE

Removal/Installation

1. Place the bike on the centerstand; remove the right- and left-hand side covers (**Figure 2**), and accessories such as fairings and crash bars.

2. Remove the seat and disconnect the battery negative lead.

3. Remove the rear bolt (A, **Figure 3**) securing the fuel tank. Disconnect the fuel gauge electrical connector (B, **Figure 3**).

4. Turn both fuel shutoff valves to the ON or RES position. Lift up on the rear of the tank and remove the fuel lines to the carburetors and vacuum lines to the intake manifolds.

5. Pull the fuel tank to the rear and remove it.

6. Drain the engine oil as described under *Changing Oil and Filter* in Chapter Three.

7. Disconnect the spark plug wires and tie them up out of the way.

8. Remove the exhaust system as described under *Exhaust System Removal/Installation* in Chapter Six.

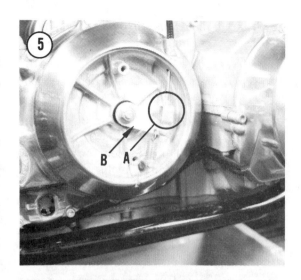

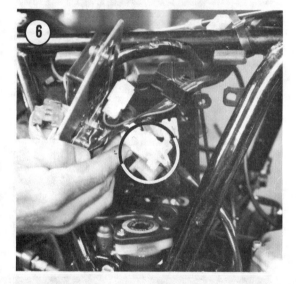

9. Remove the footpegs as described under *Footpeg Removal/Installation* in Chapter Eleven.

10. Loosen the clutch cable at the hand grip.

11. Remove the 2 screws (**Figure 4**) securing the clutch release mechanism cover and remove it.

12. Straighten out the retaining clip (A, **Figure 5**), push up on the release arm (B, **Figure 5**) and remove the cable from the arm. Remove the cable from the side cover.

13. Remove the carburetor assembly as described under *Carburetor Removal/Installation* in Chapter Six.

14. Remove the electrical leads from the alternator to the electrical connector (**Figure 6**).

15. Remove the cylinder head and cylinder as described under *Cylinder Removal/Installation* in this chapter.

16. Remove the ignition advance assembly as described under *Ignition Advance Removal/Installation* in Chapter Seven.

17. Remove the gearshift mechanism as described under *Shift Mechanism Removal/Installation* in Chapter Five.

18. Remove the 3 bolts (**Figure 7**) securing the starter motor cover and remove it.

19. Carefully pull the motor to the left and disengage the gears.

20. Pull back on the rubber boot and disconnect the electrical wire (**Figure 8**) from the motor and remove the motor.

21. Remove the clutch assembly as described under *Clutch Removal/Installation* in Chapter Five.

22. Remove the coil spring retainer on the front of the drive shaft coupling rubber boot.

23. Pull back the rubber boot and remove the four bolts (A, **Figure 9**) securing the drive shaft coupling.

> NOTE: *Have an assistant apply the rear brake to keep the shaft from turning.*

24. Remove the engine ground strap (B, **Figure 9**).

25. Take a final look all over the engine to make sure everything has been disconnected.

> NOTE: *Place wooden blocks under the crankcase to support the engine after mounting bolts have been removed.*

26. Loosen all engine mounting bolts one to two turns only. Remove the front upper through bolt (A, **Figure 10**) from the right-hand side. Remove the 2 lower bolts and nuts (B, **Figure 10**). Remove the bolts (C, **Figure 10**) securing the engine mounting brackets to the frame and remove them.

27. Withdraw the rear through bolt (**Figure 11**) from the right-hand side.

28. Have an assistant help you remove the engine from the frame through the right-hand side.

29. Install by reversing the removal steps.

> NOTE: *Due to the weight of the complete engine assembly it is suggested that all components removed in the preceding procedure be left off until the crankcase and middle gear assembly are reinstalled into the frame. If you choose to install a completed engine assembly it requires a **minimum of three people**. It must be installed into the frame from the right-hand side and the oil filter housing must be removed.*

30. After the engine is positioned correctly, install the rear through-bolt from the right-hand side and install the 2 front bolts and plates. Start the nuts but *do not tighten now*.

31. Install the 4 bolts securing the drive shaft coupling and tighten them evenly in two stages to 79 ft.-lb. (110 N•m).

32. Tighten the front and rear through-bolt nuts to 72 ft.-lb. (100 N•m) and the front mounting brackets and lower mounting bolts and nuts to 48 ft.-lb. (67 N•m).

33. Fill the crankcase with the recommended type and quantity of engine oil. Refer to Chapter Three.

34. Start the engine and check for leaks.

CYLINDER HEAD

Removal

The cylinder head can be removed with the engine in the frame.

1. Place the bike on the centerstand; remove the right- and left-hand side covers, and accessories such as fairings and crash bars.

2. Remove the seat and disconnect the battery negative led.

3. Disconnect the spark plug wires (**Figure 12**) and tie them up and out of the way.

4. Remove the rear bolt (A, **Figure 13**) securing the fuel tank. Disconnect the fuel gauge electrical connector (B, **Figure 13**).

5. Turn both fuel shutoff valves to the ON or RES position.

6. Lift up on the rear of the tank and remove the fuel lines to the carburetors and the vacuum lines to the intake manifolds (**Figure 14**).

7. Pull the fuel tank to the rear and remove it.

8. Remove the exhaust system as described under *Exhaust System Removal/Installation* in Chapter Six.

9. Remove the carburetor assembly as described under *Carburetor Assembly Removal/Installation* in Chapter Six.

19. Remove the upper and lower union bolts **(Figure 24)** securing the oil pipe and remove it. Note the location of the copper washers — do not lose them.

20. Remove the valve lifters and pads at this time to avoid the accidental mix up if they should come out while removing the head. Remove them one cylinder at a time with a suction cup tool **(Figure 25)** and place them into a container (like an egg carton, see **Figure 26**) marked with the specific cylinder and intake

and exhaust. No. 1 cylinder is on the left-hand side.

CAUTION
The lifters must be reinstalled into their original cylinder positions upon assembly.

21. Remove the 14 cylinder head nuts and washers. Loosen all nuts ½ turn in the sequence

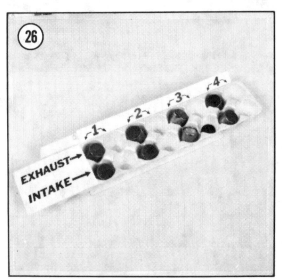

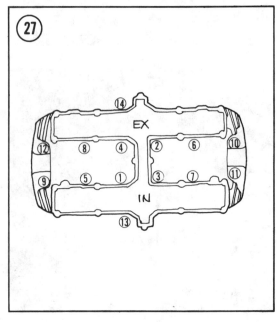

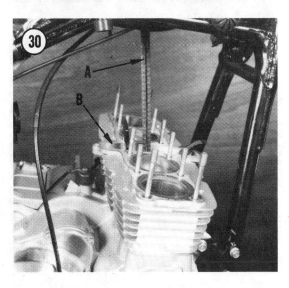

shown in **Figure 27**. Do not forget the No. 13 nut (**Figure 28**) and No. 14 nut (**Figure 29**) under the front and rear of the head.

22. Loosen the head by tapping around the perimeter with a rubber or plastic mallet. If necessary, *gently* pry the head loose with a broad-tipped screwdriver only in the ribbed areas of the fins.

CAUTION
Remember the cooling fins are fragile and may be damaged if tapped or pryed on too hard. Never use a metal hammer.

NOTE: *Sometimes it is possible to loosen the head with engine compression. Rotate the engine with the kickstarter (make sure the spark plugs are installed but the wires are not attached). As the pistons reach* TDC *on the compression stroke, they will pop the head loose.*

23. Remove the head by pulling straight up and off the cylinder studs. Tie the cam chain up to the frame with a piece of wire (A, **Figure 30**). Place a clean shop rag into the cam chain opening in the cylinder (B, **Figure 30**) to prevent the entry of foreign matter.

Inspection

1. Remove all traces of gasket from head and cylinder mating surface.

2. Without removing the valves, remove all carbon deposits from the combustion chambers with a wire brush. A blunt screwdriver or chisel may be used if care is taken not to damage the head, valves, and spark plug threads.

3. After all carbon is removed from combustion chambers and valve intake and exhaust ports, clean the entire head in solvent.

4. Clean away all carbon on the piston crowns. Do not remove carbon ridge at the top of the cylinder bore.

5. Check for cracks in the combustion chamber and exhaust ports. A cracked head must be replaced.

6. After the head has been thoroughly cleaned, place a straightedge across the gasket surface at

several points **(Figure 31)**. Measure warp by inserting a feeler gauge between the straightedge and cylinder head at each location. There should be no warpage; if a small amount is present, it can be resurfaced by a Yamaha dealer or qualified machine shop.

7. Check the cam cover mating surface using the procedure in Step 6. There should be no warpage.

8. Check the condition of the valves and valve guides as described under *Valve and Valve Components* in this chapter.

9. Check condition of the end seals **(Figure 32)**. Make sure they fit tight; if not, replace them.

Installation

1. Install a new head gasket (A, **Figure 33**).

2. Install a new cam chain cavity seal with the tabs (B, **Figure 33**) facing down.

3. Install the locating dowels **(Figure 34)** on the 2 rear outside studs.

4. Rotate the engine until No. 1 cylinder (left-hand side) is at top dead center (TDC).

> NOTE: *The cylinder is at TDC when the "T" mark on the timing plate aligns with the stationary pointer (Figure 35) and the piston is at its uppermost point of travel.*

5. Carefully slide the cylinder head over the studs and onto the cylinder.

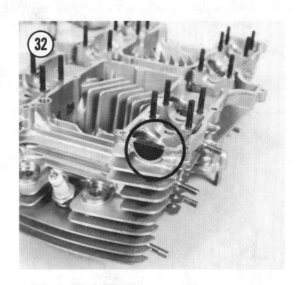

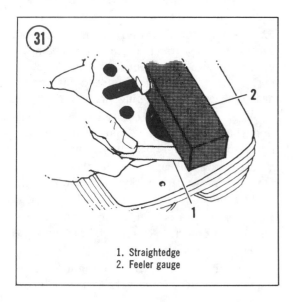

1. Straightedge
2. Feeler gauge

6. Lightly oil the stud threads and install the 12 washers and acorn nuts; tighten finger-tight only.

7. Install the 2 nuts and washers under the front and rear of the head. See **Figures 28 and 29**.

8. Tighten all 12 upper acorn nuts in the sequence shown in **Figure 27**, in 2 stages. In the first stage, tighten them to 11 ft.-lb. (15 N•m) and in the second to 25 ft.-lb. (34 N•m). Tighten the lower nuts to 7 ft.-lb. (9 N•m) and then to 14.5 ft.-lb. (20 N•m).

9. Install the oil delivery pipe. Install new copper washers and make sure they are placed on each side of each end of the pipe. The larger bolt with the dished head is to be installed at the top. Tighten the bolts to 14.5 ft.-lb. (20 N•m).

10. Install the valve lifters and pads.

NOTE: *They must be installed into their original positions (Figure 26) as removed in Step 20 in the removal sequence.*

11. Lubricate all cam bearing surfaces in the cylinder head (**Figure 36**) and bearing caps with assembly oil.

12. Make sure the No. 1 cylinder is still at TDC as set up in Step 4.

13. Slide the cam chain sprockets onto each cam and install the exhaust cam (EX) and intake cam (IN) through the cam chain. Refer to the identification marks (**Figure 37**) cast into them. Be sure to install the exhaust cam toward the front of the bike.

NOTE: *Install the cams with the sprocket flanges toward the left-hand side and the sprockets on the right-hand side (Figure 38).*

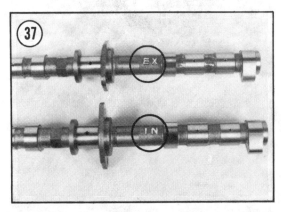

14. Temporarily position both cams in the head so that the dot on the cam boss, next to the center cam bearing cap, is almost straight up.

15. Install the intake cam bearing caps, washers, and nuts in the correct number sequence. From left to right (intake cam): I1, I2, I3, I4, and I5 with the arrows pointing to the right (**Figure 39**). Tighten the nuts only finger-tight.

> NOTE: *Be sure to install the 2 locating dowels on the center bearing cap (No. 3) studs prior to installing the cap.*

CAUTION
The bearing caps must be installed correctly as they were matched and machined together with the cylinder head at the time of manufacture.

16. Repeat Step 15 for the exhaust cam. Make sure the bearing caps are installed in the correct sequence. From left to right (exhaust cam): E1, E2, E3, E4, and E5.

> NOTE: *Don't forget to install the 2 locating dowels on the center bearing cap studs.*

17. Tighten the nuts working from the center toward the outside in the following order: No. 3, 4, 2, 5, and 1 for both cams. Tighten the nuts gradually in 2 stages to a final torque of 7.2 ft.-lb. (10 N•m).

18. Carefully rotate each cam slightly, with an open end wrench, until the dot on the cam aligns with the arrow (A, **Figure 40**) on the center bearing cap.

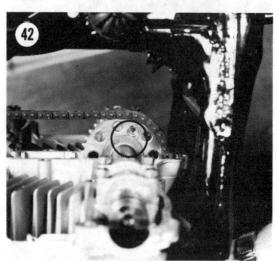

CAUTION
Extreme care must be taken when rotating the cam using the hex shoulder (B, Figure 40) on each cam. Make sure the open end wrench does not come in contact with the cylinder head as it may fracture it. Also do not rotate either cam more than 1/8 turn or valves and pistons may be damaged.

19. Carefully lift the cam chain off the intake cam sprocket. Make sure it properly engages with the sprocket on the crankshaft. Align the holes in the sprocket with the holes in the cam flange. Pull up on the chain to remove any slack and place the chain onto the sprocket.

20. Repeat for the exhaust cam.

21. Hold onto each sprocket and chain and place them up onto the shoulder on each cam.

Maintain tension on the cam chain between the *crankshaft and intake cam sprocket.* Slightly rotate the sprockets to align them with the bolt holes.

NOTE: *Make sure that the cam chain rollers are centered in both the front and rear chain tensioner slippers located in the cylinder chain cavity.*

22. Install one bolt into the intake cam sprocket, only finger-tight at this time.

CAUTION
The cam sprocket bolts are specially hardened shoulder bolts. Use only these specified for this one; substitution of bolts of lesser quality may cause severe engine damage if they break or work loose.

23. Push in on the cam chain with your finger (**Figure 41**) through the tensioner hole in the cylinder. This will help align the bolt hole in the exhaust sprocket (**Figure 42**). Install one bolt; see CAUTION after Step 22.

24. Rotate the crankshaft *clockwise* (**Figure 43**) approximately 45° and align the "C" mark on the timing plate with the fixed pointer (**Figure 44**).

25. Loosen the cam chain tensioner holding bolt, compress the tensioner and tighten the bolt to lock it in the retracted position.

26. Push in again on the chain with your finger to make sure the chain is properly seated.

27. Install the cam chain tensioner with a new gasket (**Figure 45**). Tighten the 2 bolts to 7.5 ft.-lb. (10 N•m).

28. Loosen the holding bolt on the chain tensioner. There should be an audible click as the tensioner is released and comes in contact with the chain. Make sure it does move into the chain; if not, remove it and correct any binding. Tighten the holding bolt to 4.3 ft.-lb. (6 N•m) and the locknut to 6.5 ft.-lb. (9 N•m).

29. Rotate the crankshaft *clockwise* (**Figure 43**) 2 complete rotations and align the "T" mark on the timing plate with the fixed pointer (**Figure 35**). Check the alignment of the dot on both cams to the arrow on the center caps (**Figure 46**).

> CAUTION
> *If there is any binding while rotating the crankshaft, **stop**. Determine the cause before proceeding.*
>
> *If one or both cams are misaligned when the "T" mark is aligned, disassemble and repeat Steps 18-28 until all three alignments are correct. This alignment is absolutely necessary for correct valve timing and to prevent expensive damage to the pistons and valve train.*

30. Rotate the crankshaft *clockwise* and install the 2 remaining cam sprocket bolts and tighten to 14.5 ft.-lb. (20 N•m).

31. Install the cam chain guide (**Figure 47**).

32. Make sure the end seals are in place (**Figure 48**).

33. Continue installation by reversing *Cylinder Head Removal*, Steps 1-10.

34. Adjust the valves as described under *Valve Adjustment* in Chapter Three.

35. Start the engine and check for leaks.

VALVES AND VALVE COMPONENTS

Refer to **Figure 49** for this procedure.

1. Remove the cylinder head as described under *Cylinder Head Removal* in this chapter.

2. Remove the valve lifters and adjustment pads.

3. Compress springs with a valve spring compression tool (**Figure 50**); remove the valve keepers and release compression.

> NOTE: *To prevent scratching the lifter cavity walls, wrap the surface of the valve removal tool with masking tape (Figure 51).*

4. Remove the valve spring caps, springs, and valves (**Figure 52**).

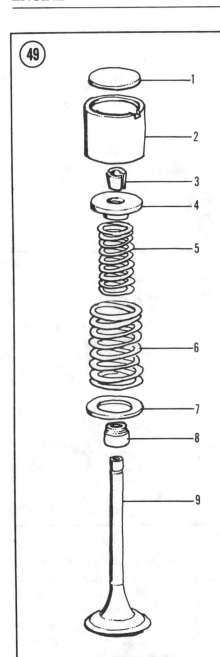

VALVE ASSEMBLY

1. Adjuster pad
2. Valve lifter
3. Keepers
4. Spring collar
5. Inner spring
6. Outer spring
7. Seat
8. Oil seal
9. Valve—intake and exhaust

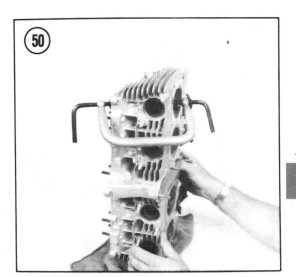

4

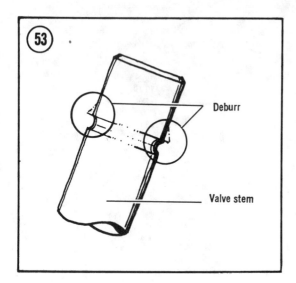

Deburr

Valve stem

CAUTION
Remove any burrs from the valve stem
grooves before removing the valve
(Figure 53). Otherwise the valve guides
will be damaged.

Inspection

1. Clean valves with a wire brush and solvent.
2. Inspect the contact surface of each valve for burning (**Figure 54**). Minor roughness and pitting can be removed by lapping the valve as described under *Valve Lapping* in this chapter. Excessive unevenness to the contact surface is an indication that the valve is not serviceable. The contact surface of the valve may be ground on a valve grinding machine, but it is best to replace a burned or damaged valve with a new one.
3. Inspect the valve stems for wear and roughness and measure the vertical runout of the valve stem as shown in **Figure 55**. The runout should not exceed 0.0012 in. (0.03mm).
4. Measure valve stems for wear (**Figure 56**). Compare with specifications in **Table 1** at the end of the chapter.
5. Remove all carbon and varnish from the valve guides with a stiff spiral wire brush.
6. Insert each valve in its guide. Hold the valve just slightly off its seat and rock it sideways. If it rocks more than slightly, the guide is probably worn and should be replaced. As a final check, take the head to a dealer and have the valve guides measured.

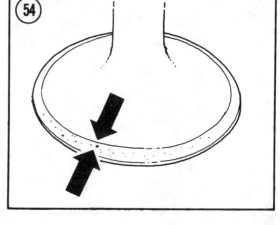

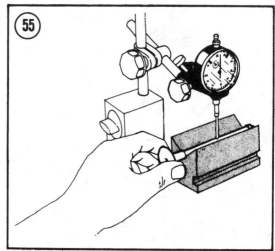

7. Measure the valve spring heights with a vernier caliper (**Figure 57**). All should be of length specified in **Table 1** with no bends or other distortion. Replace defective springs.
8. Measure the tilt of all valve springs as shown in **Figure 58**. Compare with specifications shown in **Table 1**.
9. Check the valve spring retainer and valve keepers. If they are in good condition, they may be reused.
10. Inspect valve seats. If worn or burned, they must be reconditioned. This could be performed by your dealer or local machine shop, although the procedure is described later in this section. Seats and valves in near-perfect condition can be reconditioned by lapping with fine carborundum paste. Lapping, however, is always inferior to precision grinding.

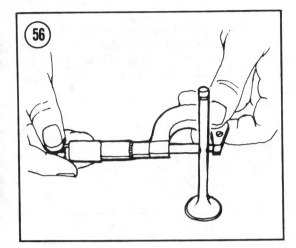

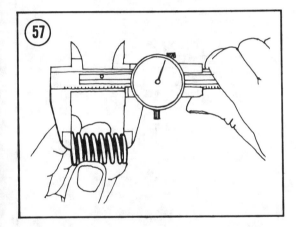

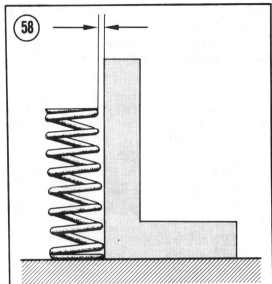

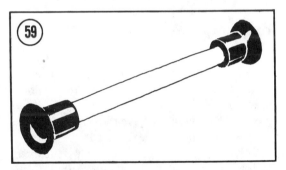

Installation

1. Coat the valve stems with molybdenum disulphide paste and insert into cylinder head.

2. Install bottom spring retainers and new seals.

3. Install valve springs with the narrow pitch end (end with coils closest together) facing the head, and install upper valve spring retainers.

4. Push down on upper valve spring retainers with the valve spring compressor and install valve keepers.

Valve Guide Replacement

When guides are worn so that there is excessive stem-to-guide clearance or valve tipping, they must be replaced. Replace all, even if only one is worn. This job should only be done by a Yamaha dealer as special tools are required.

Valve Seat Reconditioning

This job is best left to your dealer or local machine shop. They have the special equipment and knowledge for this exacting job. You can still save considerable money by removing the cylinder head and taking just the head to the shop.

Valve Lapping

Valve lapping is a simple operation which can restore the valve seal without machining if the amount of wear or distortion is not too great.

1. Coat the valve seating area in the head with a lapping compound such as Carborundum or Clover Brand.

2. Insert the valve into the head.

3. Wet the suction cup of the lapping stick (**Figure 59**) and stick it onto the head of the valve. Lap the valve to the seat by rotating the

lapping stick in both directions. Every 5 to 10 seconds, rotate the valve 180° in the seat, continue lapping until the contact surfaces of the valve and the valve seat are a uniform grey. Stop as soon as they are, to avoid removing too much material.

4. Thoroughly clean the valves and cylinder head in solvent to remove all grinding compound. Any compound left on the valves or the cylinder head will end up in the engine and will cause damage.

After the lapping has been completed and the valve assemblies have been reinstalled into the head the valve seal should be tested. Check the seal of each valve by pouring solvent into each of the intake and exhaust ports. There should be no leakage past the seat. If fluid leaks past any of the seats, disassemble that valve assembly and repeat the lapping procedure until there is no leakage.

Valve Lifters and Pads

Inspect the sides of the lifter body for scratches and scoring. If it is damaged in any way, inspect the lifter cavity in the cylinder head in which it travels. If the damage is severe the cylinder head may have to be replaced. The lifter will also have to be replaced.

Check the top ridge that retains the lifter pad. Make sure the pad seats correctly into the recess but is not too loose. Replace any parts as necessary.

CAUTION
The lifters and pads must be reinstalled into their original cylinder positions upon assembly. Refer to Cylinder Head Removal Step No. 20 in this chapter.

CAMSHAFTS

Removal/Installation

The camshafts can be removed with the engine in the frame.

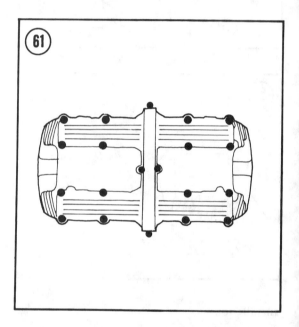

1. Place the bike on the centerstand. Remove the right- and left-hand side covers, and accessories such as fairings and crash bars.

2. Remove the seat and disconnect the battery negative lead (**Figure 60**).

3. Disconnect the spark plug wires and tie them up out of the way.

4. Remove the rear bolt securing the fuel tank. Disconnect the fuel gauge electrical connector.

5. Turn both fuel shutoff valves to the ON or RES position.

6. Lift up on the rear of the tank and remove the fuel lines to the carburetor and to the intake manifolds.

7. Pull the tank to the rear and remove it.

8. Remove the 20 Allen bolts (**Figure 61**) securing the cam cover and remove it and the gasket.

9. Remove the 2 Allen bolts (**Figure 62**) securing the cam tensioner and remove it.

10. Remove the ignition cover (**Figure 63**) and rotate the crankshaft clockwise with a 19mm wrench on the nut (A, **Figure 64**) until the No. 1 cylinder (left-hand side) is at top dead center (TDC) on the compression stroke.

NOTE: *Figures 61-69 are shown with the exhaust system and carburetor assembly removed. It is not necessary to remove them for this procedure.*

NOTE: *The cylinder is at TDC when the "T" mark on the timing plate aligns with the stationary pointer (B, Figure 64) and both valves are completely closed on the compression stroke (cam lobes off both valve lifters).*

11. Remove the cam chain guide (A, **Figure 65**).

12. Remove the 2 exposed cam sprocket bolts (B, **Figure 65**).

13. Rotate the engine 180° *clockwise* and remove the 2 remaining sprocket bolts. *Do not rotate either cam.*

CAUTION
Severe damage can be caused to the cams, valves, cylinder head, and pistons if the cams are rotated after the sprocket bolts have been removed.

14. Slide the cam sprockets to the right (**Figure 66**) off the cam shoulders.

15. Remove all nuts, flat washers, and bearing caps (**Figure 67**). The bearing caps must be loosened, then removed, working from the center toward the outside in the following order: No. 3, 4, 2, 5, 1.

> NOTE: *The bearing caps are numbered 1-5 from left to right, and with an I (intake) or E (exhaust).*

16. Carefully lift out the cams, one at a time (**Figure 68**).

> NOTE: *Tie up the chain to the frame with a piece of wire (**Figure 69**) to prevent it from falling into the crankcase.*

17. Place a clean shop cloth into the cam chain cavity to prevent the entry of foreign matter.

18. Install the camshafts. Perform Steps 11-35, *Cylinder Head Installation* in this chapter.

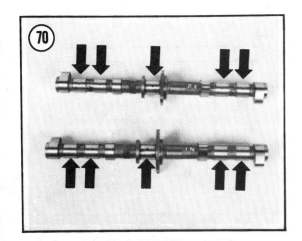

Camshaft Inspection

1. Check the bearing journals for wear and scoring (**Figure 70**).

2. Check cam lobes for wear. The lobes should not be scored and the edges should be square. Slight damage may be removed with a silicon carbide oilstone. Use No. 100-120 grit initially, then polish with a No. 280-320 grit.

3. Even though the cam lobe surface appears to be satisfactory, with no visible signs of wear, they must be measured with a micrometer as shown in **Figure 71**. Replace the shaft(s) if worn beyond the service limits (measurements less than those given in **Table 1**).

4. Check the bearing bores in the cylinder head and bearing caps. They should not be scored or excessively worn.

5. Inspect the sprockets for wear, replace if necessary.

6. Check the condition of the chain guide (**Figure 72**). If it is worn or disintegrating it must be replaced. This may indicate a worn chain or improper chain adjustment.

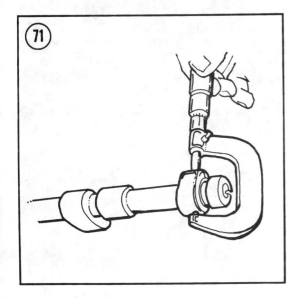

Camshaft Bearing Clearance

This procedure requires the use of a Plastigage set.

1. Rotate the engine until No. 1 cylinder (left-hand side) is at top dead center (TDC).

> NOTE: *The cylinder is at* TDC *when the "T" mark on the timing plate aligns with the stationary pointer (**Figure 73**) and the piston is at its uppermost point of travel.*

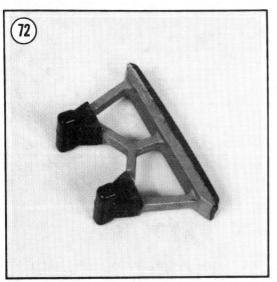

2. Install both cams into position in the head without the chain sprockets seated on the cam shoulders.

> NOTE: *Position them so that the dot on the cam boss, next to the center cam bearing cap, is almost straight up.*

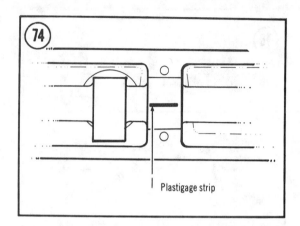

Plastigage strip

3. Place a strip of Plastigage between the cam and cam bearing cap, lengthwise with the cam, as shown in **Figure 74**.

4. Install the cam bearing caps in the correct number sequence. From left to right: E1-5 (exhaust cam) and I1-5 (intake cam) with the arrows pointing toward the right-hand side (**Figure 75**).

5. Install all flat washers and nuts to the studs and tighten them working from the center toward the outside in the following order: No. 3, 4, 2, 5, and 1 for both cams. Tighten the nuts gradually in 2 stages to a final torque of 7.2 ft.-lb. (10 N•m).

> NOTE: *Do not rotate either cam with the Plastigage material in place.*

6. Remove the bearing caps in the reverse order they were installed.

7. Measure the width of the flattened Plastigage according to manufacturer's instructions (**Figure 76**).

8. If the clearance exceeds the wear limit in **Table 1**, measure the cam bearing journals with a micrometer and compare to the wear limits in **Table 1**. If the cam bearing is less than the dimension specified, replace the cam. If the cam is within specifications, the cylinder head must be replaced.

Chain Guide

Check the condition of the top surface of the guide. If it is worn or disintegrating it must be replaced. This may indicate a worn chain or improper chain adjustment.

If its condition is very bad, check the condition of the two vertical chain tensioner slippers by looking into the chain cavity with a flashlight. If they look bad they should be replaced.

Remove the cylinder as described under *Cylinder Removal* in this chapter. Remove the 4

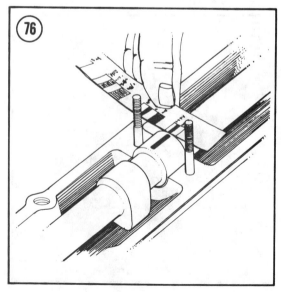

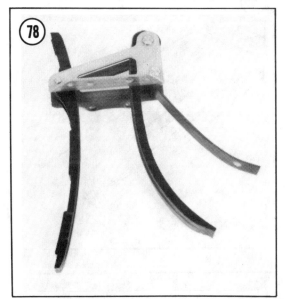

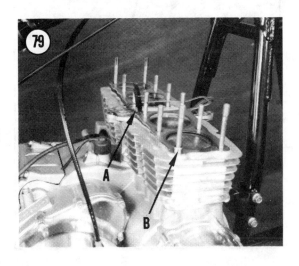

bolts and washers (**Figure 77**) securing the assembly and remove it. Inspect the condition carefully of all parts (**Figure 78**) after removal and replace if necessary.

Camshaft Chain Replacement

The chain is continuous with no master link. In order to replace the chain it is necessary to split the crankcase halves. Refer to *Crankcase Disassembly* in this chapter.

4

CYLINDER

Removal

1. Remove the cylinder head as described under *Cylinder Head Removal/Installation* in this chapter.

2. Remove the head gasket (A, **Figure 79**), cam chain cavity seal, and 2 locating dowels (B, **Figure 79**).

3. Loosen the cylinder by tapping around the perimeter with a rubber or plastic mallet. If necessary, *gently* pry the cylinder loose with a broad-tipped screwdriver only in the area of the 2 pry points (**Figure 80**).

CAUTION
Remember cooling fins are fragile and may be damaged if tapped or pryed on too hard. Do not use a metal hammer.

4. Pull the cylinder straight up and off the pistons and cylinder studs.

> NOTE: *Be sure to keep the cam chain wired up to prevent it from falling into the left-hand crankcase cover (A, Figure 81).*

5. Install a piston holding fixture under the 2 pistons (B, **Figure 81**) protruding out of the crankcase opening.

> NOTE: *These fixtures may be purchased or homemade of wood. See Figure 82 for dimensions.*

Inspection

1. Measure the cylinder bores, with a cylinder gauge (**Figure 83**) or inside micrometer at the points shown in **Figure 84**.

2. Measure in 2 axes — in line with the wrist pin and at 90° to the pin. If the taper or out-of-round is greater than 0.0004 in. (0.01mm), the cylinders must be rebored to the next oversize and new pistons and rings installed. Rebore all cylinders even though only one may be faulty.

> NOTE: *The new pistons should be obtained first before the cylinders are bored so that pistons can be measured; slight manufacturing tolerances must be taken into account to determine the actual size and the working clearance. Piston-to-cylinder clearance should be 0.0016-0.0018 in. (0.040-0.045mm).*

3. Check the cylinder walls for scratches; if evident the cylinders should be rebored.

> NOTE: *The maximum wear limit on a cylinder is 2.819 in. (71.6mm). If any cylinder is worn to this limit, the cylinder assembly must be replaced. Never rebore a cylinder if the finished rebore diameter will be this dimension or larger.*

Installation

1. Check that the top surface of the crankcase and the bottom surface of the cylinder are clean (**Figure 85**) prior to installing new gaskets.

2. Install a new cylinder base gasket (A, **Figure 86**) to the crankcase. Make sure all holes align.

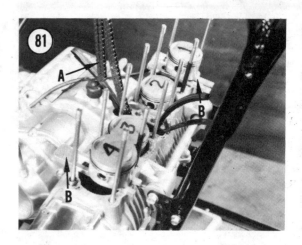

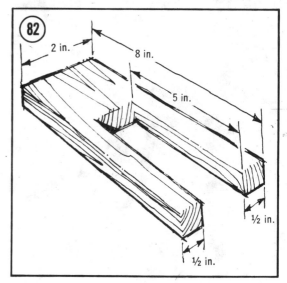

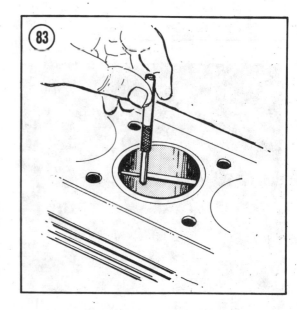

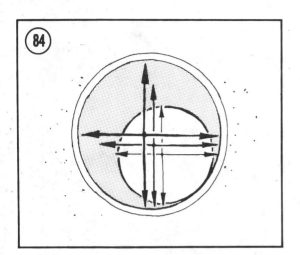

3. Install the 2 locating dowels (B, **Figure 86**) onto the rear outside studs.

4. Install a piston holding fixture under the 2 pistons protruding out of the crankcase (**Figure 87**).

5. Tie the ends of the cam chain tensioner slippers together with masking tape or wire. Otherwise the front one has a tendency to go into the cam chain tensioner hole in the front of the cylinder.

6. Carefully install the cylinder onto the cylinder studs (**Figure 88**) and slide it down over the pistons. Lubricate cylinder bores and pistons liberally with engine oil prior to installation.

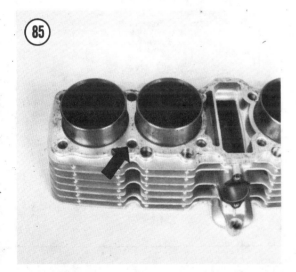

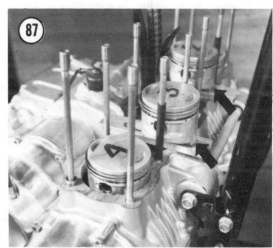

NOTE: *Rotate the crankshaft until 2 pistons are at* TDC; *this will make installation easier.*

7. Compress each ring as it enters the cylinder either with your fingers or by using aircraft type hose clamps **(Figure 89)** of appropriate diameter.

8. Remove the piston holding fixtures and push the cylinder all the way down **(Figure 90)**.

> CAUTION
> *Don't tighten the clamp any more than necessary to compress the rings. If the rings can't slip through easily, the clamp may gouge the rings.*

9. Remove the masking tape or wire from the cam chain tensioner slippers and install the cylinder head as described under *Cylinder Head Installation* in this chapter.

PISTONS AND CONNECTING RODS

The pistons may be removed with the engine in the frame by removing the cylinder head and the cylinder. To remove the rods, the crankcase has to split in order to gain access to the rod bearing caps.

Piston Removal

1. Remove the cylinder head and cylinder as described under *Cylinder Removal/Installation* in this chapter.

2. Lightly mark top of the piston with a 1, 2, 3, and 4 **(Figure 91)** so that they will be installed into the correct cylinder. Remember No. 1 is on the left-hand side.

3. Remove the top ring first by spreading the ends with your thumbs just enough to slide it up over the piston **(Figure 92)**. Repeat for the remaining rings.

4. Before removing the piston, hold the rod tightly and rock piston as shown in **Figure 93**. Any rocking motion (do not confuse with the normal sliding motion) indicates wear on the wrist pin, rod bushing, pin bore, or more likely, a combination of all three. Mark the piston, pin, and rod so that they will be reassembled into the same set.

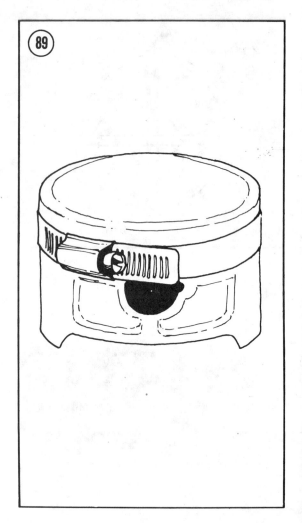

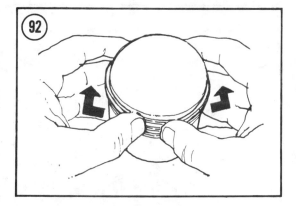

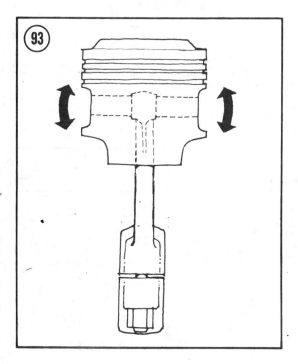

5. Remove the circlips from the wrist pin bores (**Figure 94**). Wrap a clean shop cloth under the piston so that the clips will not fall into the crankcase.

6. Heat the piston and pin with a small butane torch. The pin will probably drop right out. If it doesn't, heat the piston to about 140°F (60°C), i.e., until it is too warm to touch, but not excessively hot. If the pin is still difficult to push out, use a homemade tool as shown in **Figure 95**.

4

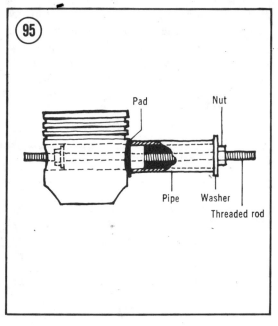

Piston Inspection

1. Carefully clean the carbon from the piston crown with a chemical remover or with a soft scraper **(Figure 96)**. Do not remove or damage the carbon ridge around the circumference of the piston above the top ring. If the pistons, rings, and cylinders are found to be dimensionally correct and can be reused, removal of the carbon ring from the tops of pistons or the carbon ridges from the tops of cylinders will promote excessive oil consumption.

> WARNING
> *The rail portions of the oil scraper can be very sharp. Be careful when handling them to avoid cut fingers.*

> CAUTION
> *Do not wire brush piston skirts.*

2. Examine each ring groove for burrs, dented edges, and wide wear. Pay particular attention to the top compression ring groove, as it usually wears more than the others.

3. Measure piston-to-cylinder clearance as described under *Piston Clearance* in this chapter.

4. If damage or wear indicate piston replacement, select a new piston as described under *Piston Clearance* in this chapter.

5. Measure all parts marked in Step 4 of the *Piston Removal* procedure with a micrometer and dial bore gauge to determine which part or parts are worn. Check against measurements given in **Table 1**. Any machinist can do this for you if you do not have micrometers. Replace piston/pin set as a unit if either or both are worn.

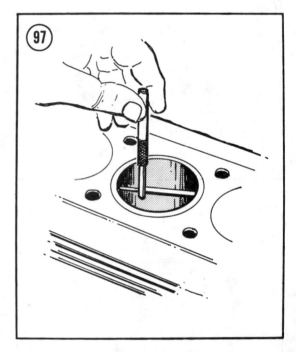

Table 3   PISTON AND RING SIZES

Piston Size	Piston Diameter	Compression Rings*
Standard	2.8130-2.8134 in. (71.45-71.46mm)	—
Oversize 1	2.8248 in. (71.75mm)	0.0098 in. (0.25mm)
Oversize 2	2.8346 in. (72.00mm)	0.0197 in. (0.50mm)
Oversize 3	2.8445 in. (72.25mm)	0.0295 in. (0.75mm)
Oversize 4	2.8543 in. (72.50mm)	0.0394 in. (1.00mm)
*Oversize number is stamped on the top of the ring.		

Piston Clearance

1. Make sure the piston and cylinder walls are clean and dry.

2. Measure the inside diameter of the cylinder bore at a point ½ in. (13mm) from the upper edge with a bore gauge (**Figure 97**).

3. Measure the outside diameter of the piston at a point ⅜ in. (10mm) from the lower edge of the piston 90° to piston pin axis (**Figure 98**). Check against measurement given in **Table 1**. Refer to **Table 3** for piston oversize numbers and dimensions.

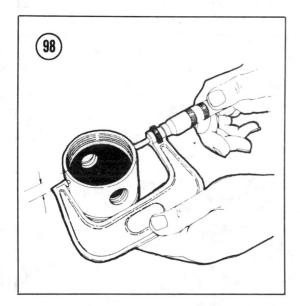

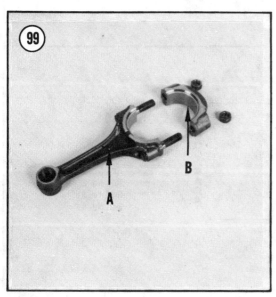

Connecting Rod Removal

In order to remove the rods, the crankcase has to be split. Refer to *Crankcase Disassembly* in this chapter.

Connecting Rod Inspection

1. Check each rod for obvious damage such as cracks and burns (A, **Figure 99**).

2. Check the piston pin bushing for wear or scoring.

3. Take the rods to a machine shop and check the alignment for twisting and bending.

4. Examine the bearing inserts (B, **Figure 99**) for wear, scoring, or burning. They are reusable if in good condition. Make a note of the bearing size (if any) stamped on the back of the insert if the bearing is to be discarded; a previous owner may have used undersize bearings.

5. Check bearing clearance and connecting rod side play as described under *Connecting Rod Bearing and Crankpin Inspection*.

Connecting Rod Bearing and Crankpin Inspection

Disassembly

1. Split crankcase as described under *Crankcase Disassembly/Assembly* in this chapter.

2. Remove the rods from crankshaft if not already removed. Install bearing inserts in rod and cap.

NOTE: *Prior to disassembly, mark the rods and caps. Number them 1, 2, 3, and 4 starting from the left-hand side. The left-hand side refers to the engine as it sits in the bike frame — not as it sits on your workbench.*

CAUTION
If the old bearings are reused, be sure that they are installed in their exact original locations.

3. Wipe bearing inserts and crankpins clean. Check again that inserts and crankpins are in good condition.

4. Place a piece of Plastigage on one crankpin parallel to the crankshaft.

5. Install rod cap and tighten nuts to 28 ft.-lb. (39 N•m).

CAUTION
Do not rotate crankshaft while Plastigage is in place.

6. Remove rod cap.

7. Measure width of flattened Plastigage according to the manufacturer's instructions. Measure at both ends of the strip. A difference of 0.001 in. (0.025mm) or more indicates a tapered crankpin, indicating that the crankshaft must be reground or replaced.

8. If the crankpin taper is within tolerance, measure the bearing clearance with the same strip of Plastigage. New bearing clearance should be 0.0017-0.0025 in. (0.042-0.064mm). Remove the Plastigage strips.

9. If the bearing clearance is greater than specified, use the following steps for new bearing selection.

10. The connecting rods and caps are marked with number 4, 5, or 6 (**Figure 100**). The crankshaft is marked on the left-hand counterbalancer with number 1, 2, or 3 (**Figure 101**). The group of 4 numbers relates to the crankshaft connecting rod journals (the group of 5 numbers relates to the crankshaft main bearing journals; *do not* refer to these 5 numbers).

11. To select the proper bearing insert number and color, subtract the crankshaft connecting rod journal number from the connecting rod and cap number.

Example:

Connecting rod and Cap No.	4
Crankshaft connecting rod journal No.	− 2
New bearing insert No. and color	2 (black)

12. After new bearings have been installed, recheck clearance to the specifications given in Step 8.

13. Repeat Steps 3-12 for the other 3 cylinders.

14. Measure the inside diameter of the small ends of the connecting rods with an inside dial gauge (**Figure 102**). Check against measurements given in **Table 1** at the end of this chapter.

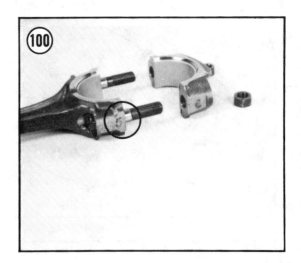

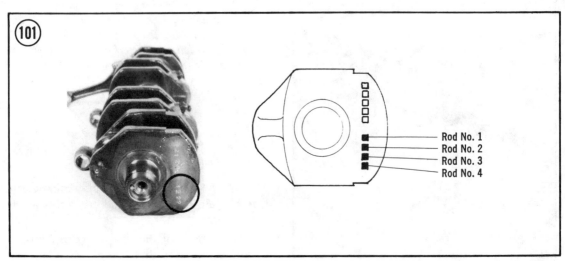

15. Insert the bearing shells into each connecting rod and cap. Make sure they are locked in place correctly.

CAUTION
If the old bearings are reused, be sure they are installed in their exact original positions.

16. Lubricate the bearings and crankpins with assembly oil and install the rods. Apply molybdenum disulfide grease to the threads of the connecting rods. Install the caps and tighten the cap nuts evenly, in a couple of steps to 28 ft.-lb. (39 N•m).

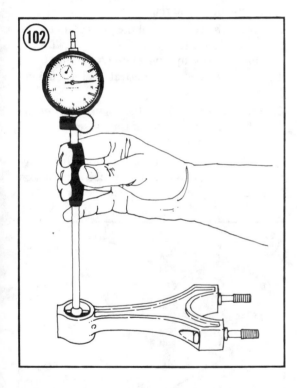

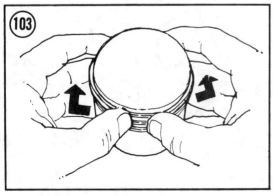

CAUTION
*On the final tightening sequence, if a torque of 24 ft.-lb. (33 N•m) is reached, **do not stop** until the final torque value is achieved. If the tightening is interrupted between 24-27 ft.-lb. (33-36 N•m), loosen the nut to less than 24 ft.-lb. (33 N•m), start again and tighten to the final torque value.*

17. Rotate the crankshaft a couple of times to make sure the bearings are not too tight.

Assembly

1. Coat the connecting rod bushing, piston pin, and piston holes with assembly oil.

CAUTION
Be sure to install the correct piston onto the same rod from which it was removed, No. 1, 2, 3, or 4.

2. Place the piston over the connecting rod. If you are reusing the same piston and connecting rods, match the piston to the rod from which it came and orient it in the same way. Make sure the arrow on the piston crown is facing forward in the engine.

3. Insert the piston pin and tap it with a plastic mallet until it starts into the connecting rod bushing. If it does not slide easily, heat the piston until it is too warm to touch but not excessively hot (140°F or 60°C). Continue to drive the piston in while holding the piston so that the rod does not have to take any shock. Otherwise, it may be bent. Drive the pin in until it is centered in the rod. If pin is still difficult to install, use the homemade tool (**Figure 95**) but eliminate the piece of pipe.

4. Install rings as described in Steps 3-8 under *Piston Ring Replacement*.

PISTON RINGS

Replacement

1. Remove old rings with a ring expander tool or by spreading the ring ends with your thumbs and lifting the rings up evenly (**Figure 103**).

2. Carefully remove all carbon from the ring grooves. Inspect grooves carefully for burrs, nicks, or broken and cracked lands. Recondition or replace piston if necessary.

3. Check end gap of each ring. To check ring, insert the ring into the bottom of the cylinder bore and square it with the wall by tapping with the piston. The ring should be in about ⅝ in. (15mm). Insert a feeler gauge as shown in **Figure 104**. Compare gap with **Table 1**. If the gap is smaller than specified, hold a small file in a vise, grip the ends of the ring with your fingers, and enlarge the gap. See **Figure 105**.

4. Roll each ring around its piston groove as shown in **Figure 106** to check for binding. Minor binding may be cleaned up with a fine cut file.

> NOTE: *Install all rings with their markings facing up.*

5. Install oil ring in oil ring groove with a ring expander tool or spread the ends with your thumbs.

6. Install 2 compression rings carefully with a ring expander tool or spread the ends with your thumbs.

7. Check side clearance of each ring as shown in **Figure 107**. Compare with specifictions in **Table 1**.

8. Distribute ring gaps around piston as shown in **Figure 108**. The important thing is that the ring gaps are not aligned with each other when installed.

9. Refer to **Table 3** for compression ring oversize numbers and dimensions.

IGNITION ADVANCE MECHANISM

Removal/Installation

1. Disconnect the negative battery lead from the battery.

2. Remove the left-hand side of the exhaust system as described under *Exhaust System Removal/Installation* in Chapter Six.

3. Remove the bolts securing the ignition cover and remove it.

4. Remove the Allen bolt (**Figure 109**) securing the timing plate and remove it.

5. Rotate the engine until the projection on the centrifugal advance mechanism aligns with the slot on the pick-up coil plate (A, **Figure 110**). This is necessary for removal of the backing plate.

6. Remove the 2 screws (B, **Figure 110**) securing the advance mechanism assembly and carefully let it hang down.

7. Disconnect the electrical connector (**Figure 111**) to the ignition advance mechanism located under the right-hand side cover.

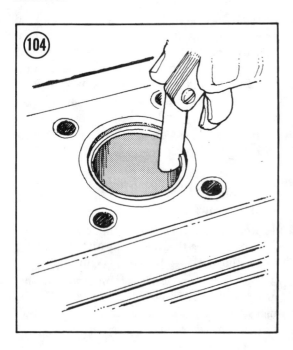

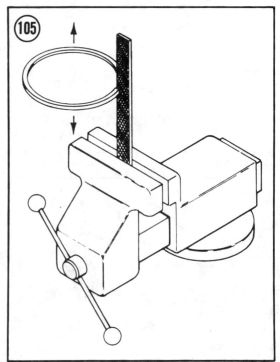

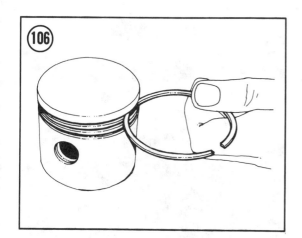

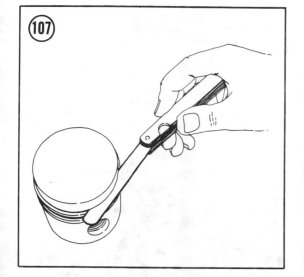

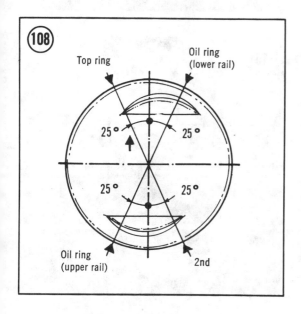

Top ring

Oil ring
(lower rail)

25°   25°

25°   25°

Oil ring
(upper rail)   2nd

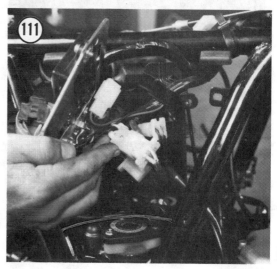

8. Remove the electrical cable clips (A, **Figure 112**) from the left-hand crankcase cover and remove the cable.

9. Disconnect the electrical wire to the neutral safety switch (B, **Figure 112**). Remove the advance mechanism assembly and electrical harness.

> NOTE: *Make a drawing of the routing of the electrical cable so it will be installed in the same position.*

10. Remove the centrifugal advance mechanism (**Figure 113**).

11. Inspect the condition of all components as described under *Ignition Advance Mechanism* in Chapter Seven.

12. Install by reversing these removal steps. Be sure to align the pin (A, **Figure 114**) on the crankshaft with the notch (B, **Figure 114**) on the centrifugal advance mechanism.

> NOTE: *Rotate the engine so the projection on the centrifugal advance mechanism (**Figure 115**) is positioned at the 10 o'clock position so the pick-up plate can be installed.*

13. Be sure to route the electrical wires in the same location especially in the clips shown in **Figure 112**.

14. Tighten the Allen bolt (**Figure 109**) to 14.5 ft.-lb. (20 N•m).

ALTERNATOR

Removal/Installation

This procedure is shown with the engine partially disassembled; it is not necessary to remove any of these components to perform this procedure.

1. Remove the seat and both side covers.

2. Disconnect the battery negative cable.

3. Remove the 2 Phillips head screws (**Figure 116**) securing the electrical panel in place.

4. Carefully pull the forward edge of the panel out and disconnect the alternator electrical connectors. The field coil contains 2 wires — 1 brown and 1 green. The stator contains 4 wires — 1 yellow and 3 white.

5. Remove the 5 Allen bolts (**Figure 117**) securing the alternator cover/coil assembly. Straighten the wire clamps securing the two electrical cables in place.

> NOTE: *Do not remove the 3 Allen bolts (Figure 118) on the cover.*

6. Remove the alternator cover/coil assembly and electrical cables.

7. Remove the bolt and washer (**Figure 119**) securing the alternator rotor.

NOTE: *If necessary use a strap wrench (Figure 120) to keep the rotor from turning while removing the bolt.*

8. Screw in a flywheel puller (**Figure 121**) until it stops. Use a wrench on the puller and tap on the end of it with your hand or a plastic mallet until the rotor disengages. Remove the puller and rotor.

9. Install by reversing these removal steps. Secure the rotor bolt to 47 ft.-lb. (65 N•m).

NOTE: *Be sure to install a new gasket (A, Figure 122) and install the 2 locating dowels (B, Figure 122). Install the cable in the wire clamps (Figure 117).*

OIL PUMP

Figure 123 illustrates the oil flow through the entire engine. Oil pressure is supplied by the oil pump, which is driven by the gear on the backside of the clutch assembly.

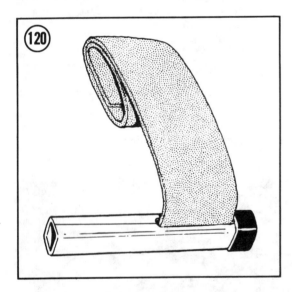

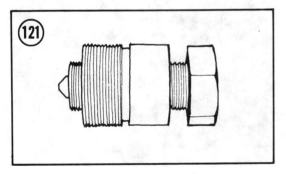

Removal/Installation

1. Remove the engine from the frame as described under *Engine Removal/Installtion* in this chapter.

2. Turn the engine upside down on the workbench.

CAUTION
If the cylinder and head have been removed, place the engine on blocks of wood to protect the cylinder studs.

3. Remove the 14 Allen bolts (**Figure 124**) securing the pan and remove it. Be sure to in-

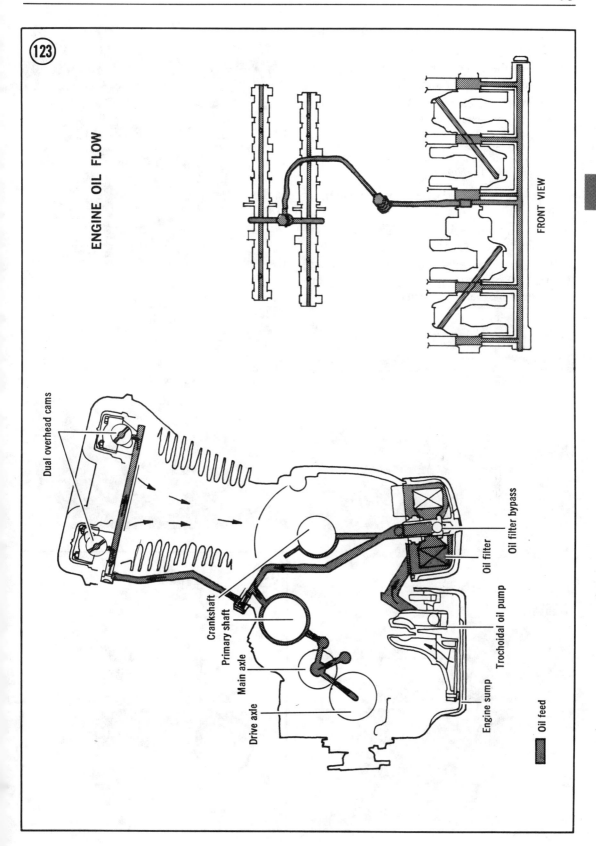

(123)

ENGINE OIL FLOW

FRONT VIEW

Dual overhead cams

Crankshaft

Primary shaft

Main axle

Drive axle

Engine sump

Trochoidal oil pump

Oil filter

Oil filter bypass

Oil feed

4

stall the electrical wire clip (**Figure 125**) in the same location upon installation.

4. Remove the 3 screws (**Figure 126**) securing the pick-up screen and remove it.

5. Remove the 3 Allen bolts (**Figure 127**) securing the oil pump assembly and remove it.

> NOTE: *Do not lose the 2 locating dowels nor the O-ring seal on the crankcase (A, Figure 128).*

6. Install by reversing the removal steps, noting the following.

7. Make sure the O-ring seal (**Figure 129**) is in good condition; replace if necessary.

8. Pour some new engine oil into the opening (**Figure 130**) of the oil pump to prime it, prior to installing the pick-up screen assembly.

9. Remove the 6 screws (**Figure 131**) securing the baffle plates in the oil pan and remove them. Thoroughly clean out the pan with solvent and dry with compressed air. Reinstall the baffle plates. Make sure there is no solvent residue left in the pan as it will contaminate the engine oil.

10. Clean the pick-up screen with solvent and dry with compressed air.

11. Remove all traces of old gasket material from the pan and lower crankcase.

12. Install a new pan gasket and install the pan.

> NOTE: *Apply Loctite Lock 'N' Seal to the pan bolts prior to installation.*

Disassembly/Inspection/Assembly

Refer to **Figure 132** for this procedure.

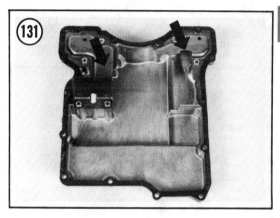

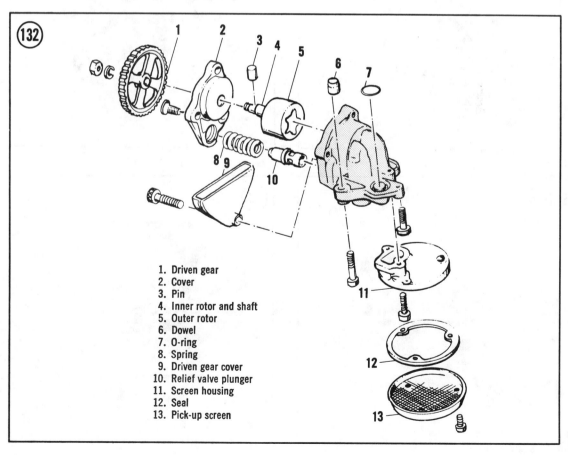

1. Driven gear
2. Cover
3. Pin
4. Inner rotor and shaft
5. Outer rotor
6. Dowel
7. O-ring
8. Spring
9. Driven gear cover
10. Relief valve plunger
11. Screen housing
12. Seal
13. Pick-up screen

1. Inspect the outer housing for cracks.

2. Remove the 2 Allen bolts (**Figure 133**) securing the strainer cover and remove it.

3. Remove the Allen bolt (**Figure 134**) and remove the gear cover.

4. Remove the nut and lockwasher (**Figure 135**) and remove the driven gear and dowel pin (**Figure 136**).

5. Remove the 3 Torx bolts (A, **Figure 137**) with a T-30 Torx wrench (B, **Figure 137**) and remove the cover and gasket.

NOTE: *Refer to front of this chapter for information on availability of Torx wrenches.*

6. Remove the spring (**Figure 138**) and relief valve plunger (A, **Figure 139**).

7. Remove the inner and outer rotor and check for scratches or abrasions. Replace both parts if evidence of this is found.

8. Clean all parts in solvent and thoroughly dry with compressed air. Coat all parts with fresh engine oil prior to assembly.

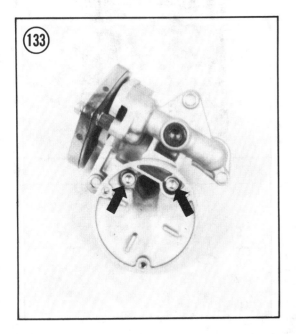

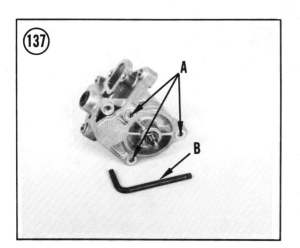

(137)

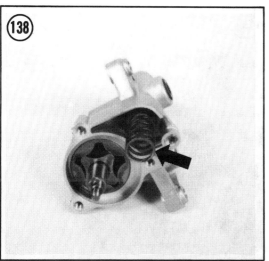
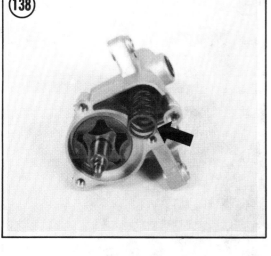

(138)

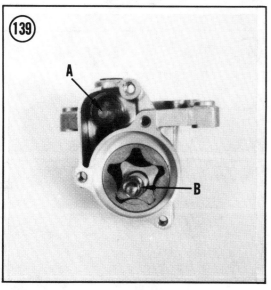

(139)

9. Install the inner and outer rotor (B, **Figure 139**).

10. Check the clearance between the housing and outer rotor **(Figure 140)** with a flat feeler gauge. The clearance should be between 0.0035-0.0059 in. (0.090-0.150mm). If the clearance is greater, replace the work part.

11. Check the clearance between the inner and outer rotor **(Figure 141)** with a flat feeler gauge. The clearance should be 0.0047 in. (0.12mm). If the clearance is greater, replace the worn part.

4

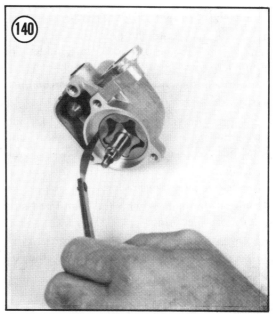

(140)

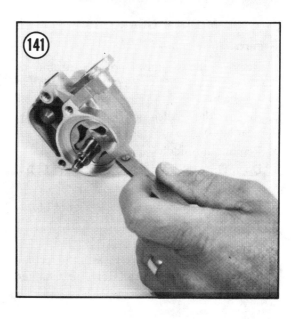

(141)

12. Continue assembling by reversing Steps 1-5.

13. After assembly, rotate the shaft and rotor to make sure it rotates freely.

14. Install the oil pump assembly.

15. Make sure the O-ring (**Figure 129**) at the pump outlet is in good condition. Replace it if it has lost its resiliency or is deteriorating. Make sure the 2 locating dowels (B, **Figure 128**) and O-ring seal (A, **Figure 128**) are in place.

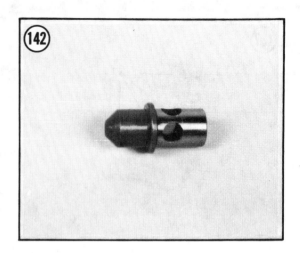

OIL PRESSURE RELIEF VALVE

Removal/Inspection/Installation

1. To gain access to the pressure relief valve, remove the oil pump as described under *Oil Pump Removal/Installation* in this chapter.

2. Perform Steps 1-6, *Oil Pump Disassembly/Inspection/Assembly* in this chapter.

3. Inspect the valve plunger (**Figure 142**) and the cylinder that it rides in for wear and scratches. Replace if found defective.

4. Make sure the spring is not broken or distorted; replace if necessary.

5. Install the plunger with the chamfered side out toward the spring.

6. Reverse Steps 1-6, *Oil Pump Disassembly/Inspection/Assembly*, and assemble the oil pump.

7. Install the oil pump assembly.

MIDDLE GEAR CASE

Removal/Installation

1. Remove the engine from the frame as described under *Engine Removal/Installation* in this chapter.

2. Remove the 7 Allen bolts securing the middle gear housing to the crankcase.

3. Remove the middle gear case.

4. Do not lose the locating dowel (**Figure 143**).

5. Install by reversing these removal steps.

6. Be sure to use a new gasket (A, **Figure 144**).

7. Tighten all Allen bolts to 16 ft.-lb. (22 N•m).

8. If the oil was drained, refill with the recommended type and quantity. Refer to Chapter Three.

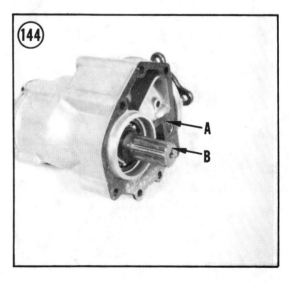

Inspection

Visually inspect the outer case for cracks and signs of oil leakage; check condition of splines (B, **Figure 144**) and the output drive flange.

Although it may be practical for you to disassemble the case assembly for inspection, it requires special tools and equipment to replace the bearings and seals. If there is trouble with the middle gear unit, take it to your Yamaha dealer and let them overhaul it. They are also better equipped to check and adjust gear lash.

SECONDARY SHAFT AND STARTER MOTOR CLUTCH ASSEMBLY

Removal

1. Remove the engine as described under *Engine Removal/Installation* in this chapter.

2. Split the crankcase as described under *Crankcase Disassembly* in this chapter.

3. Remove the middle gear assembly (A, **Figure 145**) and transmission main shaft assembly (B, **Figure 145**).

4. Straighten the locking tab (A, **Figure 146**) and remove the large nut securing the gear to the primary shaft.

> NOTE: *To prevent the gear from turning, insert a large flat-bladed screwdriver into the slot (B, Figure 146) and into the gear teeth.*

5. Remove the nut, lockwasher, spring washer, gear and spacer.

6. Remove the 3 Allen bolts (**Figure 147**) securing the left-hand bearing support and remove it.

> NOTE: *The left-hand side refers to the engine as it sits in the bike frame — not as it sits on your workbench.*

7. Gently tap on the left-hand end of the shaft with a plastic or rubber mallet and withdraw the primary shaft assembly (**Figure 148**) from the left-hand side.

8. Lift up on the Hy-Vo primary chain and remove the starter clutch assembly from it.

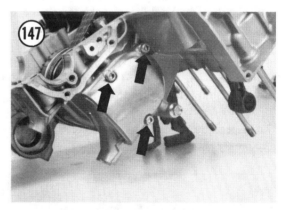

Inspection

1. Visually inspect the bearing surfaces of the rollers, the starter gear hub and the slots in the clutch body, for wear or damage (**Figure 149**). Replace worn or damaged components or the complete assembly.

2. Check each Allen bolt (**Figure 150**) for tightness. If any are loose, remove them and replace with *new* bolts. Apply Loctite Lock 'N' Seal to the threads prior to installation.

3. Check the functioning of the plungers and springs in the clutch body for binding or sag. Replace any weak springs with new ones. Relieve any binds with emery cloth, or by replacing the plungers with new ones.

4. Install the bushing and starter gear into the starter clutch assembly and slide it onto the primary shaft.

5. Spin the assembly fast clockwise, and stop the starter gear suddenly. The clutch body should continue spinning momentarily. Repeat the operation, spinning the assembly clockwise. The clutch body should stop at the same time as the gear. If either of these tests fail to perform correctly, the roller mechanism is at fault.

6. Inspect the condition of the teeth on the starter gear (A, **Figure 151**) and the condition of the bushing (B, **Figure 151**). Replace as a set if either is faulty.

7. Inspect the condition of the teeth on the secondary sprocket (A, **Figure 152**). Light

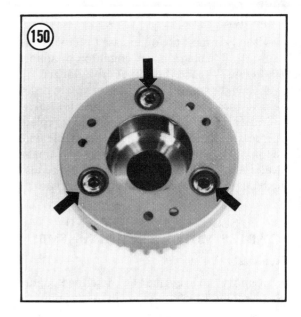

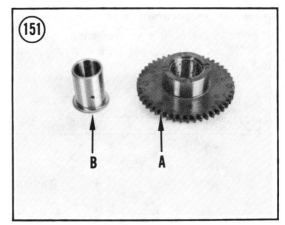

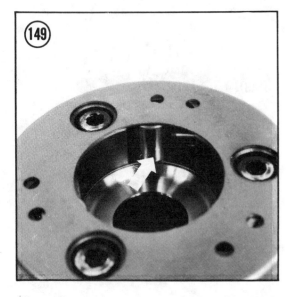

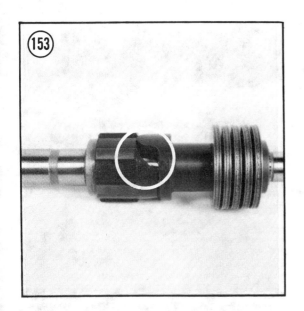

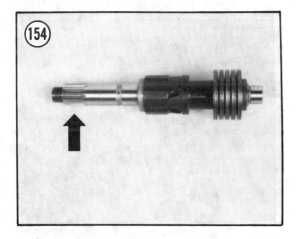

damage may be removed with an oilstone, but if damage is severe, the sprocket must be replaced. Also check the condition of the Hy-Vo chain as it may be damaged also; replace if necessary.

8. Inspect the condition of the interior splines (B, **Figure 152**) in the starter clutch assembly for wear or damage.

9. Inspect the condition of the damper cam surface (**Figure 153**). They must be smooth and without extreme wear. If damaged or worn, replace the primary shaft assembly.

> NOTE: *Do not try to disassemble the primary shaft assembly as special tools and a press are required in order to remove the circlip. This should be entrusted to a Yamaha dealer or qualified machine shop.*

10. Inspect the condition of the splines (**Figure 154**) on the end of the primary shaft assembly for wear or damage; replace if necessary.

11. Inspect the condition of the bearing (A **Figure 155**) in the left-hand bearing support. Make sure it rotates smoothly with no signs of wear or damage. To replace the bearing, remove the circlip (B, **Figure 155**), turn the housing upside down and tap it until the bearing comes out.

12. Remove and replace the two O-ring seals (**Figure 156**) with new ones.

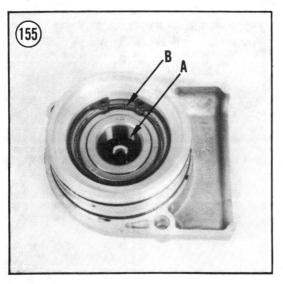

Installation

1. Install the assembled starter clutch assembly into the Hy-Vo primary chain (**Figure 157**). Make sure it is properly engaged in the chain.

2. Push the starter clutch assembly into position and insert the primary shaft assembly (**Figure 148**). Tap it lightly with a plastic or rubber mallet until it is completely seated.

3. Ensure that new O-ring seals (**Figure 156**) are installed. Apply clean engine oil to the bearing housing, install it and secure it with the 3 Allen bolts (**Figure 147**).

4. Install the spacer (**Figure 158**) and gear onto the shaft.

5. Install the spring washer (**Figure 159**) with the *cupped side of the washer facing the gear*.

6. Install a new lockwasher and make sure the 2 locking tabs (**Figure 160**) are correctly seated into the 2 holes in the gear.

7. Install the nut and tighten to 51 ft.-lb. (70 N•m).

> NOTE: *To prevent the gear from turning, insert a large flat-bladed screwdriver into the slot (B, **Figure 146**) and into the gear teeth.*

8. Bend up one side of the lockwasher against one side of the nut (A, **Figure 146**).

9. Install the middle driven gear assembly and main shaft assembly as described under *Transmission Installation* in Chapter Five.

10. Assemble the crankcases as described under *Crankcase Assembly* in this chapter.

11. Install the engine as described under *Engine Removal/Installation* in this chapter.

CRANKCASE

Service to the lower end requires that the crankcase assembly be removed from the motorcycle frame.

While the engine is still in the frame it is easier to remove the cylinder head, cylinder, pistons, electric starter, alternator, and clutch. In addition, the decrease of engine weight makes it easier to remove the crankcase from the frame.

Disassembly

1. Remove the engine as described under *Engine Removal* in this chapter. Remove all exterior assemblies from the crankcase. Set the engine on the workbench right side up.

> NOTE: *Be sure to remove the special oil nozzle assembly. Remove the 3 Torx bolts (Figure 161) securing the assembly. These bolts have been Loctited in place and it may be difficult to break them loose. A special tool (Figure 162) is required to remove these bolts and the size is T-30. Detailed information regarding this tool is covered at the front of this chapter.*

2. Remove the 4 Allen bolts (**Figure 163**) securing the crankcase breather cover and remove it. This will expose bolt No. 32 (**Figure 164**).

> CAUTION
> *Always remove this cover and bolt before trying to separate the crankcase halves.*

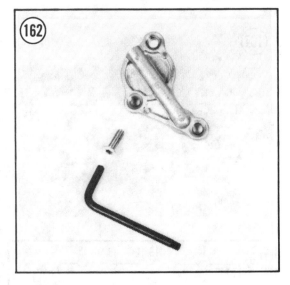

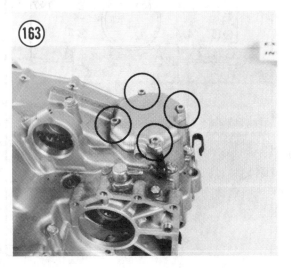

3. Loosen by ½ turn all number bolts (34-23) in the upper crankcase half (**Figure 165**); start with the highest number first. The numbers are cast into the case adjacent to the bolt hole (**Figure 166**). After all bolts have been loosened, remove all of them (don't forget No. 32).

> NOTE: *All bolts have washers under them with the exception of the 2 within the oil filter cavity (**Figure 167**).*

4. Turn the crankcase over. Set it on wooden blocks to prevent damage to the cylinder studs.

5. Loosen by ½ turn all number bolts (22-1), starting with the highest number first (**Figure 168**). After loosening all bolts, remove all of them.

> CAUTION
> *Always remove the bolts in the crankshaft area (No. 10-1) last.*

6. Carefully tap around the perimeter of the crankcase with a plastic mallet — do not use a metal hammer — to help separate the 2 case halves.

> CAUTION
> *If it is necessary to pry the halves apart, do it very carefully so that you do not mar the gasket surfaces. If you do, the cases will leak and must be replaced. They cannot be repaired.*

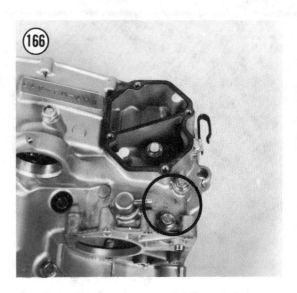

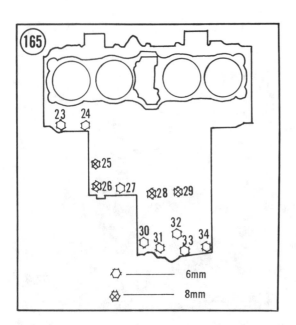

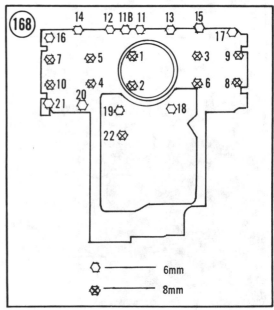

7. Lift up on the lower crankcase and separate it from the upper. The transmission and crankshaft assemblies should stay with the upper crankcase. After removal, check that the lower crankshaft bearings are still in place. If they are loose or have fallen out, reinstall them immediately in their original positions.

8. Don't lose the rubber O-ring and locating dowel (**Figure 169**) in the upper crankcase half.

9. Remove the secondary shaft and starter motor clutch assembly and crankshaft assembly as described in this chapter.

10. Remove transmission assemblies, shift forks, shift drum, and related items as described in Chapter Five.

11. Remove the bolts securing the kickstarter engagement assembly and remove it. See **Figures 170 and 171**.

12. Remove the crankcase main bearing inserts from the upper and lower crankcase halves. Mark the backside of the inserts with No. 1, 2, 3, 4, and 5 U (upper) and L (lower) starting from the left-hand side, so they will be installed into the same position.

> NOTE: *The No. 4 bearing (Figure 172) in the upper crankcase is a special side thrust bearing.*

> NOTE: *The left-hand side refers to the engine as it sits in the bike frame — not as it sits on your workbench.*

13. Remove the 2 bolts (**Figure 173**) securing the oil baffle plate and remove it.

Inspection

Thoroughly clean the inside and outside of both crankcase halves with cleaning solvent. Dry with compressed air. Make sure there is no solvent residue left in the cases as it will contaminate the engine oil.

Make sure all oil passages are clean; be sure to blow them out with compressed air.

Check the crankcases for possible damage such as cracks or other damage. Inspect the mating surfaces of both halves (**Figure 174**). They must be free of gouges, burrs, or any damage that could cause an oil leak.

Make sure the cylinder studs are not bent and the threads are in good condition. Make sure they are screwed into the crankcase tightly.

Assembly

Prior to installation of all parts, coat surfaces with assembly oil or engine oil.

1. Install the main bearing inserts in both the upper and lower crankcase halves. If reusing the old bearings, make sure that they are installed in the same location. Refer to marks made in *Disassembly*, Step 12.

2. Install the oil baffle in the upper crankcase (**Figure 173**).

3. Install the kickstarter assembly.

4. Install the transmission assemblies, shift drum and forks, and all related parts as described in Chapter Five.

5. Apply assembly oil to the main bearing insert and install the crankshaft assembly. Make sure the oil seals (**Figure 175**) are properly positioned in the groove at each end of the crankshaft.

6. Be sure both locating dowels at each side (A, **Figure 176**) and the locating dowel and oil gallery O-ring in the center (B, **Figure 176**) are installed.

7. Clean the crankcase mating surfaces of both halves adjacent to the crankshaft bearings with contact cleaner (**Figure 177**).

8. Apply a thin coat of Yamabond No. 4 to each surface adjacent to the bearings. Apply sealant to within 0.10 in. (2.5mm) of the insert (**Figure 178**).

Table 4   CRANKCASE BOLT SIZES

Bolt Number	Diameter (mm)	Length (mm)
— Lower crankcase —		
1-10	8	115
11B	6	45
11-17	6	45
18	6	85
19-21	6	65
22	8	75
— Upper crankcase —		
23-24	6	65
25	8	125
26	8	45
27	6	45
28	8	45
29	8	125
30-32	6	65
33-34	6	45

CAUTION
Failure to apply sealant to these areas may result in reduced oil pressure and the possibility of crankshaft seizure.

9. Make sure case half sealing surfaces are perfectly clean and dry.

10. Apply a light coat of gasket sealer to the sealing surfaces of both halves. Cover only flat surfaces, not curved bearing surfaces. Make the coating as thin as possible or the case can shift; hammer out the bearings.

> NOTE: *Make sure the upper crankcase main bearing inserts are in place and correctly positioned.*

> NOTE: *Use Gasgacinch Gasket Sealer, Yamabond No. 4, or equivalent. When selecting an equivalent, avoid thick and hard setting materials.*

CAUTION
Make sure no sealant comes in contact with the oil gallery O-ring (B, Figure 176) as it will destroy its sealing effectiveness.

11. Join both halves and tap together lightly with a plastic mallet — do not use a metal hammer as it will damage the cases.

> NOTE: *Make sure the No. 2 shift fork engages in the correct slot in the transmission.*

12. Refer to **Table 4** for the crankcase bolt numbers and their respective size and lengths.

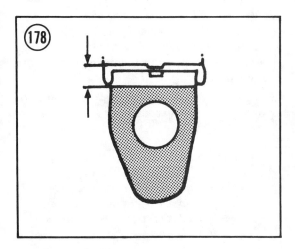

NOTE: *Bolt numbers 1 and 2* ***do not*** *have washers under them.*

13. Apply oil to the threads of all bolts. Install all bolts in both crankcase halves and tighten in two stages to a final torque as follows:

    a. 6mm bolts — 8.7 ft.-lb. (12 N•m)

    b. 8mm bolts — 17.4 ft.-lb. (24 N•m)

Tighten bolts No. 1-22 (lower crankcase) first, then No. 23-34 (upper crankcase). The torque pattern is indicated by the bolt number adjacent to the bolt hole. See **Figure 165** for the upper crankcase and **Figure 168** for the lower crankcase.

> CAUTION
> *Don't forget No. 32 within the crankcase breather housing.*

14. Install the crankcase breather cover along with a new gasket (**Figure 163**). Install the special oil nozzle assembly (**Figure 161**). Apply Loctite Lock 'N' Seal to the threads prior to installation.

15. Install all engine assemblies that were removed.

16. Install the engine as described under *Engine Removal/Installation* in this chapter.

17. Fill the crankcase with the recommended type and quantity of engine oil. Refer to Chapter Three.

CRANKSHAFT

Removal/Installation

1. Split the crankcase as described under *Crankcase Disassembly* in this chapter.

2. Remove the secondary shaft assembly as described under *Secondary Shaft and Starter Motor Clutch Assembly Removal/Installation* in this chapter.

3. Remove the crankshaft assembly and remove the connecting rods.

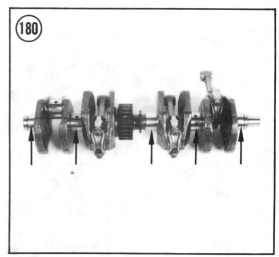

NOTE: *Prior to disassembly, mark the rods and caps. Number them 1, 2, 3, and 4 starting from the left-hand side. The left-hand side refers to the engine as it sits in the bike frame — not as it sits on your workbench.*

4. Install by reversing these removal steps, noting the following procedures.

5. Insert the bearing shells into each connecting rod and cap. Make sure they are locked in place correctly.

CAUTION
If the old bearings are reused, be sure they are installed in their exact original positions.

6. Lubricate the bearings and crankpins with assembly oil and install the rods. Apply molybdenum disulfide grease to the threads of the connecting rods. Install the caps and tighten the cap nuts evenly, in a couple of steps, to 28 ft.-lb. (39 N•m).

CAUTION
*On the final tightening sequence, if a torque of 24 ft.-lb. (33 N•m) is reached, **do not stop** until the final torque value is achieved. If the tightening is interrupted between 24-27 ft.-lb. (33-36 N•m), loosen the nut to less than 24 ft.-lb. (33 N•m), start again, and tighten to the final torque value.*

7. Be sure to install the crankshaft oil seals with the larger OD seal on the left-hand side (**Figure 179**).

8. After crankshaft has been reinstalled, rotate it several times to make sure the bearings are not too tight.

Crankshaft Inspection

1. Clean crankshaft thoroughly with solvent. Clean oil holes with rifle cleaning brushes; flush

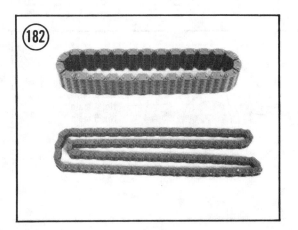

thoroughly and dry with compressed air. Lightly oil all journal surfaces immediately to prevent rust.

2. Carefully inspect each journal (**Figure 180**) for scratches, ridges, scoring, nicks, etc. Very small nicks and scratches may be removed with crocus cloth. More serious damage must be removed by grinding — a job for a machine shop.

3. If the surface on all journals is satisfactory, take the crankshaft to your dealer or local machines shop. They can check out-of-roundness, taper, and wear on the journals. They can also check crankshaft alignment and inspect for cracks. Check against measurements given in **Table 1**.

4. Inspect the condition of the cam chain and primary chain drive sprockets (**Figure 181**). If they are worn or damaged, the crankshaft will have to be replaced. Also inspect the condition of both chains (**Figure 182**); replace if necessary.

Main Bearing and Journal Inspection

1. Check the inside and outside surfaces of the bearing inserts for wear, bluish tint (burned), flaking, abrasion, and scoring. If the bearings are good, they may be reused. If any insert is questionable, replace the entire set.

2. Measure the main bearing oil clearance. Clean the bearing surfaces of the crankshaft and the main bearing inserts.

3. Set the upper crankcase upside down on the workbench. Set it on wood blocks to prevent damage to the cylinder studs.

4. Install the existing inserts into the upper crankcase.

5. Install the crankshaft into the upper crankcase.

6. Place a strip of Plastigage over each main bearing journal parallel to the crankshaft.

NOTE: *Do not rotate the crankshaft while the Plastigage strips are in place.*

7. Install the existing bearing inserts into the lower crankcase.

8. Carefully turn the crankcase over and install it onto the upper crankcase.

9. Apply oil to the bolt threads and install bolts No. 1-10; remember there are no washers under No. 1 and 2.

10. Tighten to 17.4 ft.-lb. (24 N•m) in two stages. Use the torque pattern as indicated by the bolt number adjacent to the bolt hole (**Figure 183**).

11. Remove bolts No. 1-10 in the reverse order of installation.

12. Carefully remove the lower crankcase. Do not move the crankshaft.

13. Measure the width of the flattened Plastigage according to manufacturer's instructions. Measure both ends of Plastigage strip (**Figure 184**). A difference of 0.001 in. (0.025mm) or more indicates a tapered journal. Confirm with a micrometer. Main bearing oil clearance should be 0.0014-0.0023 in. (0.035-0.059mm). Remove the Plastigage strips.

14. If the bearing clearance is greater than specified, use the following steps for new bearing selection.

15. The crankshaft is marked on the left-hand counterbalancer with the numbers 1, 2, or 3 (**Figure 185**). The group of 5 numbers relates to the crankshaft main bearing journals (the group of 4 numbers relates to the crankshaft connecting rod journals — *do not* refer to these four numbers). Each crankcase bearing journal is marked with numbers 4, 5, or 6 (**Figure 186**). These numbers are stamped on the front mating surface of both halves.

16. To select the proper bearing insert number and color, subtract the crankshaft bearing journal number from the crankcase bearing journal number.

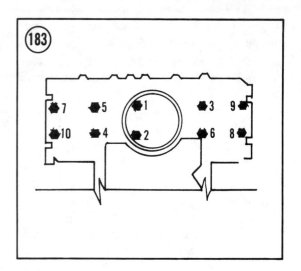

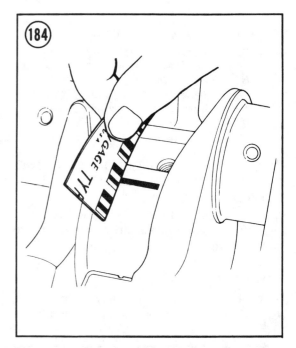

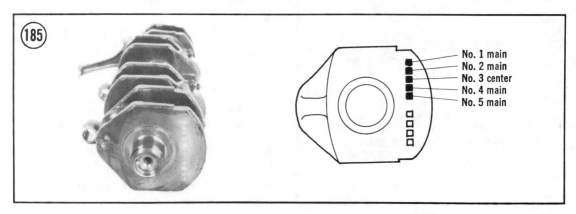

Example:

Crankcase journal number	5
Crankshaft bearing journal number	– 2
New bearing insert number and color	3 (brown)

Repeat for all four bearings.

NOTE: *Bearing selection for the special side thrust bearing (Figure 187) is the same as for the others. This bearing takes up side thrust of the crankshaft.*

17. After new bearings have been installed, recheck the clearance to the specifications given in Step 13.

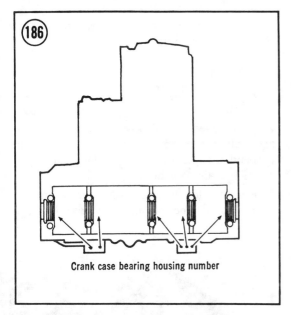

Crank case bearing housing number

4

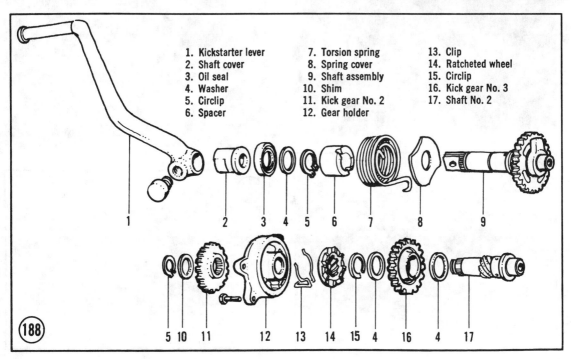

1. Kickstarter lever
2. Shaft cover
3. Oil seal
4. Washer
5. Circlip
6. Spacer
7. Torsion spring
8. Spring cover
9. Shaft assembly
10. Shim
11. Kick gear No. 2
12. Gear holder
13. Clip
14. Ratcheted wheel
15. Circlip
16. Kick gear No. 3
17. Shaft No. 2

KICKSTARTER

Removal/Installation

Refer to **Figure 188** for this procedure.

1. Perform Steps 1-8, *Clutch Removal* in Chapter Five.

2. Unhook the return spring (**Figure 189**) from the lug on the crankcase housing and remove the external kickstarter assembly.

> NOTE: *Figure 189 is shown with the clutch assembly removed. It is not necessary to remove it if only the external kickstarter assembly is to be removed.*

3. If the internal kickstarter gear assembly is at fault, remove the engine and split the crankcase as described under *Crankcase Disassembly* in this chapter.

4. Remove the 3 bolts (**Figure 190**) and straighten the locking tab and remove the internal bolt (**Figure 191**). Withdraw the kickstarter assembly.

Inspection

1. Check for broken, chipped, or missing teeth (**Figure 192**) on all gears. Replace any if necessary.

2. Make sure the engagement gear operates smoothly on its shaft.

3. Be sure the retaining clip rides snug in the groove in the shaft. If it is loose, tighten by bending it a little.

4. Check all parts for uneven wear; replace any that are questionable.

Installation

1. Apply assembly oil to all sliding surfaces of all parts.

2. If removed, install the internal kickstarter assembly into the lower crankcase half. Be sure to bend up one side of the lockwasher (**Figure 191**) against the bolt.

3. Reassemble the crankcases and install the engine as described under *Crankcase Assembly* in this chapter.

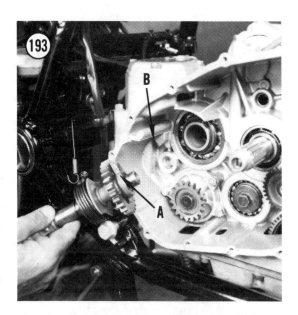

4. Install the external kickstarter assembly partially into the crankcase. Hook return spring onto the lug on the crankcase and temporarily install the kickstarter lever. Rotate the assembly 180° *counterclockwise* or until the kickstarter gear engages with the idle gear No. 2.

> NOTE: *Make sure the lug (A, Figure 193) on the backside of the kickstarter assembly is positioned correctly below the lug (B, Figure 193) on the crankcase. Figure 193 is shown with the clutch assembly removed for clarity only.*

5. Check the operation of the assembly; remove the kickstarter lever.

6. Install the clutch components as described under *Clutch Installation* in Chapter Five.

BREAK-IN

Following cylinder servicing (boring, honing, new rings, etc.) and major lower end work, the engine should be broken in just as if it were new. The performance and service life of the engine depend greatly on a careful and sensible break-in.

For the first 500 miles, no more than one-third throttle should be used and speed should be varied as much as possible within the one-third throttle limit. Prolonged, steady running at one speed, no matter how moderate, is to be avoided, as is hard acceleration.

Following the 500-mile service, increasingly more throttle can be used but full throttle should not be used until the motorcycle has covered at least 1,000 miles and then it should be limited to short bursts until 1,500 miles have been logged.

The mono-grade oils recommended for break-in and normal use provide a more superior bedding pattern for rings and cylinders than do multi-grade oils. As a result, piston ring and cylinder bore life are greatly increased. During this period, oil consumption will be higher than normal. It is therefore important to frequently check and correct the oil level. At no time, during break-in or later, should the oil level be allowed to drop below the bottom line on the dipstick; if the oil level is low, the oil will become overheated resulting in insufficient lubrication and increased wear.

500-Mile Service

It is essential that oil and filter be changed after the first 500 miles. In addition, it is a good idea to change the oil and filter at the completion of break-in (about 1,500 miles) to ensure that all of the particles produced during break-in are removed from the lubrication system. The small added expense may be considered a smart investment that will pay off in increased engine life.

CHAPTER FIVE

CLUTCH AND TRANSMISSION

CLUTCH

The clutch on the Yamaha XS1100 is a wet multi-plate type which operates immersed in the engine oil.

All clutch parts can be removed with the engine in the frame. Refer to **Figure 1** for all clutch components.

Refer to **Table 1** for all clutch torque specifications.

Removal

This procedure is shown with the engine partially disassembled. It is not necessary to do so for clutch removal.

1. Place the bike on the centerstand.

2. Remove the brake lever and front footpeg **(Figure 2)**.

3. Remove the exhaust system on the right-hand side as described under *Exhaust System Removal/Installation* in Chapter Six.

4. Drain the engine oil as described under *Changing Engine Oil and Filter* in Chapter Three.

5. Slacken the clutch cable at the hand lever **(Figure 3)**.

6. Remove the 2 screws **(Figure 4)** securing the clutch release mechanism cover and remove it.

7. Straighten out the retaining clip (A, **Figure 5**), push up on the release arm (B, **Figure 5**) and remove the cable from the arm **(Figure 6)**.

8. Remove the 13 Allen bolts **(Figure 7)** securing the right-hand side cover in place and remove it. Remove the clutch cable from the side cover.

9. Remove the 6 clutch bolts **(Figure 8)** and remove the pressure plate No. 1 **(Figure 9)**.

10. Remove the 6 clutch springs **(Figure 10)**.

11. Straighten out the locking tab **(Figure 11)** on the clutch nut and remove the clutch nut with an impact driver and socket.

12. Remove the lockwasher **(Figure 12)** and spring washer **(Figure 13)**.

13. Remove the clutch boss assembly, clutch discs, and plates and pressure plate No. 2.

Table 1   CLUTCH AND TRANSMISSION TORQUE SPECIFICATIONS

Item	Foot-Pounds (Ft.-lb.)	Newton Meters (N•m)
Clutch boss assembly nut	51	70
Clutch spring bolts	7.5	10
Left-hand side cover bolts	7.2	10
Shift cam detent	7.2	10
Shift drum locating bolt	14	20
Countershaft retaining washer/bolt	51	70

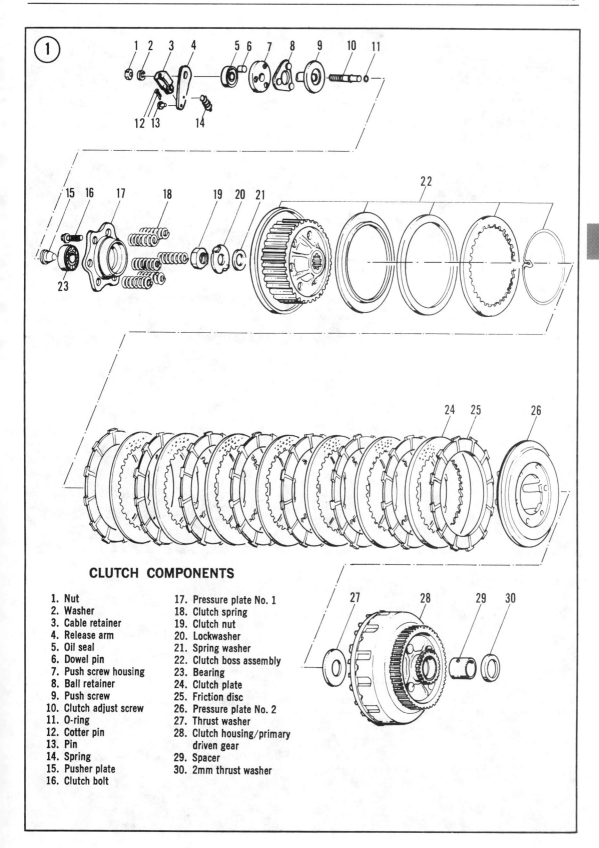

CLUTCH COMPONENTS

1. Nut
2. Washer
3. Cable retainer
4. Release arm
5. Oil seal
6. Dowel pin
7. Push screw housing
8. Ball retainer
9. Push screw
10. Clutch adjust screw
11. O-ring
12. Cotter pin
13. Pin
14. Spring
15. Pusher plate
16. Clutch bolt
17. Pressure plate No. 1
18. Clutch spring
19. Clutch nut
20. Lockwasher
21. Spring washer
22. Clutch boss assembly
23. Bearing
24. Clutch plate
25. Friction disc
26. Pressure plate No. 2
27. Thrust washer
28. Clutch housing/primary driven gear
29. Spacer
30. 2mm thrust washer

5

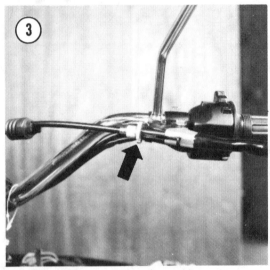

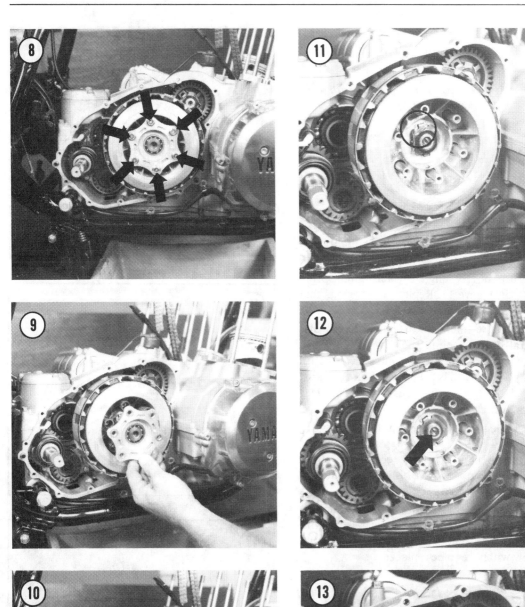

5

14. Remove the thrust washer (A, **Figure 14**) and clutch housing/primary driven gear (B, **Figure 14**).

> NOTE: *The spacer may come off with the clutch housing or may stay on the transmission shaft. Don't let it fall out onto the ground as it may be damaged.*

15. Remove the spacer and the 2mm thrust washer (**Figure 15**).

Inspection

1. Clean all clutch parts in petroleum-based solvent such as kerosene, and thoroughly dry with compressed air.

2. Measure the free length of each clutch spring as shown in **Figure 16**. Replace the springs that are 1.646 in. (41.8mm) or less.

3. Measure the thickness of each friction disc at several places around the disc as shown in **Figure 17**. The standard thickness is 0.12 in. (3.0mm). If any disc is 0.11 in. (2.8mm) or less, replace the entire set of discs, do not replace only 1 or 2 discs.

4. Check the metal clutch plates for warpage as shown in **Figure 18**. If any plate is warped 0.0039 in. (0.1mm) or more, replace the entire set of plates; do not replace only 1 or 2 plates.

5. Inspect the condition of the teeth on the primary driven gear (**Figure 19**) for damage. Remove any small nicks on the gear teeth with an oilstone. If damage is severe, the entire assembly will have to be replaced.

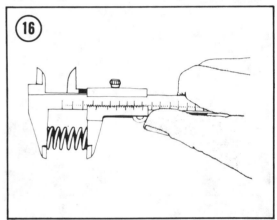

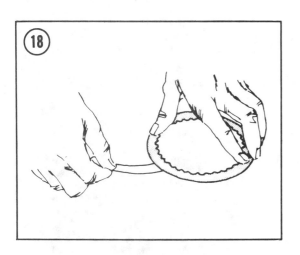

NOTE: *If the primary driven gear/clutch housing or spacer are to be replaced they must be sized to each other. Each part is marked with either one or two lines (Figure 20). A primary drive with one line may be used with a spacer having either one or two lines, but a primary drive marked with two lines **must be used** with a spacer having two lines.*

6. Also check the condition of the gear teeth on the primary drive gear (A, **Figure 21**) and the oil pump gear (B, **Figure 21**).

7. Inspect the clutch outer housing (**Figure 22**)

5

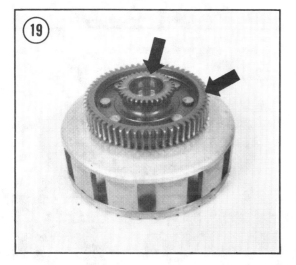

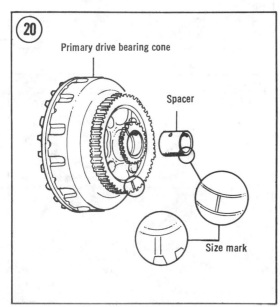

Primary drive bearing cone

Spacer

Size mark

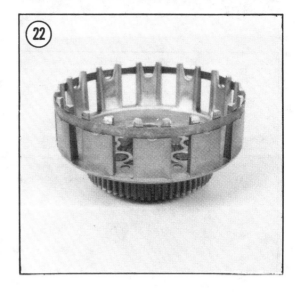

and clutch boss assembly **(Figure 23)** for cracks or galling in the grooves where the clutch friction disc tabs slide. They must be smooth for chatter-free clutch operation.

8. Inspect the condition of the splines **(Figure 24)** in the clutch boss assembly. If damage is only a slight amount, remove any small burrs with a fine cut file; if damage is severe, replace the assembly.

> NOTE: *The clutch boss is a sub-assembly with a built-in damper located inside the first clutch plate. Do not disassemble this unit unless there is severe clutch chatter. Make sure the retaining ring end (**Figure 25**) is securely in place.*

9. Inspect the condition of the notches (A, **Figure 26**) and the spring bosses (B, **Figure 26**) in the pressure plate No. 2.

10. Inspect the condition of the ball-bearing in the pressure plate No. 1. Make sure it rotates smoothly with no signs of wear or damage. If necessary, replace the pressure plate.

11. Inspect the condition of the end of the clutch push screw for any signs of indentation. Make sure the push screw assembly moves smoothly. If the end is indented or the operation of the assembly is not smooth, replace the push screw assembly.

Installation

1. Install the 2mm thrust washer and spacer **(Figure 27)**.

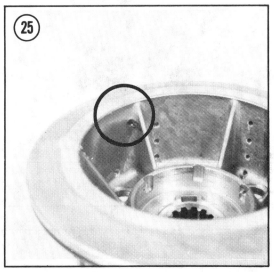

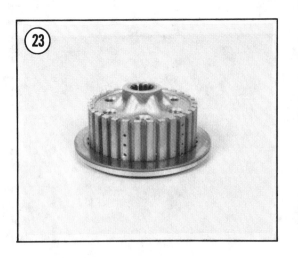

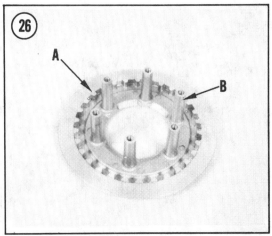

NOTE: *Prior to installing them, coat the transmission shaft and the inside and outside of the spacer with new engine oil.*

2. Install the clutch housing/primary driven gear. Make sure it meshes properly with both the primary drive gear and oil pump gear (**Figure 28**).

NOTE: *While pushing the clutch housing/primary driven gear on, slightly rotate it back and forth until the gears mesh properly. Push it on until it bottoms out.*

3. Install the thrust washer (**Figure 29**).

4. Install the 8 friction discs and 7 clutch plates. Install a friction plate first and then a clutch plate; alternate until all are installed, ending up with a friction plate installed last.

NOTE: *If either or both friction and clutch plates have been replaced with new ones, coat all surfaces with new engine oil. This will prevent the clutch from locking up when it is used for the first time.*

5. Install the pressure plate No. 2 onto the assembled clutch boss assembly. Install one spring and bolt, only finger-tight, to hold this assembly together for installation (**Figure 30**).

6. Install the clutch boss assembly into the clutch housing/primary driven gear (**Figure 31**). Push in slowly while aligning the tabs on the friction plates into the clutch housing. Push it in until it bottoms out.

> **CAUTION**
> *Be careful not to damage or bend the friction plate tabs during installation.*

7. Install the spring washer (A, **Figure 32**) with the dome-shaped side facing toward the outside.

8. Install a new lockwasher. Make sure the locking tabs (B, **Figure 32**) on the lockwasher are inserted into the slots in the pressure plate (C, **Figure 32**). Push the lockwasher all the way on (**Figure 33**).

9. Install the clutch nut and tighten to 51 ft.-lb. (70 N•m). Use a torque wrench and socket (**Figure 34**) and bend up the lockwasher against one side of the nut (**Figure 35**).

10. Remove the bolt and spring installed in Step 5 and install the 6 clutch springs, pressure plate No. 1 and 6 clutch bolts. Tighten the bolts in a crisscross pattern (**Figure 36**) to 7.5 ft.-lb. (10 N•m).

11. Continue installation by reversing *Removal* Steps 1-8.

12. Adjust the clutch mechanism and cable as described under *Clutch Adjustment* in Chapter Three.

13. Refill the crankcase with the recommended type and quantity of engine oil; refer to Chapter Three.

CLUTCH CABLE

Replacement

In time, the cable will stretch to the point where it is no longer useful and will have to be replaced.

1. Remove the seat and remove the rear bolt securing the fuel tank. Disconnect the fuel gauge electrical connector.

2. Turn both fuel shutoff valves to the ON or RES position. Lift up on the rear of the fuel tank and remove the fuel lines to the carburetors and the vacuum lines to the intake manifolds.

3. Pull the tank to the rear and remove it.

4. Loosen the adjustment nut (**Figure 37**) and remove the cable from the hand lever.

5. Remove the 2 screws (**Figure 38**) securing the clutch release mechanism cover and remove it.

6. Straighten out the retaining clip (A, **Figure 39**), push up on the release arm (B, **Figure 39**) and remove the cable from the arm.

5

7. Remove the cable from the right-hand side cover.

8. Slip the cable out from the retaining clip on the right-hand carburetor (**Figure 40**).

> NOTE: *Prior to removing the cable, make a drawing of the cable routing through the frame. It is very easy to forget how it was, once it has been removed. Replace it exactly as it was, avoiding any sharp turns.*

9. Remove the cable from the frame and replace with a new one.

10. Adjust the cable free play as described under *Clutch Adjustment* in Chapter Three.

SHIFT MECHANISM

Removal

1. Place the bike on the centerstand and drain the engine oil as described in Chapter Three.

2. Remove the exhaust system on the left-hand side as described under *Exhaust System Removal/Installation* in Chapter Six.

3. Remove the front footpeg.

4. Remove the bolt (**Figure 41**) clamping the shift lever and remove the lever.

5. Remove the 9 Allen bolts (**Figure 42**) securing the left-hand side cover in place and remove it and the gasket.

> NOTE: *Remove the ignition wire harness from the 3 clips, and disconnect the neutral indicator switch wire.*

6. Remove the shift shaft No. 1 assembly (**Figure 43**).

7. Remove the circlip (**Figure 44**) on the shift shaft No. 2.

8. Flip the shift pawl up and out of the shift drum (**Figure 45**) and remove the shift lever.

Installation

1. Install the shift lever and position the shift pawl onto the shift drum.

2. Install a new circlip (**Figure 44**).

3. Install the shift shaft No. 1 with the tension spring correctly located (**Figure 46**) on the stopper bolt.

4. The punch marks (**Figure 47**) must align on each lever.

> NOTE: *This alignment is necessary for proper gear shifting.*

5

5. Shift the transmission into second gear. Make sure the line on the shift drum aligns with the line on the shift lever (A, **Figure 48**). If alignment is incorrect, adjust by loosening the locknut and turning the eccentric screw (B, **Figure 48**). After alignment is correct, tighten the locknut.

6. Make sure the 2 locating dowels (A, **Figure 49**) are in place, and install a new gasket (B, **Figure 49**).

7. Install the left-hand side cover, making sure the 3 wire clips are properly positioned (A, **Figure 50**). Attach the neutral indicator switch wire (B, **Figure 50**). Tighten all Allen screws to 7.2 ft.-lb. (10 N•m).

8. Install the shift lever, footpeg, and exhaust system.

9. Refill the crankcase with the recommended type and quantity engine oil; refer to Chapter Three.

TRANSMISSION

The crankcase must be split to gain access to the transmission components.

Refer to **Table 1** for transmission torque specifications.

Removal

1. Perform Steps 1-8 in *Crankcase Disassembly* in Chapter Four.

2. Remove the middle driven gear assembly (**Figure 51**).

3. Remove the main shaft assembly (**Figure 52**).

4. Remove the circlip (**Figure 53**) on the shift fork shaft.

5. Withdraw the shift fork shaft (**Figure 54**) and remove the shift forks.

6. Remove the 3 Torx bolts (**Figure 55**) securing the countershaft bearing housing and remove the housing. These bolts have been Loctited in place so it may be difficult to remove them.

> NOTE: *A special tool is required to remove the Torx bolts. The size is T-30 and it is available as shown in* **Figure 56** *or shaped similar to a screwdriver.*

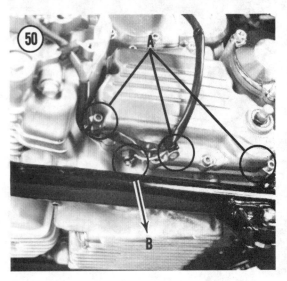

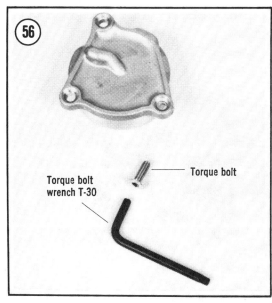

Torque bolt

Torque bolt
wrench T-30

These tools are manufactured by Proto and Apex and are available at most large hardware, automotive, or motorcycle supply stores.

7. Remove the washer/bolt (**Figure 57**) on the opposite end of the countershaft with an impact driver.

> NOTE: *Have an assistant place a shop cloth on the gears and hold it while removing the bolt.*

8. Pivot the countershaft assembly up and carefully remove it.

Installation

Prior to installation, coat all bearings and bearing surfaces with assembly oil.

1. Install the countershaft assembly.

2. Install the washer/bolt (**Figure 57**) and tighten to 51 ft.-lb. (70 N•m).

> NOTE: *Have an assistant place a shop cloth on the gears and hold it while tightening the bolt.*

3. Install the countershaft bearing housing (**Figure 58**). Apply Loctite Lock 'N' Seal, or equivalent, to the Torx bolts prior to installation.

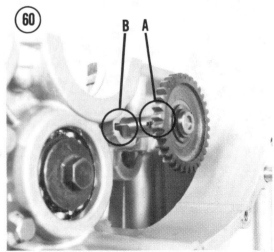

4. Position the No. 1 and No. 3 shift forks onto the countershaft assembly and shift drum. Slide the shift fork shaft in all the way. Each shift fork has its number cast into it (No. 1, 2, 3). Refer to **Figure 59** for correct placement.

NOTE: *Make sure the pin followers are installed into each shift fork prior to installation. The No. 2 shift fork must be positioned **up** as it fits into the main shaft assembly.*

*Align the pin in the shift fork shaft (A, **Figure 60**) with the slot in the crankcase (B, **Figure 60**) when installing it. After installing it, check that the relief on the shaft (**Figure 61**) is positioned correctly so that the middle drive gear on the countershaft clears it.*

5. Install a new circlip (**Figure 53**) on the shift fork shaft.

6. Install the main shaft assembly in the lower crankcase half (**Figure 62**).

NOTE: *Make sure the circlips are properly seated in the slots in the crankcase and that the locating pin on the bearing is positioned correctly in the locating notch in the crankcase (**Figure 63**).*

7. Install the middle driven gear assembly (**Figure 64**). Apply grease to the lips of the seal prior to installation.

NOTE: *Make sure the circlips are properly positioned (Figure 65) and that they seat properly in the slots in the crankcase.*

8. Perform Steps 1-17, *Crankcase Assembly* in Chapter Four.

Main Shaft Disassembly/Assembly

Refer to **Figure 66** for this procedure.

1. Slide off the bearing/circlip (**Figure 67**).
2. Remove the circlip and washer (**Figure 68**).
3. Slide off the 5th gear (**Figure 69**).
4. Remove the thrust washer (**Figure 70**) and circlip (**Figure 71**).
5. Slide off the 2nd/3rd combination gear (**Figure 72**).

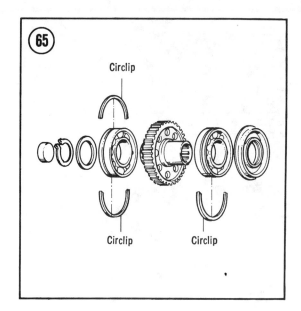

Circlip

Circlip   Circlip

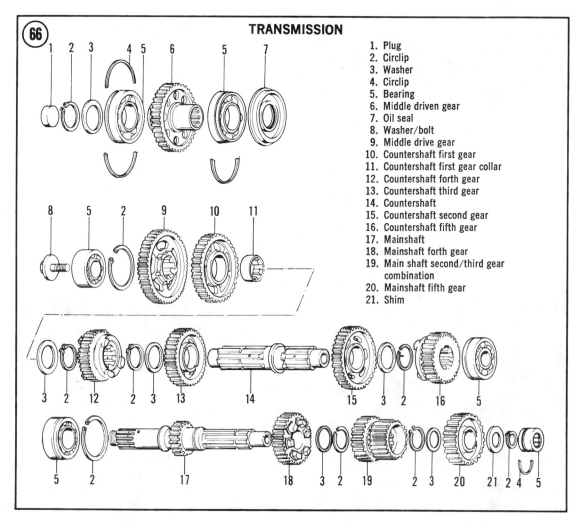

TRANSMISSION

1. Plug
2. Circlip
3. Washer
4. Circlip
5. Bearing
6. Middle driven gear
7. Oil seal
8. Washer/bolt
9. Middle drive gear
10. Countershaft first gear
11. Countershaft first gear collar
12. Countershaft forth gear
13. Countershaft third gear
14. Countershaft
15. Countershaft second gear
16. Countershaft fifth gear
17. Mainshaft
18. Mainshaft forth gear
19. Main shaft second/third gear combination
20. Mainshaft fifth gear
21. Shim

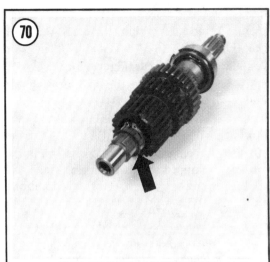

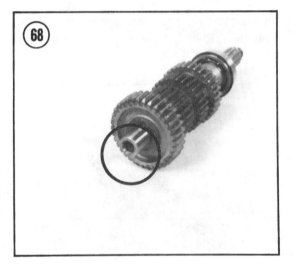

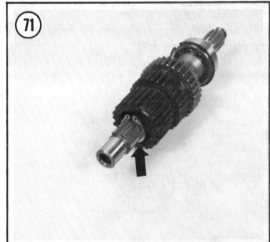

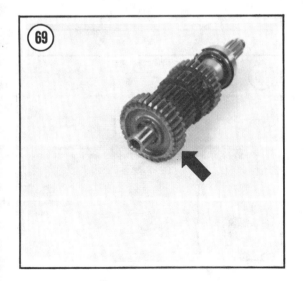

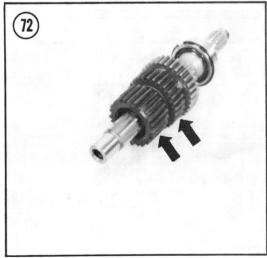

5

6. Remove the circlip and thrust washer (**Figure 73**) located within the recess in the 4th gear (**Figure 74**).

7. Slide off the 4th gear (**Figure 75**).

8. If necessary remove the ball bearing (A, **Figure 76**) from the shaft.

9. Clean all parts in cleaning solvent and thoroughly dry.

10. Check each gear for excessive wear, burrs, pitting, or chipped or missing teeth. Make sure the lugs on ends of gears are in good condition.

> NOTE: *Defective gears should be replaced, and it is a good idea to replace the mating gear on the countershaft even though it may not show as much wear or damage.*

11. Make sure that all gears slide smoothly on the main shaft splines. Inspect the condition of the splines (B, **Figure 76**).

12. Check the condition of the large bearing (A, **Figure 76**) and the smaller end bearing (**Figure 77**). Make sure they rotate smoothly (**Figure 78**) without signs of wear or damage. Replace if necessary.

13. Assemble by reversing these removal steps. Refer to **Figure 79** for correct placement of the gears. Make sure that all circlips are seated correctly in the main shaft grooves.

14. Make sure each gear engages properly to the adjoining gear where applicable.

Countershaft Disassembly/Assembly

Refer to **Figure 66** for this procedure.

1. Slide off the middle drive gear (**Figure 80**).

2. Slide off the 1st gear collar and 1st gear (**Figure 81**).

3. Remove the thrust washer (**Figure 82**) and circlip (**Figure 83**).

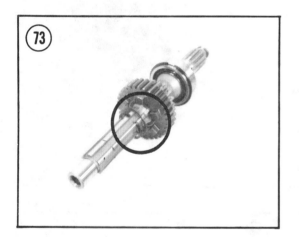

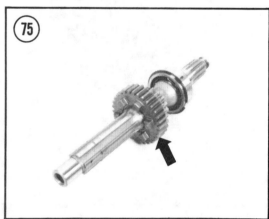

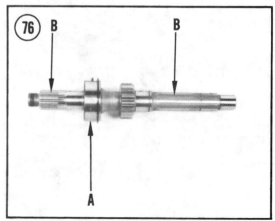

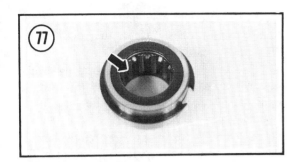

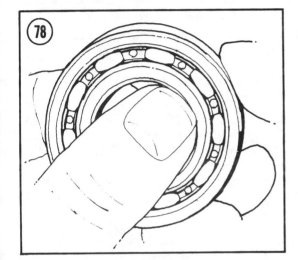

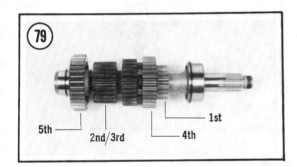

5th —— 2nd/3rd —— 4th —— 1st

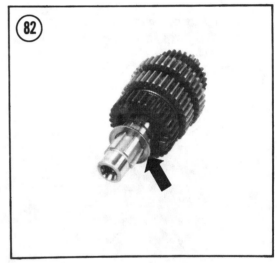

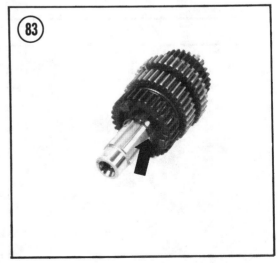

4. Slide off the 4th gear (**Figure 84**).

5. Remove the circlip and thrust washer (**Figure 85**) located within the recess in the 3rd gear (**Figure 86**).

6. Slide off the 3rd gear (**Figure 87**).

7. Slide off the 5th gear (**Figure 88**).

8. Remove the thrust washer and circlip (**Figure 89**).

9. Slide off the 2nd gear (**Figure 90**).

10. Clean all parts in cleaning solvent and thoroughly dry.

11. Check each gear for excessive wear, burrs, pitting, or chipped or missing teeth. Make sure the lugs on ends of gears are in good condition.

> NOTE: *Defective gears should be replaced, and it is a good idea to replace the mating gear on the main shaft and middle driven gear assembly even though it may not show signs of wear or damage.*

12. Make sure all gears slide smoothly on the countershaft splines. Inspect the condition of the splines (**Figure 91**).

13. Check the condition of the bearing. Make sure it rotates smoothly (**Figure 78**) with no signs of wear or damage. Replace it if necessary.

14. Assemble by reversing these removal steps. Refer to **Figure 92** for correct placement of the gears. Make sure all circlips are seated correctly in the countershaft grooves.

15. Make sure each gear engages properly to the adjoining gear where applicable.

Middle Driven Gear Assembly Inspection

1. Inspect the condition of the gear teeth (A, **Figure 93**) for excessive wear, burrs, pitting, or chipped or missing teeth.

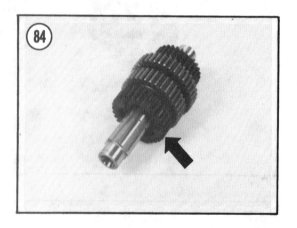

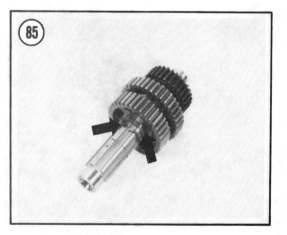

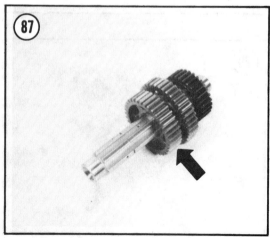

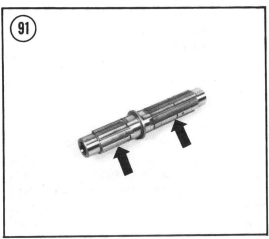

5

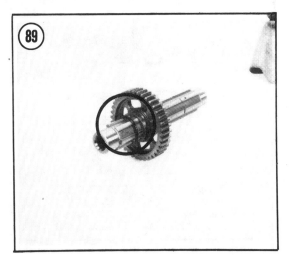

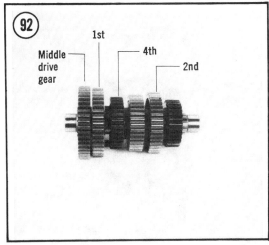

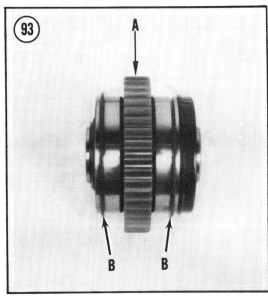

NOTE: *If the gear is defective it should be replaced and it is a good idea to replace the mating gear on the counter-shaft even though it may not show signs of wear or damage.*

2. Check the condition of the internal splines (A, **Figure 94**). Make sure it engages properly with the splined shaft on the middle gear case.

3. Inspect the condition of the bearings. Make sure they rotate smoothly with no signs of wear or damage. If bearing replacement is necessary, remove the circlip (**Figure 95**) and washer and

remove the bearing from the right-hand side. To remove the left-hand bearing, slide off the oil seal (B, **Figure 94**) and the bearing.

NOTE: *Replace the oil seal at the same time. Be sure to apply a small amount of grease to the seal lips prior to sliding it onto the shaft.*

4. Install the bearings by reversing Step 3.

5. Make sure the circlips (B, **Figure 93**) are snug in the grooves in the bearings, if not they should be replaced.

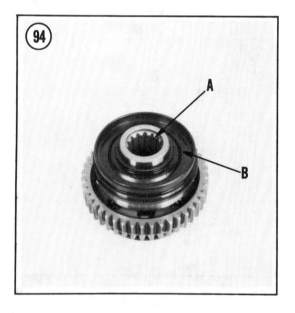

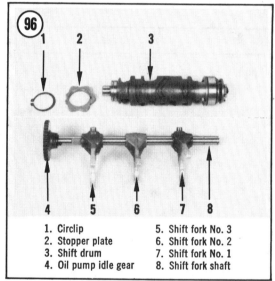

1. Circlip
2. Stopper plate
3. Shift drum
4. Oil pump idle gear
5. Shift fork No. 3
6. Shift fork No. 2
7. Shift fork No. 1
8. Shift fork shaft

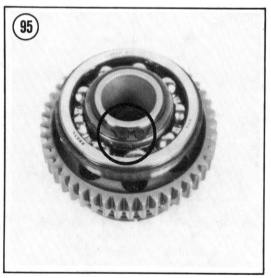

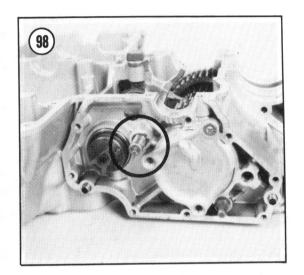

GEARSHIFT DRUM AND FORKS

Removal

Refer to **Figure 96** for this procedure.

1. Perform Steps 1-9, *Crankcase Disassembly* in Chapter Four.

2. Remove middle gear assembly (A, **Figure 97**).

3. Remove mainshaft assembly (B, **Figure 97**).

4. Remove the circlip (**Figure 98**) on the shift fork shaft.

5. Withdraw the shift fork shaft (**Figure 99**) and remove the shift forks.

6. Straighten out the lock tab on the lockwasher (**Figure 100**) and remove the shift cam detent (**Figure 101**).

7. Remove neutral safety switch (**Figure 102**).

5

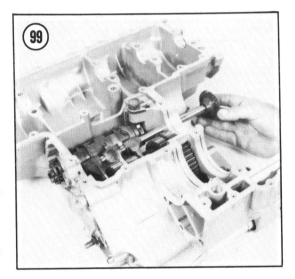

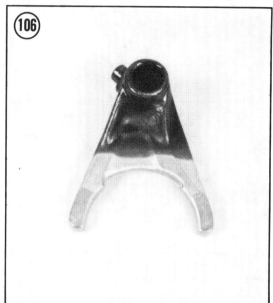

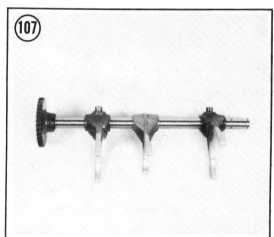

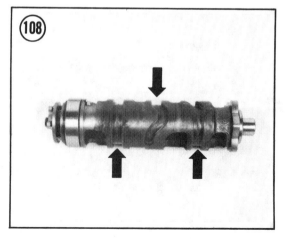

8. Remove the shift drum locating bolt and retainer (**Figure 103**) and remove the guide pin (**Figure 104**).

9. Partially withdraw the shift drum and remove circlip and stopper plate (**Figure 105**). Remove the shift drum.

10. Wash all parts in solvent and thoroughly dry with compressed air.

Inspection

1. Inspect each shift fork for signs of wear or cracking (**Figure 106**). Make sure the forks slide smoothly on the shaft (**Figure 107**). Make sure the shaft is not bent.

> NOTE: *Check for any arc shaped wear marks on the shift forks. If this is apparent, the shift fork has come in contact with the gear, indicating the fingers are worn beyond use and the fork must be replaced.*

2. Check grooves in the shift drum (**Figure 108**) for wear or roughness.

3. Check the shift drum bearing (**Figure 109**). Make sure it operates smoothly with no signs of wear or damage.

4. Check the cam pin followers in each shift fork. It should fit snugly but not too tightly. Check the end that rides in the shift drum for wear or burrs. Replace as necessary.

5. Check the stopper plate (**Figure 110**) for wear; replace if necessary.

Assembly

1. Coat all of the bearing surfaces with assembly oil.

2. Install the shift drum from the right-hand side and install the stopper plate and circlip (**Figure 105**).

3. Install the shift cam detent (**Figure 101**) and tighten to 7.2 ft.-lb. (10 N•m).

4. Install the neutral safety switch (**Figure 102**).

5. Install shift drum locating bolt (**Figure 103**) and tighten to 14 ft.-lb. (20 N•m).

> CAUTION
> *Be sure to bend up the locking tab onto the side of the bolt.*

> NOTE: *Make sure that the pin followers are installed in each shift fork prior to installation.*

6. Partially insert the shift fork shaft and position the No. 3 shift fork onto the countershaft assembly. Push shaft through it (**Figure 111**).

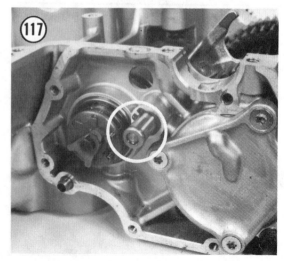

7. Position No. 2 shift fork in the UP position and slide the shaft through it (**Figure 112**).

> NOTE: *Make sure shift fork is up as it will be inserted into the main shaft assembly.*

8. Position the No. 1 shift fork into the countershaft assembly and slide the shaft through it (**Figure 113**).

> NOTE: *Make sure the pin followers are all riding correctly in the shift drum grooves (**Figure 114**) and that all shift forks are positioned as shown.*

9. Align the pin in the shift fork shaft (A, **Figure 115**) with the slot in the crankcase (B, **Figure 115**) when installing it. After installation, check that the relief on shaft (**Figure 116**) is positioned correctly so that the middle drive gear, on the countershaft, clears it.

10. Install a new circlip (**Figure 117**) on the shift fork shaft.

11. Complete installation by performing Steps 6-8, *Transmission Installation* in this chapter.

5

NOTE: If you own a 1980 or 1981 model, first check the Supplement at the back of the book for any new service information.

CHAPTER SIX

FUEL AND EXHAUST SYSTEMS

The fuel system consists of the fuel tank, two shutoff valves with fuel filters, four Mikuni constant velocity carburetors, and an air cleaner.

The exhaust system consists of four exhaust pipes, a crossover pipe, and two mufflers.

This chapter includes service procedures for all parts of the fuel and exhaust system.

AIR CLEANER

The air cleaner must be cleaned every 1,000 miles (1,600km) or more frequently in dusty areas.

Service the air cleaner element as described under *Air Cleaner* in Chapter Three.

CARBURETORS

Basic Principles

An understanding of the function of each of the carburetor components and their relationship to one another is a valuable aid for pinpointing a source of carburetor trouble.

The carburetor's purpose is to supply and atomize fuel and mix it in correct proportions with air that is drawn in through the air intake. At the primary throttle opening — at idle — a small amount of fuel is siphoned through the

pilot jet by the incoming air. As the throttle is opened further, the air stream begins to siphon fuel through the main jet and needle jet. The tapered needle increases the effective flow capacity of the needle jet, as it is lifted with the air slide, in that it occupies decreasingly less of the area of the jet. In addition, the amount of cutaway in the leading edge of the throttle slide aids in controlling the fuel/air mixture during partial throttle openings.

At full throttle, the carburetor venturi is fully open and the needle is lifted far enough to permit the main jet to flow at full capacity.

Air flow through the carburetor is controlled by the throttle slide (vacuum piston). The throttle slide is moved by engine vacuum rather than the throttle cable. By working this way, the carburetor automatically compensates for any change in atmospheric pressure. This is usually encountered when riding at high altitudes.

The two-position type starter jet (choke) is designed to provide an even mixture of fuel/air for the engine during the entire warm-up period until the engine reaches normal operating temperature.

Starter Jet Operation (Choke)

Refer to **Figure 1** along with this description.

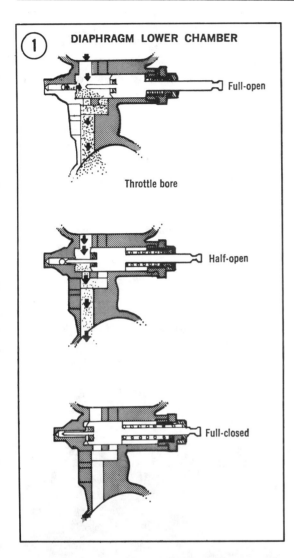

DIAPHRAGM LOWER CHAMBER

Full-open

Throttle bore

Half-open

Full-closed

Full open

A rich mixture is needed to start a cold engine. Pull the choke lever all the way out so the needle regulating the fuel flow allows the fuel to flow at its maximum rate. This fuel is mixed with the air supplied from the diaphragm lower chamber and creates a rich mixture.

Half open

A slightly rich mixture is needed halfway through the warm-up period. Push the choke lever in halfway and the fuel flow rate is decreased as the needle moves back in. This fuel is mixed with the air from the diaphragm lower chamber and is only slightly rich.

Full closed

When the engine reaches the normal operating temperature this additional slightly rich mixture is no longer needed. Push the choke lever all the way in, thus closing the needle and shutting off any additional fuel supply from this system. The carburetor will now operate on its regular fuel/air mixture.

> NOTE: *Do not run a warm engine with the choke lever in the half or fully open position* (***Figure 2***). *This will result in excessive exhaust emission and will give poor performance and gas mileage.*

Service

The carburetor service recommended at 10,000-mile intervals involves routine removal, disassembly, cleaning, and inspection. Alterations in jet size, throttle slide cutaway, changes in needle position, etc., should be attempted only if you are experienced in this type of "tuning" work; a bad guess could result in costly engine damage or, at the very least, poor performance. If after servicing the carburetors and making the adjustments described in Chapter Three, the motorcycle does not perform correctly (and assuming that other factors affecting performance are correct, such as ignition timing and condition, valve adjustment, etc.) the motorcycle should be checked by a Yamaha dealer or a qualified performance tuning specialist.

Refer to **Table 1** for fuel and exhaust torque specifications and to **Table 2** for complete carburetor specifications.

Removal/Installation

1. Place the bike on the centerstand; remove the right- and left-hand side covers.

2. Remove the seat and disconnect the battery negative lead.

3. Remove the rear bolt (A, **Figure 3**) securing the fuel tank. Disconnect the fuel gauge electrical connector (B, **Figure 3**).

4. Turn both fuel shutoff valves to the ON or RES position, lift up on the rear of the tank and remove the fuel lines to the carburetors and vacuum lines to the intake manifolds (**Figure 4**).

5. Pull the tank to the rear and remove it.

6. Remove the 4 wing nuts (**Figure 5**) securing the air cleaner base and remove it and the element.

7. Loosen the 4 clamping screws on the front rubber intake tubes (A, **Figure 6**) and slide the clamps away from the carburetors.

8. Loosen the 4 clamping screws on the rear rubber boots (B, **Figure 6**) and slide the clamps away from the carburetors.

9. Remove the crankcase breather and carburetor ventilation hoses (**Figure 7**) from the air cleaner box.

10. Remove the vacuum advance hose from the No. 2 carburetor.

> NOTE: *The carburetors are numbered in the same sequence as the engine cylinders, with No. 1 on the left-hand side and No. 2, 3, and 4 from left to right.*

11. Remove the top bolt (A, **Figure 8**) and 2 side bolts (B, **Figure 8**), there is one on each side, securing the air cleaner box to the frame.

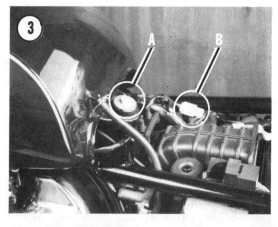

NOTE: *Do not loosen or remove any of the Phillips head screws on top of the air cleaner box (Figure 9). There are many internal washers, sleeves, brackets, etc., that will come apart. It is very time consuming and frustrating to reassemble these little monsters, so leave them alone.*

Table 1   FUEL TANK AND EXHAUST TORQUE SPECIFICATIONS

Item	Foot-Pounds	Newton Meters
Fuel tank mounting bolt	3.6	5.0
Exhaust flange bolts	14.5	20
Crossover pipe	7.5	1.0
Muffler to exhaust pipe	7.5	1.0
Muffler rear bracket	28	3.8

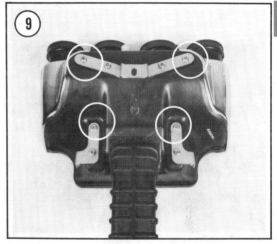

Table 2   CARBURETOR SPECIFICATIONS

	XS1100/E	XS1100/F	XS1100/SF
Manufacturer	Mikuni	Mikuni	Mikuni
Model No.	BS34-11 2H7-00	BS34-11 2H7-00	BS34-11 3H3-00
Main jet No.	137.5	137.5	137.5
Needle jet No.	X-2	X-2	X-2
Starter jet No.	40	32.5	32.5
Pilot jet No.	42.5	42.5	42.5
Air jet — main	140	140	140
Air jet — pilot	180	180	180
Jet needle	5GZ6	5GZ6	5GZ6
Jet needle position	3	3	3
Float height*	1.012 ± 0.04 in. (25.7 ± 1.0mm)	1.012 ± 0.04 in. (25.7 ± 1.0mm)	1.012 ± 0.04 in. (25.7 ± 1.0mm)
Idle mixture screw**	Pre-set	Pre-set	Pre-set
Fuel valve seat	0.079 in. (2.0mm)	0.079 in. (2.0mm)	0.079 in. (2.0mm)
Throttle valve No.	135	135	135
Engine idle speed	950-1,050rpm	1,050-1,150rpm	1,050-1,150rpm

*Above gasket surface
**Preset at the factory — do not reset (if disturbed the setting is 1¼ turns out)

12. Pull the air cleaner box to the rear, separating it from the rear of the carburetor assembly.

13. Remove the clutch cable from the clip (**Figure 10**) on the No. 4 carburetor.

14. Pull the carburetor assembly back to free it from the rubber intake tubes.

15. Slacken the throttle cable at the handlebar and remove the cable from the carburetor assembly (**Figure 11**).

16. Pull the carburetor assembly to the left and remove it.

> NOTE: *Drain most of the gasoline from the carburetor assembly and place it in a clean heavy-duty plastic bag to keep it clean until it is worked on or reinstalled.*

17. Install by reversing these removal steps.

Disassembly/Assembly

Refer to **Figure 12** for this procedure.

It is recommended that only one carburetor be disassembled at a time. This will prevent intermixing of parts.

1. Loosen the 4 setscrews (A, **Figure 13**) on the choke start shaft and remove the shaft from all 4 carburetors.

> NOTE: *Do not lose the 2 small steel positioning balls on the outboard carburetors (No. 1 and 4) when the shaft is removed.*

2. Remove the upper (**Figure 14**) and the lower

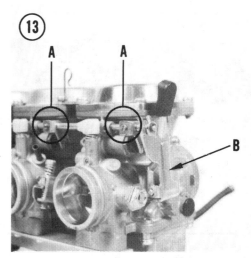

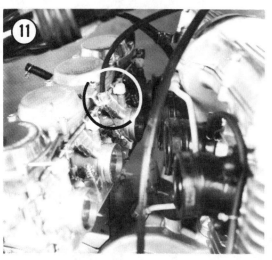

⑫ **CARBURETOR**

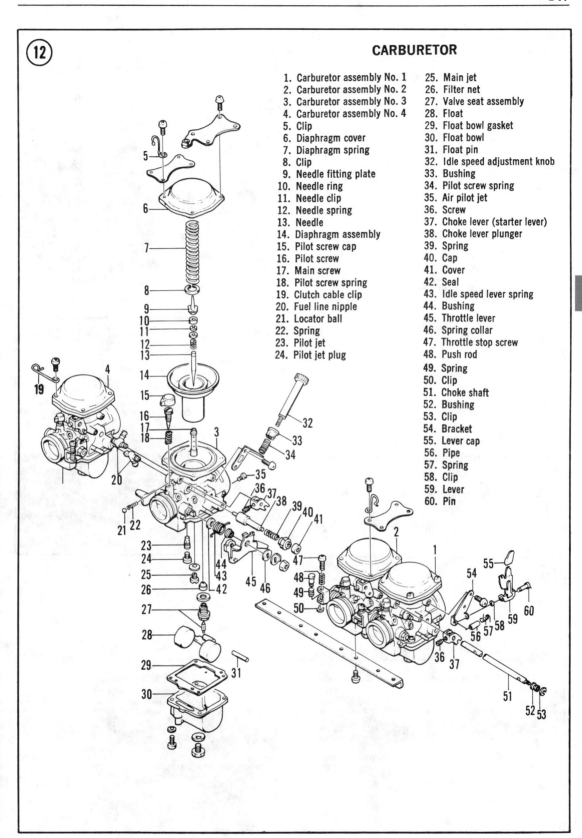

1. Carburetor assembly No. 1
2. Carburetor assembly No. 2
3. Carburetor assembly No. 3
4. Carburetor assembly No. 4
5. Clip
6. Diaphragm cover
7. Diaphragm spring
8. Clip
9. Needle fitting plate
10. Needle ring
11. Needle clip
12. Needle spring
13. Needle
14. Diaphragm assembly
15. Pilot screw cap
16. Pilot screw
17. Main screw
18. Pilot screw spring
19. Clutch cable clip
20. Fuel line nipple
21. Locator ball
22. Spring
23. Pilot jet
24. Pilot jet plug
25. Main jet
26. Filter net
27. Valve seat assembly
28. Float
29. Float bowl gasket
30. Float bowl
31. Float pin
32. Idle speed adjustment knob
33. Bushing
34. Pilot screw spring
35. Air pilot jet
36. Screw
37. Choke lever (starter lever)
38. Choke lever plunger
39. Spring
40. Cap
41. Cover
42. Seal
43. Idle speed lever spring
44. Bushing
45. Throttle lever
46. Spring collar
47. Throttle stop screw
48. Push rod
49. Spring
50. Clip
51. Choke shaft
52. Bushing
53. Clip
54. Bracket
55. Lever cap
56. Pipe
57. Spring
58. Clip
59. Lever
60. Pin

6

(**Figure 15**) assembly brackets and separate the carburetors. Remove air pilot jet (**Figure 16**).

> NOTE: *The carburetors are not separated in this procedure to help simplify the presentation of the material.*

3. Remove the 4 screws (**Figure 17**) securing the diaphragm cover and remove it and any brackets.

> NOTE: *Only the two outboard carburetors (No. 1 and 4) are fitted with polished diaphragm covers. Be sure to install them this way when reassembling. This is for **appearance only** and has no effect on performance or operation of the carburetors.*

4. Remove the starter jet assembly (B, **Figure 13**).

5. Remove the spring (**Figure 18**), diaphragm (vacuum piston) and needle jet (**Figure 19**).

6. Remove the 4 screws (**Figure 20**) securing the float bowl and remove it and the gasket.

7. Remove the main jet (**Figure 21**) and washer (**Figure 22**).

8. Carefully remove main nozzle (**Figure 23**) with needle nose pliers.

9. Remove screw plug and pilot jet (**Figure 24**).

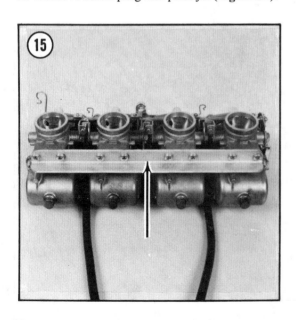

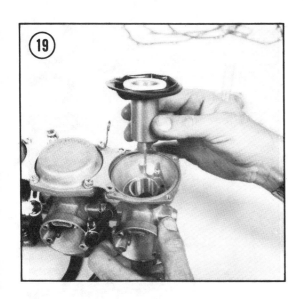

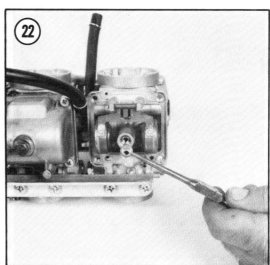

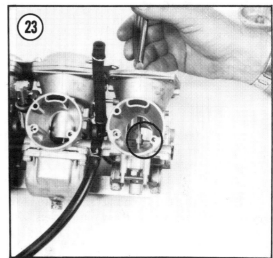

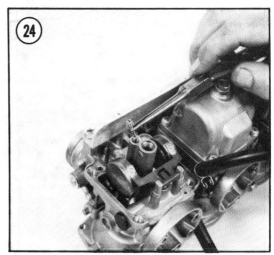

10. Remove the float pin (**Figure 25**) and remove the float.

11. Remove the valve needle (**Figure 26**) and seat (**Figure 27**).

> NOTE: *The idle mixture (**Figure 28**) is pre-set at the factory with the use of special equipment.* **It must not be reset.** *If it has been tampered with, the setting is approximately 1-1/4 turns out from a lightly seated position. After resetting, the carburetors should be checked by a Yamaha dealer so they will be within the required emissions standards.*

12. Clean all parts, except rubber or plastic parts, in a good grade of carburetor cleaner. This solution is available at most automotive or motorcycle supply stores, in a small, resealable tank with a dip basket, for just a few dollars (**Figure 29**). If it is tightly sealed when not in use, the solution will last for several cleanings. Follow the manufacturer's instructions for correct soaking time (usually about ½ hour).

> NOTE: *It is recommended that one carburetor be cleaned at a time to avoid the interchange of parts.*

13. Remove all parts from the cleaner and blow dry with compressed air. Blow out the jets with

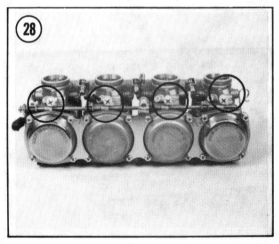

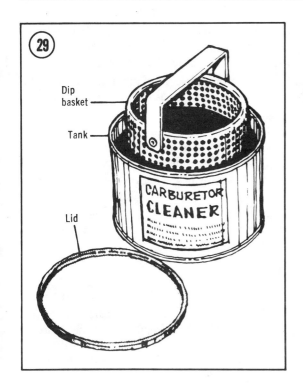

Dip basket

Tank

Lid

CARBURETOR CLEANER

compressed air. *Do not* use a piece of wire to clean them as minor gouges in a jet can alter the flow rate and upset the fuel/air mixture.

14. Repeat Steps 3-11 for the other 3 carburetors. Do not intermix the parts — keep them separated.

15. Prior to assembly, check the float height as described under *Float Height Adjustment* in this chapter.

16. Assemble by reversing these disassembly steps. Be sure to position the tab on the diaphragm (**Figure 30**) correctly into the recess in the carburetor body.

17. Make sure the 4 setscrews (**Figure 13**) seat properly into the detents in the choke start shaft.

18. Be sure to correctly position the small balls in the outboard carburetors (**Figure 31**).

6

Float Adjustment

The carburetor assembly has to be removed and partially disassembled for this adjustment.

1. Remove carburetor assembly as described under *Carburetor Removal/Installation* in this chapter.

2. Remove lower bracket assembly (A, **Figure 32**) only. It is not necessary to remove the upper ones.

3. Remove the float bowls (B, **Figure 32**) from the main body.

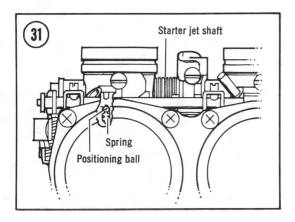

Starter jet shaft

Spring

Positioning ball

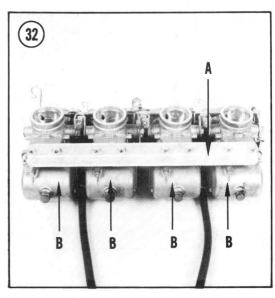

A

B   B   B   B

4. Turn the carburetor assembly upside down.

5. Measure the distance from the bottom of the float to the float bowl gasket surface. See **Figure 33**. The correct height is 1.012 ± 0.04 in. (25.7 ± 1.0mm).

6. Adjust by carefully bending the tang on the float arm (**Figure 33**).

> NOTE: *Both floats within the same carburetor must be at the same height.*

> CAUTION
> *The floats in all 4 carburetors must be adjusted to exactly the same height to maintain the same fuel/air mixture to all 4 cylinders.*

7. If the float level is set too high, the result will be a rich fuel/air mixture. If it is set too low, the mixture will be too lean.

8. Reassemble and install the carburetors by reversing these steps.

Rejetting the Carburetors

Do not try to solve a carburetion problem by rejetting if all the following conditions hold true.

1. The engine has held a good tune in the past with the standard jetting and needle positions.

2. The engine has not been modified.

3. The motorcycle is being operated in the same geographic region under the same general climatic conditions as in the past.

4. The motorcycle was and is being ridden at average highway speeds.

If those conditions all hold true, the chances are that the problem is due to a malfunction in the carburetion or in another component that needs to be adjusted or repaired. Changing the carburetion probably won't solve the problem.

Rejetting the carburetors may be needed if any of the following conditions hold true.

1. A nonstandard type of air filter element is being used.

2. A nonstandard exhaust system is being used.

3. Any of the top end components in the engine (pistons, valves, compression ratio, etc.) have been modified.

4. The motorcycle is in use at considerably higher or lower altitudes, or in a markedly hotter or colder climate, than in the past.

5. The motorcycle is being operated at considerably higher speeds than before, and changing to colder spark plugs did not solve the problem.

6. Someone has changed the jetting or the needle positions in your motorcycle.

7. The motorcycle has never held a satisfactory engine tune.

If rejetting the carburetors is needed, check with a Yamaha dealer for recommendations as to the sizes of jets to install.

Needle Jet Adjustment

Needle position can be adjusted to affect the fuel/air mixture for medium throttle openings.

The carburetor assembly will have to be removed and partially disassembled for this adjustment.

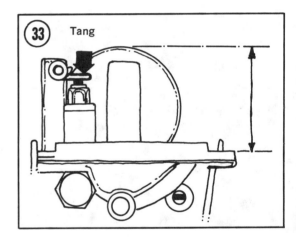

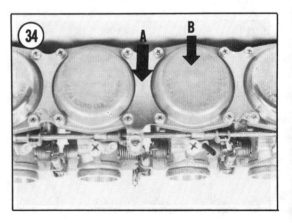

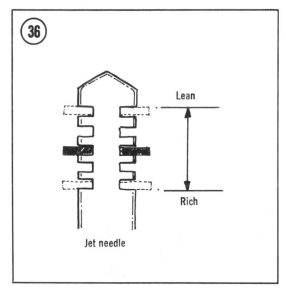

Lean

Rich

Jet needle

1. Remove the carburetors as described under *Carburetor Removal/Installation* in this chapter.

2. Remove the upper brackets (A, **Figure 34**) and remove diaphragm covers (B, **Figure 34**).

3. Remove the diaphragm spring, diaphragm, and the needle jet (**Figure 35**).

4. Note the original position of the needle clip (**Figure 36**). The standard setting is in the middle. Raising the needle (lowering the clip) will enrich the mixture during mid-throttle opening, while lowering it (raising the needle clip) will lean the mixture.

> CAUTION
> *Needle jet setting must be the same for all 3 carburetors.*

5. Reassemble and install the carburetors by reversing these steps.

FUEL SHUTOFF VALVES

Cleaning

1. Turn the valve to the ON or RESERVE position.

2. Remove the fuel and vacuum lines to the carburetors.

3. On regular valves, remove the screws (**Figure 37**) securing the drain cover and remove it. Clean the bottom of the cover with solvent and check the condition of the gasket.

4. On vacuum controlled valves, remove the fuel lines and drain screws (**Figure 38**). Clean the screws with solvent and inspect the condition of the sealing gaskets on the screws; replace if necessary.

5. Install all parts removed.

Removal/Installation and Filter Cleaning

The fuel filter removes particles which might otherwise enter into the carburetors and may cause the float needle to remain in the open position.

Refer to **Figure 39** for this procedure.

1. Turn the valve to the ON or RESERVE position.
2. Remove the fuel line and vacuum line to the valve.

> NOTE: *There is no* OFF *position on the valve. Fuel will not flow through the valve in the* ON *or* RESERVE *position without engine vacuum to open the valve.*

3. Remove seat and remove the bolt (A, **Figure 40**) securing the fuel tank at the rear. Disconnect the fuel gauge electrical connector (B, **Figure 40**). Pull the tank to the rear and remove it.

4. Set the fuel tank on a protective pad or blanket and position it so fuel will not spill out when the shutoff valve is removed.

> NOTE: *Remove only one valve at a time, thus avoiding an intermixing of parts.*

5. Remove the screws (**Figure 41**) securing the shutoff valve to the tank. Remove the valve and gasket.

6. Clean the filter with a medium soft toothbrush and carefully blow out with compressed air.

7. If the valve has been leaking, remove the screws securing the lever fitting plate and disassemble the valve assembly. Inspect all components for cracks or corrosion on all sealing surfaces. Inspect the condition of the O-ring; replace any part if condition is doubtful.

8. Reassemble the valve and install on the fuel tank. Repeat Steps 5-7 for the other valve. Do not forget the tasket between the valve and the fuel tank.

9. Install the fuel tank and seat.

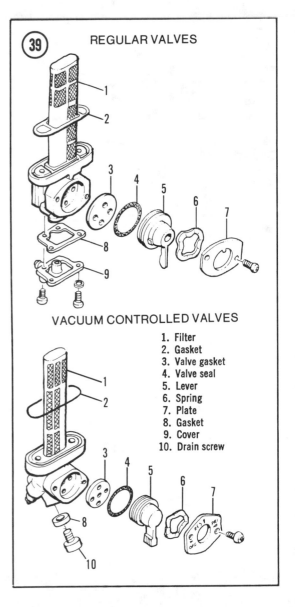

REGULAR VALVES

VACUUM CONTROLLED VALVES

1. Filter
2. Gasket
3. Valve gasket
4. Valve seal
5. Lever
6. Spring
7. Plate
8. Gasket
9. Cover
10. Drain screw

Vacuum Diaphragm

If fuel is not flowing properly to the fuel shutoff valves when the engine is running, the diaphragm may be at fault.

Refer to **Figure 42** for this procedure.

1. Remove the seat and disconnect the battery negative lead.

2. Remove the rear bolt securing the fuel tank and prop it up slightly to gain access to fuel and vacuum lines.

3. Turn both shutoff valves to either the ON or RES position.

4. Disconnect the forward fuel lines (not the rear vacuum lines) from both shutoff valves (A, **Figure 43**). *Fuel should not flow* from the fuel lines when they are removed.

5. Remove the vacuum line from the engine (B, **Figure 43**). Clean off the end and wrap the sides with a clean cloth. Place it in your mouth and suck in to simulate engine vacuum. Fuel should now flow out of both fuel lines.

> NOTE: *Figure 43 is shown with the fuel tank removed for clarity only, do not remove it for this test.*

6. If fuel flows in Step 3 and/or does not flow in Step 4, the diaphragm must be replaced.

7. Remove the fuel tank.

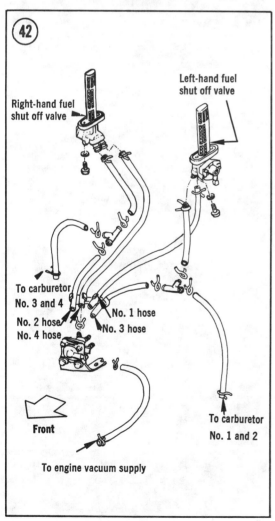

8. Remove screw and lockwasher (**Figure 44**), remove the vacuum lines to it, and remove the diaphragm.

9. When installing the new diaphragm, make sure all vacuum lines are properly routed. Refer to **Figure 42** and to the numbers (No. 1, 2, 3, and 4) on the diaphragm and fuel shutoff valves (No. 1, 2). The left-hand shutoff valve has a No. 1 and the right-hand has a No. 2 on it. Make sure they are connected to their respective numbers on the diaphragm.

FUEL TANK

Removal/Installation

1. Place the bike on the centerstand and remove the left-hand side cover (**Figure 45**).

2. Disconnect battery negative lead (**Figure 46**).

3. Remove the seat.

4. Remove the rear bolt (A, **Figure 47**) securing the fuel tank. Disconnect the fuel gauge electrical wire (B, **Figure 47**).

5. Turn both fuel shutoff valves to the ON or RES position. Lift up on the rear of the tank and remove the fuel lines to the carburetors and vacuum lines to intake manifolds (**Figure 48**).

6. Pull the tank to the rear and remove it.

7. Install by reversing these removal steps.

Sealing (Pin Hole Size)

A small pin hole size leak can be sealed with the use of a product called Thextonite Gas Tank Sealer Stick or equivalent. Follow the manufacturer's instructions.

Sealing (Small Hole Size)

This procedure requires the use of the chemical trichloroethylene, *which is flammable and toxic.*

If you feel unqualified to accomplish it, take the tank to your dealer and let him seal the tank.

> **WARNING**
> *Before attempting any service on the fuel tank, be sure to have a fire extinguisher rated for gasoline or chemical fires within reach. Do not smoke or work where there are any open flames. The work area must be well-ventilated.*

1. Remove the tank as described under *Fuel Tank Removal/Installation* in this chapter.

2. Mark the spot on the tank where the leak is visible with a grease pencil.

3. Turn the fuel shutoff valve to the RESERVE position and blow the interior of the bank completely dry with compressed air.

4. Turn the fuel shutoff valve to the OFF position and pour about one quart (one liter) of non-petroleum solvent into the tank, install the fuel fill cap and shake the tank vigorously one or two minutes. This is used to remove all fuel residue.

5. Drain the non-petroleum solvent solution into a safe storable container. This solution may be reused.

6. Remove the fuel shutoff valve by unscrewing the fitting from the tank. If necessary, plug the tank with a cork or tape it closed with duct tape.

7. Again blow the tank interior completely dry with compressed air.

8. Position the tank so that the point of the leak is located at the lowest part of the tank. This will allow the sealant to accumulate at the point of the leak.

9. Pour the sealant into the tank (a silicone rubber base sealer like Pro-Tech Fuel Tank Sealer, or equivalent, may be used). This is available at most motorcycle supply stores.

10. Let the tank set in this position for at least 48 hours.

11. After the sealant has dried, install the fuel shutoff valve, turn it to the OFF position and refill the tank with fuel.

12. After the tank has been filled, let it sit for at least 2 hours and recheck the leak area.

13. Install the tank on the motorcycle.

EXHAUST SYSTEM

The exhaust system consists of four exhaust pipes, a crossover pipe, and two mufflers.

Removal/Installation

1. Place the bike on the centerstand.

2. Loosen the bolt **(Figure 49)** securing the clamp on the crossover pipe.

3. Remove the 8 Allen bolts (**Figure 50**) securing the exhaust pipe flanges to the cylinder head.

4. Loosen the 2 clamps (**Figure 51**) securing the 2 inboard exhaust pipes to the outboard exhaust pipes.

5. Loosen the acorn nuts and bolts (**Figure 52**) securing the muffler to the footrest bracket.

6. Remove the 2 inboard exhaust pipes.

7. Separate the crossover pipe at the joint.

8. Remove the muffler attachment bolts and acorn nuts (**Figure 52**) and remove the outboard exhaust pipe and muffler as an assembly. Repeat for the other side.

9. Install by reversing these removal steps, noting the following.

10. Install a new gasket into each exhaust port in the cylinder head.

11. The exhaust pipes are numbered to correspond to the correct cylinder number (No. 1, 2, 3, and 4). These numbers are stamped on the flanged end of the exhaust pipe (**Figure 53**). The No. 1 cylinder is on the left-hand side of the bike with Nos. 2, 3, and 4 from left to right.

12. Tighten the rear muffler bolts only finger-tight until the exhaust flange bolts are securely tightened; then tighten them completely. This will minimize an exhaust leak at the cylinder head. Be sure the split keepers are correctly installed into the recesses in the cylinder head.

> NOTE: *Tighten the muffler and crossover pipe bolts to 7.5 ft.-lb. (1.0 N•m) and the exhaust flange bolts to 14.5 ft.-lb. (20 N•m).*

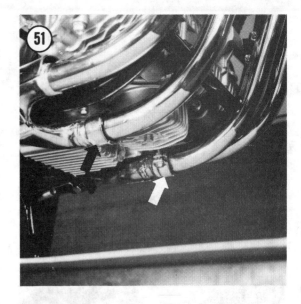

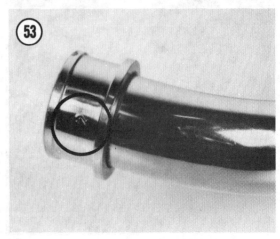

NOTE: If you own a 1980 or 1981 model, first check the Supplement at the back of the book for any new service information.

CHAPTER SEVEN

ELECTRICAL SYSTEM

The electrical system includes the following systems (each is described in detail in this chapter):

a. Charging system
b. Ignition system
c. Lighting system
d. Directional signals
e. Horn

WIRING DIAGRAMS

Full color wiring diagrams are located at the end of this book.

CHARGING SYSTEM

The charging system consists of the battery, alternator, and voltage regulator/rectifier (**Figure 1**).

The alternator generates an alternating current (AC) which the rectifier converts to direct current (DC). The regulator maintains the voltage to the battery and load (lights, ignition, etc.) at a constant voltage regardless of variations in engine speed and load.

Testing Charging System

Whenever a charging system trouble is suspected, make sure the battery is good before going any further. Clean and test the battery as described under *Battery Testing* in Chapter Three.

To test the charging system, disconnect the voltage regulator/rectifier black electrical wire, connect a 0-15 DC voltmeter and a 0-10 DC ammeter as shown in **Figure 2**. Connect the ammeter in series to the positive battery terminal. Connect the positive voltmeter terminal to the positive battery terminal and negative voltmeter terminal to ground.

> CAUTION
> *Since the ammeter is connected between the positive battery terminal and the starter cable, the ammeter will burn out if the electric starter is used. Use the kickstarter only.*

Start the engine with the kickstarter and run at 2,000 rpm. Minimum charging current should be 5 amperes. Voltmeter should read 14.5 volts.

> NOTE: *The removable kickstarter is stored on the frame, just above the rear swing arm pivot point. Remove the wing nut and cover (A, Figure 3) and remove the kickstarter arm. Remove the rubber protective cover (B, Figure 3) and insert the kickstarter arm fully onto the shaft.*

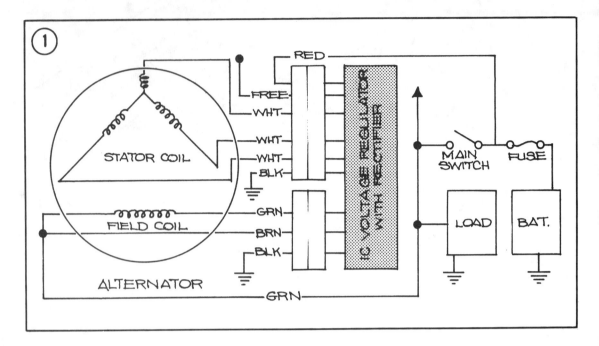

WARNING
Make sure the kickstarter arm if inserted fully onto the shaft. If not, it may be thrown off during the starting operation and injure the operator.

All of the measurements are made with lights on high beam. If charging current is considerably lower than specified, check the alternator and voltage regulator/rectifier. It is less likely that the charging current is too high; in that case, the regulator is probably at fault.

Test the separate charging system components as described under the appropriate heading in the following sections.

Battery Care, Inspection, and Testing

For complete battery information refer to *Battery* in Chapter Three.

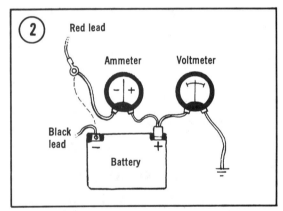

ALTERNATOR

An alternator is a form of electrical generator in which a magnetized field called a rotor revolves within a set of stationary coils called a stator. As the rotor revolves, alternating current is induced in the stator. The current is then rectified and used to operate the electrical accessories on the motorcycle and for charging the battery. Rotor is an electromagnet.

Removal/Installation

This procedure is shown with the engine partially disassembled; it is not necessary to remove any of these components to perform this procedure.

1. Remove the seat and both side covers.

2. Disconnect the battery negative cable.

3. Remove the 2 Phillips head screws (**Figure 4**) securing the electrical panel in place.

4. Carefully pull the forward edge of the panel out and disconnect the alternator electrical connectors. The field coil contains 2 wires — 1 brown and 1 green. The stator contains 4 wires — 1 yellow and 3 white.

5. Remove the 5 Allen bolts (A, **Figure 5**) securing the alternator cover/coil assembly. Straighten the wire clamps (B, **Figure 5**) securing the two electrical cables in place.

> NOTE: *Do not remove the 3 Allen bolts (Figure 6) on the cover.*

6. Remove the alternator cover/coil assembly and electrical cables.

7. Remove the bolt and washer (**Figure 7**) securing the alternator rotor.

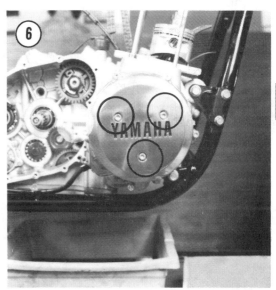

7

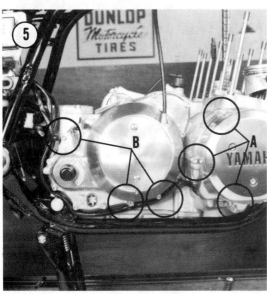

NOTE: *If necessary use a strap wrench (Figure 8) to keep the rotor from turning while removing the bolt.*

8. Screw in a flywheel puller **(Figure 9)** until it stops. Use a wrench on the puller and tap on the end of it with your hand or a plastic mallet until the rotor disengages. Remove the puller and rotor.

9. Install by reversing these removal steps. Secure the rotor bolt to 47 ft.-lb. (65 N•m) using a torque wrench and strap wrench **(Figure 10)**.

NOTE: *Be sure to install a new gasket (A, Figure 11) and install the 2 locating dowels (B, Figure 11). Install the cable in the wire clamps (Figure 5).*

Stator Testing

1. Remove the alternator as described under *Alternator Removal/Installation* in this chapter.

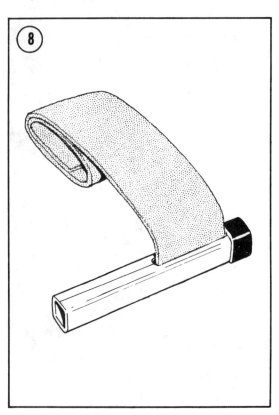

2. Visually inspect the stator **(Figure 12)** for signs of damage to the coils and electrical wires leading to it. If necessary, remove the 3 Allen bolts **(Figure 13)** securing the stator assembly to the cover.

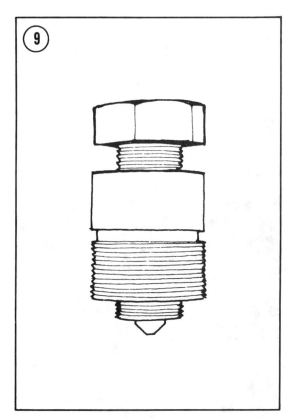

3. Use an ohmmeter and measure the resistance between the following terminals. See **Figure 14**.

   a. Field coil terminals — brown to green. The value should be 3.5 ohms ± 10% at 68°F (20°C).

   b. Stator coil terminals — check each white against the other two whites. The value should be 0.4 ohms ± 10% at 68°F (20°C).

4. If the values are not within the specified

range, check the electrical wires to and within the terminal connectors. If they are OK, then there is an open or short in the coils and the stator must be replaced.

VOLTAGE REGULATOR/RECTIFIER

Voltage Regulator Testing

Refer to **Figure 15** for this test procedure.

1. Remove the seat and fuel tank.

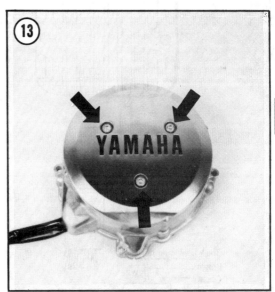

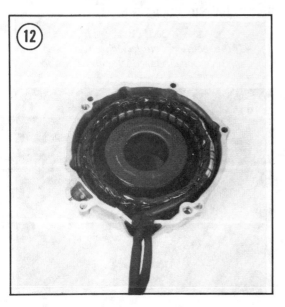

2. Tests are made on the electrical connector **(Figure 16)** containing 3 wires — 1 green, 1 black, and 1 brown.

CAUTION
Do not short-circuit the voltage regulator when connecting the test leads or it will be damaged.

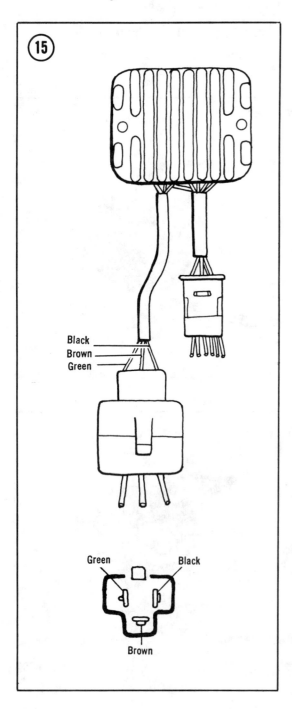

15

Black
Brown
Green

Green   Black

Brown

3. Turn the ignition switch to the ON position. Connect a 20V DC voltmeter — negative (−) lead to black and the positive (+) lead to green. The voltage should be less than 1.8 volts.

NOTE: *Do not turn on the headlight or turn signals.*

4. Start the engine and recheck. This reading should gradually increase up to 9-11 volts when the engine is started and as rpm increases.

5. Connect the voltmeter — negative (−) lead to black and positive (+) to brown. The voltage should be 14.2-14.8 volts with the engine running and should remain there as engine rpm is increased.

6. If the voltage specified in Steps 3 and 4 are not met in these tests, the voltage regulator/rectifier must be replaced. It cannot be serviced. Remove the 2 screws **(Figure 17)** and disconnect the 2 electrical connectors. Remove and replace the unit.

Rectifier Testing

Refer to **Figure 18** for this test procedure.

1. Disconnect the battery negative cable from the battery.

2. Remove the seat and fuel tank.

3. Disconnect the voltage regulator/rectifier terminal connectors **(Figure 16)**. One connector contains 5 wires — 3 white, 1 black, and 1 red. The other connector contains 3 wires — 1 brown, 1 green, and 1 black.

CAUTION
If the rectifier is subjected to overcharging it can be damaged. Be careful not to

16

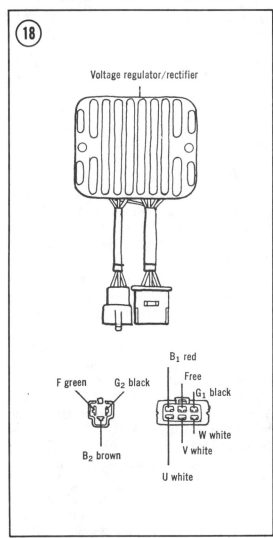

Voltage regulator/rectifier

F green   G₂ black   B₁ red

Free

G₁ black

W white

V white

B₂ brown   U white

short-circuit it or incorrectly connect the battery positive and negative leads. Never directly connect the rectifier to the battery for a continuity check.

4. Measure the resistance between each of the following terminals with an ohmmeter. Record each of the measurements.

  a. B_1 and U
  b. B_1 and V
  c. B_1 and W
  d. B_1 and B_2
  e. U and G_1
  f. V and G_1
  g. W and G_1
  h. B and G_1

5. Reverse the ohmmeter leads, then repeat Step 4. Each set of measurements must be high with the ohmmeter connected one way, and low with the ohmmeter leads reversed. It is not possible to specify exact ohmmeter readings, but each set of measurements should differ by a factor of not less than 10.

6. Even if only one of the elements is defective, the entire unit must be replaced; it cannot be serviced.

Voltage Regulator Performance Test

Connect a voltmeter to the battery terminals. Start the engine and let it idle; increase engine speed until the voltage going to the battery reaches 14.0-15.0 volts. At this point, the voltage regulator must divert the current to ground. If this does not happen, the voltage regulator/rectifier must be replaced.

IGNITION SYSTEM (FULLY TRANSISTORIZED)

All XS1100 models are equipped with a fully transistorized ignition system. This solid state system, unlike conventional ignition systems, does not use breaker points. This system provides a longer life for components and delivers a more efficient spark throughout the entire speed range of the engine. Ignition timing is maintained for a long time without periodic adjustment.

7

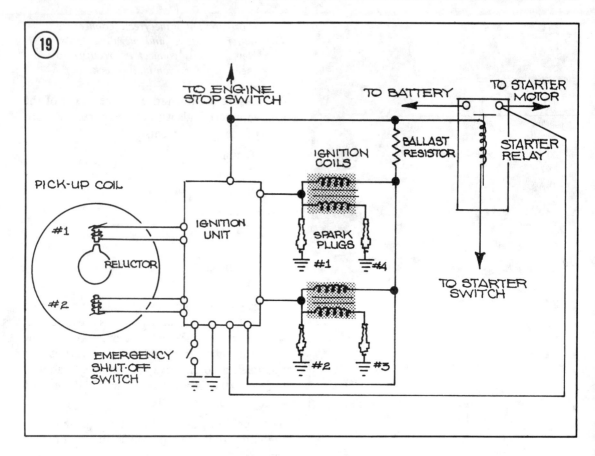

Figure 19 is a diagram of the ignition circuit.

When the raised portion on the crankshaft driven reluctor passes one of the cylinder pick-up coils, a pulse is generated within the pick-up coil. This pulse (electrical current) flows to the switching and distributing circuits in the ignition unit. The magnetic field that has built up in the coil, from the battery, is now interrupted by this pulse and causes the field to collapse. When this happens, a very high voltage is induced (up to 15,000 volts) into the secondary windings of that cylinder's ignition coil. This voltage is sufficient to jump the gap at the spark plugs of No. 1 and 4 cylinders, causing the plugs to fire. The same sequence of events happens to No. 2 and 3 cylinders and is controlled by the 180° rotation of the driven reluctor.

> NOTE: *Two plugs will fire at the same time (No. 1 and 4 or No. 2 and 3) but only one of the cylinders will be at* TDC *on the compression stroke. The other cylinder is on the exhaust stroke and the spark in that cylinder has no effect on it.*

Cautions

Certain measures must be taken to protect the transistorized ignition system. Instantaneous damage to the semiconductors in the system will occur if the following precautions are not observed.

1. Never connect the battery backwards. If the battery polarity is wrong, damage will occur to the voltage regulator/rectifier, alternator, and ignitor unit.

2. Do not disconnect the battery when the engine is running. A voltage surge will occur which will damage the voltage regulator/rectifier and possibly burn out the lights.

3. Keep all connections between the various units clean and tight. Be sure that the wiring connectors are pushed together firmly.

4. Do not substitute another type of ignition coil(s) or battery.

5. Each unit is mounted with a rubber vibration isolator. Always be sure that the isolators are in place when replacing any units.

Troubleshooting

Problems with the transistorized ignition system are usually production of a weak spark or no spark at all.

1. Check all connections to make sure they are tight and free of corrosion.

2. Check the ignition coils as described under *Ignition Coil Testing* in this chapter.

3. Check the pick-up coil assembly with an ohmmeter. The coil resistance should be 720 ohms ± 20% at 68°F (20°C).

4. If the ignition coil and pick-up coil check out OK, the ignitor unit is at fault and must be replaced. It cannot be serviced.

Ignition Unit Replacement

1. Remove the seat and disconnect the negative battery lead.

2. Disconnect the 2 electrical connectors. See A, **Figure 20** for Models E and F, **Figure 21** for Model SF.

3. Remove the attachment screws (B, **Figure 20** or B, **Figure 21**) and remove the unit.

4. Install by reversing these removal steps.

Ignition Unit Testing

Tests may be performed on the unit but a good one may be damaged by someone unfamiliar with test equipment. To play it safe, have the tests performed by your Yamaha dealer or substitute a unit suspected to be bad with one that is known to be good.

IGNITION COIL

Removal/Installation

There are two ignition coils, the one on the left-hand side fires No. 1 and 4 cylinders and the one on the right-hand side fires the No. 2 and 3 cylinders.

1. Remove the seat and left-hand side cover and disconnect negative lead from the battery (**Figure 22**).

2. Remove the rear bolt securing the fuel tank. Disconnect the fuel gauge electrical connector.

3. Turn both fuel shutoff valves to the ON or RES position, lift up on the rear of the tank and

remove the fuel lines to the carburetors and vacuum lines to intake manifolds.

4. Pull the tank to the rear and remove it.

5. Disconnect the spark plug leads and the coil primary electrical wires (**Figure 23**) at the electrical connector.

6. Remove the 2 nuts and lockwashers (**Figure 24**) securing each coil to the frame and remove them.

7. Install by reversing these removal steps. Make sure to correctly connect the primary electrical wires to the correct coils and the spark plug leads to the correct spark plug. Refer to **Figure 25**.

Testing

The ignition coil is a form of transformer which develops the high voltage required to jump the spark plug gap. The only maintenance required is that of keeping the electrical connections clean and tight, and occasionally checking to see that the coil is mounted securely.

If coil condition is doubtful, there are several checks which may be made. Disconnect coil wires before testing.

1. Measure the coil primary resistance, using an ohmmeter, between both coil primary terminals (**Figure 26**). Resistance should measure approximately 1.5 ohms ± 10% at 68°F (20°C).

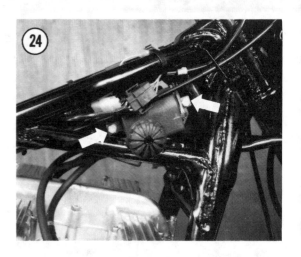

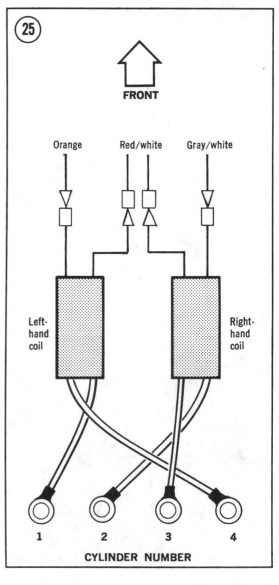

FRONT

Orange   Red/white   Gray/white

Left-hand coil

Right-hand coil

1   2   3   4

CYLINDER NUMBER

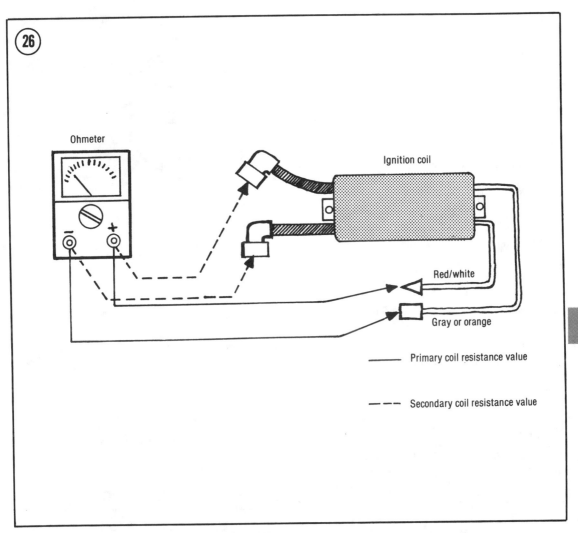

(26)

Ohmeter

Ignition coil

Red/white

Gray or orange

——— Primary coil resistance value

– – – Secondary coil resistance value

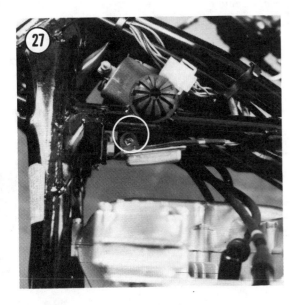

(27)

2. Measure the coil secondary resistance between both primary leads. Resistance should be approximately 15k ohm ± 10% at 68°F (20°C).

3. Replace any coil if the spark plug lead exhibits visible damage and/or if they do not meet the preceding test specifications.

IGNITION BALLAST RESISTOR

The ballast resistor is used in the ignition circuit to drop the voltage and current to the ignition coils, for normal ignition operation, after engine starting has been completed.

To remove the ballast resistor, remove the screw (**Figure 27**) securing it to the frame and disconnect the electrical connector.

IGNITION ADVANCE MECHANISM

Ignition advance is achieved by both centrifugal and vacuum mechanisms. Remove the advance mechanism as described under *Ignition Advance Mechanism Removal/Installation* in Chapter Four.

Centrifugal Advance

1. Inspect the pivoting action of the weights (A, **Figure 28**). They must be able to pivot smoothly all the way to the extent of their travel. Apply a small amount of molybdenum disulfide grease to the pivot points (B, **Figure 28**) and pin slots (C, **Figure 28**).

2. The reluctor (D, **Figure 28**) must rotate smoothly on the shaft. If it does not, remove the circlip (E, **Figure 28**), slide the reluctor up off the shaft, and apply molybdenum disulfide grease to the rotating surfaces of both parts and reassemble.

3. Make sure the centrifugal advance weights return springs (F, **Figure 28**) completely retract the weights. If not replace the reluctor unit.

Vacuum Advance

1. Rotate the pick-up coil assembly (A, **Figure 29**) by hand. It should rotate smoothly. If there is any binding, remove the 3 screws and holding tabs (B, **Figure 29**). Also remove the E-clip (C, **Figure 29**) securing the arm and remove and replace the pick-up coil assembly.

2. Inspect the vacuum advance diaphragm. Connect a hand-operated vacuum pump and vacuum gauge (**Figure 30**) to the vacuum advance inlet (A, **Figure 31**). Apply a vacuum. The mechanism should fully advance at 5.9 in. Hg (150mm Hg). If it does not, remove the screw (B, **Figure 31**) and the E-clip (C, **Figure 31**) and remove and replace the vacuum unit (D, **Figure 31**).

IGNITION EMERGENCY SHUTOFF SWITCH

The emergency shut off switch will shutoff the ignition if the bike reaches a lean angle of 60° or more from vertical. In case you spill the bike, it will automaticaly shut it off.

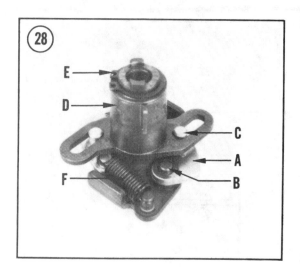

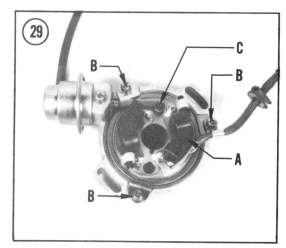

Replacement

1. Remove the seat and disconnect the battery negative lead from the battery.

2. Remove the rear bolt securing the fuel tank. Disconnect the electrical connector to the fuel gauge.

3. Turn the fuel shutoff valves to the ON or RES position. Lift up on the rear of the tank and remove the fuel lines to the carburetors and vacuum lines to the intake manifolds.

4. Pull the tank to the rear and remove it.

5. Disconnect the electrical connector going to the emergency shutoff switch (A, **Figure 32**).

6. Remove the switch assembly from the rubber mount (B, **Figure 32**) on the frame.

7. Install by reversing these removal steps. Make sure all electrical connections are tight.

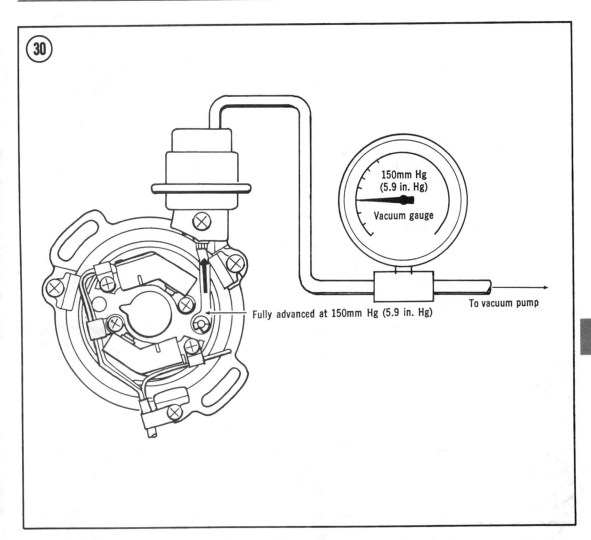

30

150mm Hg
(5.9 in. Hg)

Vacuum gauge

To vacuum pump

Fully advanced at 150mm Hg (5.9 in. Hg)

7

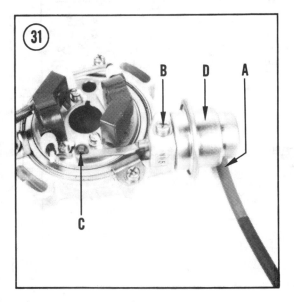

31

B   D   A

C

32

Testing

1. Use an ohmmeter, set at R X100, and check the switch as shown in **Figure 33**.

2. Position the switch vertically — the reading should be infinity (∞). If the reading is 0 ohms, replace the switch.

3. Position the switch leaning approximately 60° to both right and then to the left and check both ways. The reading should be 0 ohms, if the reading is infinity (∞), replace the switch.

SPARK PLUGS

The spark plugs recommended by the factory are usually the most suitable for your machine. If riding conditions are mild, it may be advisable to go to spark plugs one step hotter than normal. Unusually severe riding conditions may require slightly colder plugs. See Chapter Three for details.

STARTING SYSTEM

The starting system consists of the starter motor, starter solenoid, and the starter button.

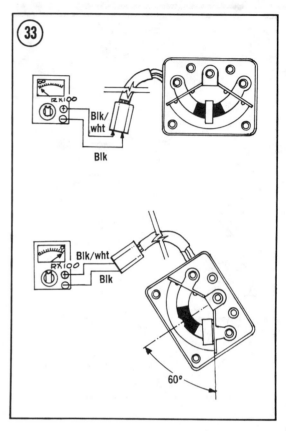

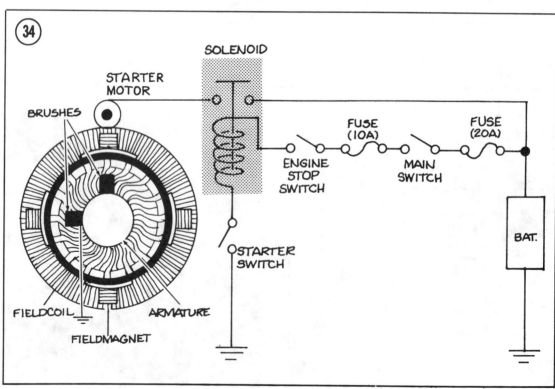

The layout of the starting system is shown in **Figure 34**. When the starter button is pressed, it engages the solenoid switch that closes the circuit. The electricity flows from battery to the starter motor.

CAUTION
Do not operate the starter for more than five seconds at a time. Let it rest approximately ten seconds, then use it again.

The starter gears and kickstarter are covered in Chapter Four.

Table 1 lists possible starter problems, probable causes, and the most common remedies.

Removal/Installation

1. Place the bike on the centerstand.
2. Turn the ignition switch to the OFF position.
3. Remove the seat and disconnect the negative battery lead from battery.
4. Remove the 4 wing nuts and remove the lower air cleaner base and element (A, **Figure 35**).
5. Disconnect the crankcase breather tube (B, **Figure 35**) from the upper crankcase.
6. Remove the 3 bolts (**Figure 36**) securing the starter motor cover and remove it.

Table 1   STARTER TROUBLESHOOTING

Symptom	Probable Cause	Remedy
Starter does not work	Low battery	Recharge battery
	Worn brushes	Replace brushes
	Defective relay	Repair or replace
	Defective switch	Repair or replace
	Defective wiring or connection	Repair wire or clean connection
	Internal short circuit	Repair or replace defective component
Starter action is weak	Low battery	Recharge battery
	Pitted relay contacts	Clean or replace
	Worn brushes	Replace brushes
	Defective connection	Clean and tighten
	Short circuit in commutator	Replace armature
Starter runs continuously	Stuck relay	Replace relay
Starter turns; does not turn engine	Defective starter clutch	Replace starter clutch

7. Carefully pull the motor to the left and disengage the gears.

8. Pull back on the rubber boot and disconnect the electrical wire (**Figure 37**) from the motor and remove the motor.

> NOTE: *Figures 36 and 37 are shown with the engine partially disassembled for clarity only. It is not necessary to remove any of these components to remove the starter motor.*

9. Install by reversing these removal steps. Prior to installing the cover, position the oil pressure switch electrical wires as shown in **Figure 38**. Be sure to align the notches in the cover with the wire to prevent crimping and damaging them.

Starter Disassembly/Assembly

The overhaul of a starter motor is best left to an expert. This section shows how to determine if the unit is defective.

1. Remove the starter motor case screws (A, **Figure 39**) and separate the case.

> NOTE: *Write down how many thrust washers are used and install the same number when reassembling the starter.*

2. Clean all grease, dirt, and carbon dust from the armature, case, and end covers.

> CAUTION
> *Do not immerse brushes or the wire windings in solvent or the insulation might be damaged. Wipe the windings with a cloth lightly moistened with solvent and dry thoroughly.*

3. Remove the brushes and use a vernier caliper (**Figure 40**) to measure the length of the brush. If it is worn beyond the 0.21 in. (5.5mm), it should be replaced.

4. Inspect the condition of the commutator (**Figure 41**). The mica in the normal commutator (A) is cut below the copper. A worn commutator (B) is also shown; the copper is worn to the level of the mica. A worn commutator can be undercut, but it requires a specialist. Take the job to your Yamaha dealer or motorcycle electrical repair shop.

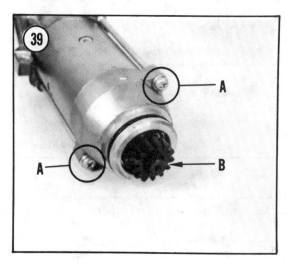

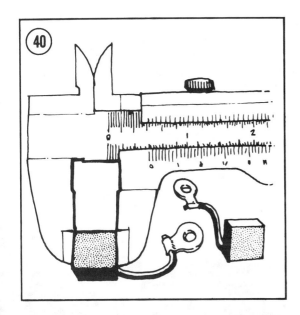

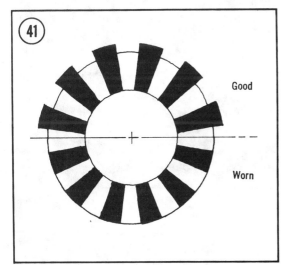

Good

Worn

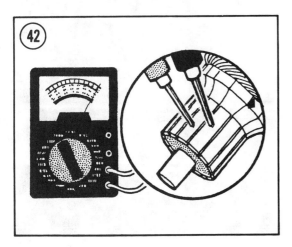

5. Inspect the commutator bars for discoloration. If a pair of bars are discolored, that indicates grounded armature coils.

6. Check the electrical continuity between pairs of armature bars and between the commutator bars and the shaft mounting (**Figures 42 and 43**). If there is a short, the armature should be replaced.

7. Inspect the field coil by checking continuity from the cable terminal to the motor case. Also check from the cable terminal to the brush wire. If there is a short or open, the case should be replaced.

8. Assemble the case together; make sure that the punch marks on the case and covers align (**Figure 44**).

9. Inspect condition of the gears (B, **Figure 39**). If they are chipped or worn, remove the circlip and replace the gear.

10. Inspect the front and rear cover bearings for damage. Replace the starter if they are worn or damaged.

7

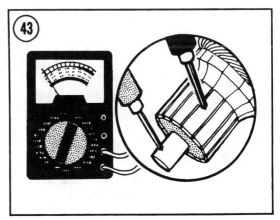

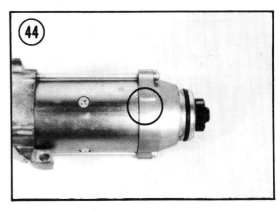

Starter Solenoid
Removal/Installation

1. Turn the ignition switch to the OFF position.

2. Remove the right-hand side cover (**Figure 45**).

3. Slide off the rubber protective boots and disconnect the 2 electrical wires from the large terminals (A, **Figure 46**). Remove the 2 mounting screws (B, **Figure 46**).

4. Remove the solenoid from the frame along with the 2 smaller electrical wires that are attached to it.

5. Install by reversing these reoval steps.

LIGHTING SYSTEM

The lighting system consists of the headlight, taillight/brakelight combination, directional signals, warning lights, and speedometer and tachometer illumination lights. **Table 2** lists replacement bulbs for these components.

The headlight circuit is equipped with a reserve lighting system that automatically switches current from the burned out headlight filament to the reserve filament. It also notifies the rider that one filament is burned out by an indicator light on the instrument cluster.

The circuit also contains a relay that turns the headlight on automatically when the ignition switch is turned on even with the headlight switch in the OFF position.

Headlight Replacement

Refer to **Figure 47** for this procedure.

1. On models except special, remove the 2 lower mounting screws (**Figure 48**) on the headlight housing.

2. On special models, remove the 2 mounting screws (**Figure 49**) on each side of the headlight housing.

3. Pull the trim bezel and headlight unit out and disconnect the electrical connector from the backside of the lens assembly.

4. Remove the socket cover and bulb holder and remove the defective bulb and install a new one.

> **WARNING**
> *If the headlight has just burned out or turned off it will be Hot! Don't touch the bulb until it cools off.*

Table 2   REPLACEMENT BULBS

Item	Wattage	Candlepower
Headlight		
Except special models	50/65	—
Special models	55/60	—
Tail/brakelight	8/27	3/32
Directional lights	27	32
Instrument lights	3.4	1
Meter light	3.4	4
Parking light	8	3

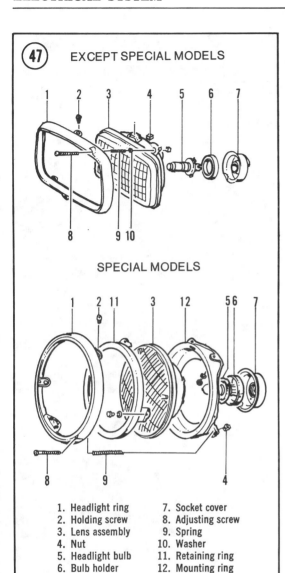

47 EXCEPT SPECIAL MODELS

SPECIAL MODELS

1. Headlight ring
2. Holding screw
3. Lens assembly
4. Nut
5. Headlight bulb
6. Bulb holder
7. Socket cover
8. Adjusting screw
9. Spring
10. Washer
11. Retaining ring
12. Mounting ring

48

CAUTION

Carefully read all instructions shipped with the replacement bulb. Do not touch the bulb glass with your fingers because of your skin oil. Any traces of oil on a quartz halogen bulb will drastically reduce the life of the bulb. Clean any traces of oil from the bulb with a cloth moistened in alcohol or lacquer thinner. Keep any flammable material or liquids and your hands away from the bulb when it's on; it is Hot.

5. Install by reversing these removal steps.

6. Adjust the headlight as described under *Headlight Adjustment* in this chapter.

Headlight Adjustment

Adjust the headlight horizontally and vertically according to Department of Motor Vehicle regulations in your area.

1. On models except special, there are 3 adjustments: horizontal, coarse vertical, and fine vertical. To adjust the headlight horizontally, turn the screw (A, **Figure 50**) *counterclockwise* to move the beam to the right and *clockwise* to move the beam to the left. Coarse vertical adjustment is with the screw (B, **Figure 50**) at the lower lefthand side and fine adjustment is with the screw (C, **Figure**

7

49

50) on the center lower headlight rim. Turn the screw *clockwise* to lower the beam and *counterclockwise* to raise it.

2. On special models, there are 2 adjustments. To adjust headlight horizontally, turn the screw (**Figure 51**). Screwing it in turns the light to the right, and loosening it will turn the light to the left. For vertical adjustment, loosen the bolt (**Figure 52**) under the headlight and move the headlight assembly up or down. After adjustment is correct, be sure to tighten the bolt.

Headlight Reserve Lighting System Removal/Installation

If the reserve lighting unit becomes defective, it must be replaced as it cannot be serviced. **Figures 53, 54, and 55** are diagrams of each system for the different models.

> NOTE: *This system relates to the headlight only, not to any of the other lights on the bike.*

1. Remove the seat and disconnect the battery negative lead from the battery.

2. Remove the rear bolt securing the fuel tank. Disconnect the electrical connector from the fuel gauge.

3. Turn the fuel shutoff valves to the ON or RES position. Lift up on the rear of the tank and remove the fuel lines to the carburetors and vacuum lines to intake manifolds.

4. Pull the tank to the rear and remove it.

5. Disconnect the electrical connectors from the reserve lighting unit and remove the 2 screws (**Figure 56**) securing it to the frame and remove it.

6. Install by reversing these removal steps. Make sure all electrical connections are tight.

Headlight Relay Replacement

1. Remove the seat and disconnect the battery negative lead from the battery.

2. Remove the rear bolt securing the fuel tank.

3. Turn the fuel shutoff valves to the ON or RES position. Lift up on the rear of the tank and remove the fuel lines to the carburetors and vacuum lines to intake manifolds.

4. Pull the tank to the rear and remove it.

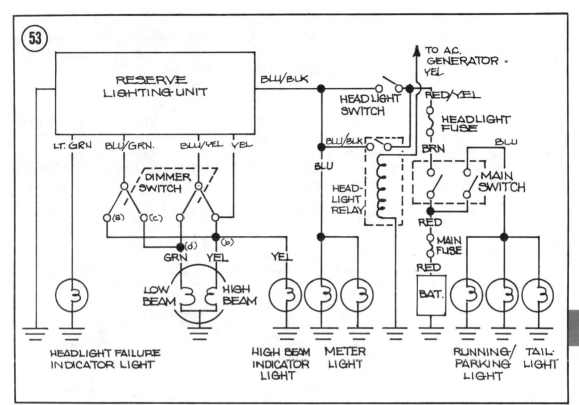

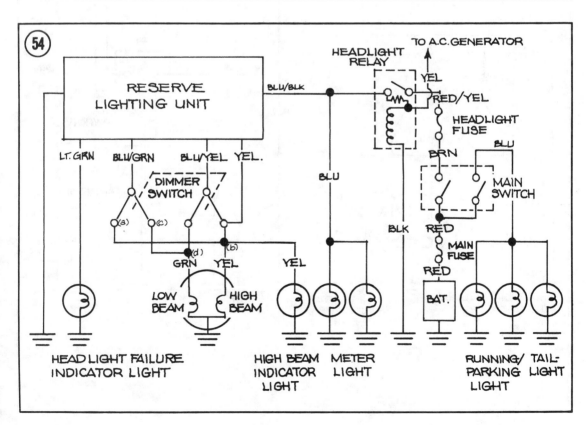

5. Disconnect the electrical connector to the headlight relay and pull it out of the rubber mounting on the frame (**Figure 57**).

6. Install by reversing these removal steps. Make sure all electrical connections are tight.

Taillight Replacement

Remove the screws securing the lens (**Figure 58**) and remove it. Wash out the inside and outside of the lens with a mild detergent and wipe dry. Wipe off the reflective base surrounding the bulb with a soft cloth. Replace the bulbs and install the lens; do not overtighten screws or the lens may crack.

Directional Signal Light Replacement

Remove the two screws securing the lens (**Figure 59**) and remove it. Wash out the inside and outside of it with a mild detergent. Replace the bulb. Install the lens; do not overtighten the screws as that will crack the lens.

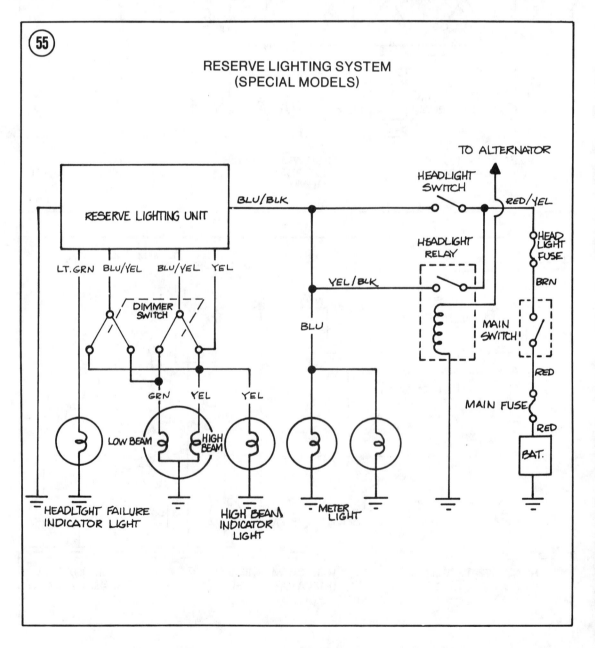

Speedometer and Tachometer Illumination Light Replacement (Except Special Models)

1. Remove the speedometer drive cable (A, **Figure 60**) from the backside of the housing.

> NOTE: *The tachometer is electronic and has no drive cable.*

2. Remove the 2 upper acorn nuts and washers (B, **Figure 60**) securing the speedometer or tachometer assembly in place.

3. Remove the top cover and replace the defective bulb(s).

7

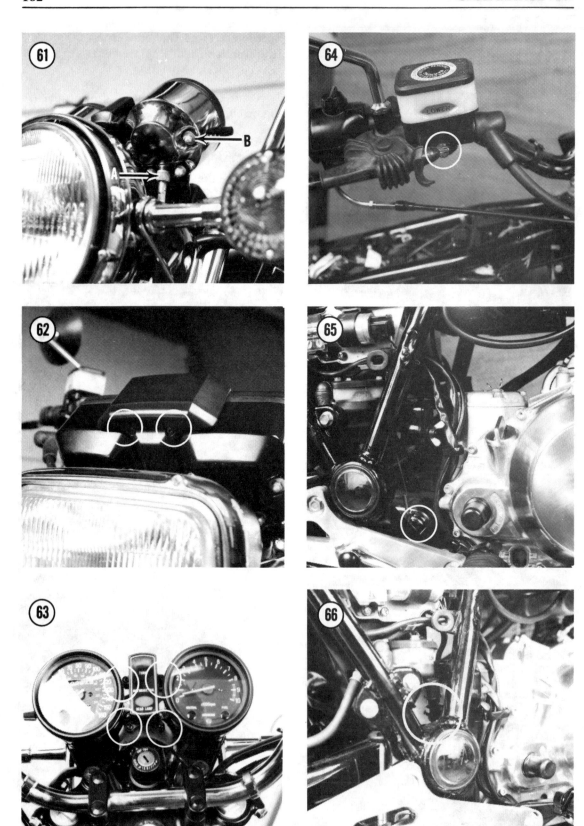

Speedometer and Tachometer Illumination Light Replacement (Special Models)

1. Disconnect the drive cable(s) from the chrome housing(s). See A, **Figure 61**.
2. Remove the acorn nuts and washers (B, **Figure 61**), 2 per unit, securing the speedometer or tachometer units into the chrome housings.
3. Pull the unit(s) and rubber rings(s) up and out of the housing(s) and remove it.
4. Replace the defective bulb(s).

Turn, High Beam, Oil Pressure, Neutral and Headlight Failure Indicator Bulb Replacement (Except Special Models)

Remove the 2 screws (**Figure 62**) securing the indicator housing in place and carefully remove it. Replace the defective bulb(s).

Neutral Indicator and High Beam Indicator Light Replacement (Special Models)

Follow the procedure for replacement of *Speedometer and Tachometer Illumination Light Replacement*, (Special Models).

Turn, Oil Pressure, Headlight Failure Indicator Replacement (Special Models)

Remove the 4 screws (**Figure 63**) securing the indicator housing to the mounting bracket and remove it. Replace the defective bulb(s).

Front Brake Light Switch Replacement

Pull back the rubber protective boot on the hand lever. Pull the rubber boot back away from the switch and remove the switch (**Figure 64**). Disconnect the electrical wires and replace the switch.

Rear Brake Light Switch Replacement

1. Unhook spring from brake arm (**Figure 65**).
2. Unscrew the switch housing and locknut from bracket (**Figure 66**).
3. Pull up the rubber boot and remove the electrical wires.

4. Replace the switch; reinstall and adjust as described under *Rear Brake Light Switch Adjustment* in this chapter.

Rear Brake Light Switch Adjustment

1. Turn the ignition switch to the ON position.
2. Depress the brake pedal. Light should come on just as the brake begins to work.
3. To make the light come on earlier, hold the switch body and turn adjusting locknut *clockwise* as viewed from the top. Turn *counterclockwise* to delay the light.

> NOTE: *Some riders prefer the light to come on a little early. This way, they can tap the pedal without braking to warn drivers who follow too closely.*

Self-cancelling Flasher System

The self-cancelling system turns the turn signals off after a period of time or after a specific distance traveled (**Figure 67**).

Flasher Cancelling Unit Replacement

Remove the seat and pull out the old unit (**Figure 68**). Disconnect the electrical wires and transfer them to the new unit. Install the new unit.

Flasher Relay Replacement

The flasher unit is located under the right-hand side cover (**Figure 69**). Pull the old flasher relay (**Figure 70**) out of the rubber mount. Transfer wires to new relay and install the relay in the rubber mount.

TACHOMETER

The tachometer on all models is electric and receives impulses from one of the stator leads from the alternator to evaluate engine rpm.

Service to this tachometer should be entrusted to a Yamaha dealer or motorcycle electric repair shop.

FUEL GAUGE (EXCEPT SPECIAL MODELS)

The fuel gauge is electronically operated and is located within the tachometer face. The

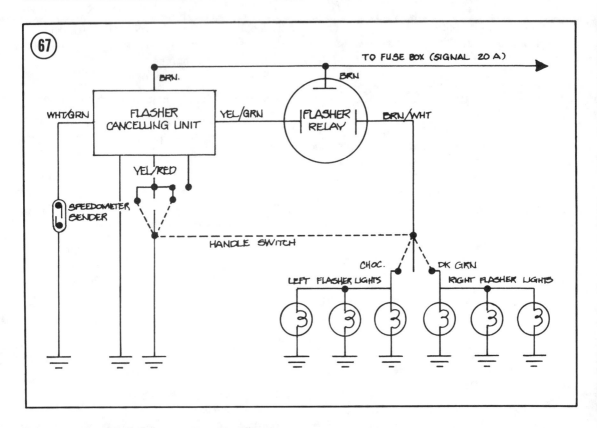

sending unit is located within the fuel tank on the lefthand side. The gauge operates only when the ignition is in the ON position.

Fuel Gauge Testing

Refer to **Figure 71** for this procedure.
1. Remove the headlight as described under *Headlight Replacement*—except special models in this chapter.

2. Inside the headlight housing, locate the electrical connector, going to the tachometer housing, containing one brown and one green wire to disconnect it.

3. Turn the ignition switch to the ON position.

4. Connect a 0-20 V DC voltmeter to the brown terminal and to ground. The reading should be 12 volts. If the reading is less, check the condition of the battery charge as described in Chapter Three.

5. Check the green terminal and to ground, the reading should be 7 volts. If the reading is more or less than specified, replace the fuel gauge.

6. Remove the seat and disconnect the fuel tank sending unit electrical connector (**Figure 72**).

7. On the wiring harness side of the connector, check voltage of the green wire. The voltage should be 7 volts, if not check for loose electrical connections, open circuit, or defective fuel gauge in the tachometer housing.

Fuel Tank Sending Unit Testing

Refer to **Figure 73** for this procedure.

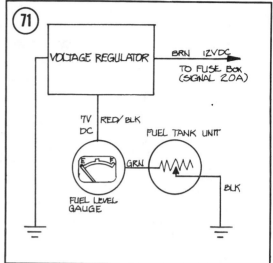

VOLTAGE REGULATOR

BRN 12VDC
TO FUSE BOX
(SIGNAL 20A)

7V DC   RED/BLK

FUEL TANK UNIT

GRN

FUEL LEVEL GAUGE

BLK

7

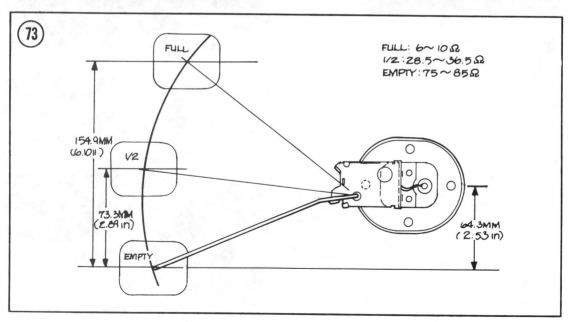

FULL: 6~10Ω
1/2: 28.5~36.5Ω
EMPTY: 75~85Ω

FULL

154.9MM
(6.10 in)

1/2

73.3MM
(2.89 in)

EMPTY

64.3MM
(2.53 in)

1. Remove the fuel tank and completely drain all gasoline from it.

2. Set the fuel tank upside down on a protective pad or blanket to protect the finish.

3. Disconnect the electrical connectors (A, **Figure 74**) from the terminals on the sending unit.

4. Remove the 4 bolts (B, **Figure 74**) and carefully remove the sending unit from the tank.

CAUTION
Be careful not to damage the float arm and float during removal and installation of the unit.

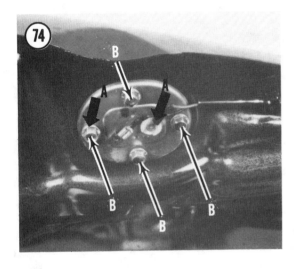

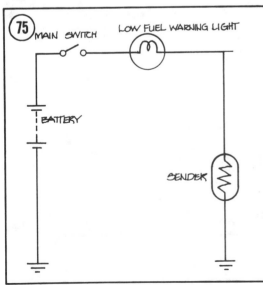

5. Temporarily secure the sending unit in a fixture so that float measurements can be made for this test.

6. Use an ohmmeter set to R X 1, and connect it to the green and black wire terminals on the sending unit. The readings should be as follows:

 a. Full — 6-10 ohms

 b. ½ — 28.5-36.5 ohms

 c. Empty — 75-85 ohms

If the sending unit does not meet these values it must be replaced.

NOTE: *Be sure to install a new gasket when reinstalling the sending unit. Partially refill with gasoline prior to installing the tank and check for leaks. Tighten the attachment bolts to 3.6 ft.-lb. (5.0 N•m).*

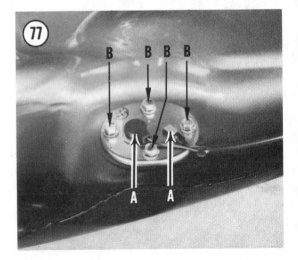

LOW FUEL WARNING LIGHT (SPECIAL MODEL)

The low fuel warning light is electrically operated and is located within the tachometer face. The warning light operates only when the ignition is in the ON position.

Fuel Warning Light Testing

Refer to **Figure 75** for this procedure.

1. Remove the headlight as described under *Headlight Replacement*—special model in this chapter.
2. Inside the headlight housing, locate the electrical connector, going to the tachometer housing, containing one brown and one green wire to disconnect it.
3. Turn the ignition switch to the ON position.
4. Connect a 0-20 V DC voltmeter to the brown terminal and to ground. The reading should be

12 volts. If the reading is less, check the condition of the battery charge as described in Chapter Three.

5. Check the voltage from the green terminal to ground; the reading should be 12 volts. If the reading is less than specified, replace the bulb and/or clean the bulb socket of any corrosion.
6. Remove the seat and disconnect the fuel gauge sending unit electrical connector (**Figure 76**).
7. On the wiring harness side of the connector, check voltage of the green wire. The voltage should be 12 volts, if not check for loose electrical connections, open circuit or defective light bulb in the tachometer housing.

Fuel Tank Sending Unit Testing

1. Remove the fuel tank and completely drain all gasoline from it.
2. Set the fuel tank upside down on a protective pad or blanket to protect the finish.
3. Disconnect the electrical connectors (A, **Figure 77**) from the terminals on the sending unit.
4. Remove the 4 bolts (B, **Figure 77**) and carefully remove the sending unit from the tank.
5. Use an ohmmeter set to R X 100, and connect it to the green and black wire terminals on the sending unit. The value should be 1,500 ± 100 ohms at 77°F (25°C). If the unit does not meet these values it must be replaced.

> NOTE: *Be sure to install a new gasket when reinstalling the sending unit. Partially refill with gasoline prior to installing the tank and check for leaks. Tighten the attachment bolts to 3.6 ft.-lb. (5.0 N•m).*

INSTRUMENT CLUSTER

Except Special Models
Removal/Installation

1. Remove the left-hand side cover and disconnect negative lead from the battery (**Figure 78**).
2. Disconnect all electrical terminals leading to the instrument cluster.
3. Remove the speedometer cable (**Figure 79**) from the backside of the housing.

4. Remove the 2 lower acorn nuts and washers (**Figure 80**) on each side, securing the instrument cluster to the mounting bracket and remove it.

5. Install by reversing these removal steps.

Special Models
Removal/Installation

1. Remove the left-hand side cover and disconnect negative lead from the battery (**Figure 78**).

2. Disconnect all electrical terminals leading to the instrument cluster.

3. Remove the speedometer cable (**Figure 81**) from the instrument cluster.

4. Remove the 2 bolts (**Figure 82**) securing the instrument cluster to brackets, and remove it.

5. Install by reversing these removal steps.

> CAUTION
> *Install the instrument cluster with the attachment bracket **below** the top fork bridge (**Figure 83**). If it is mounted above, the speedometer and tachometer drive cables will be stretched and damaged when the steering is turned to its limits.*

HORN

Removal/Installation

1. Disconnect horn connector from electrical harness (**Figure 84**).

2. Remove the bolt securing horn to bracket (**Figure 84**).

3. Installation is the reverse of these steps.

Testing

1. Disconnect horn wires from harness.

2. Connect horn wires to 12-volt battery. If it is good, it will sound.

FUSES

There are four fuses used on the XS1100. All are located in the fuse panel located under the right-hand side panel (**Figure 85**).

The main fuse (30A) is on the left side of the fuse panel and continuing from left to right are the headlight fuse (10A), turn signal fuse (20A),

and ignition fuse (10A). There are three spare fuses located within the cover; always carry spares.

Whenever a fuse blows, find out the reason for the failure before replacing the fuse. Usually, the trouble is a short circuit in the wiring. This may be caused by worn-through insulation or a disconnected wire shorting to ground.

> CAUTION
> *Never substitute tinfoil or wire for a fuse. Never use a higher amperage fuse than specified. An overload could result in fire and complete loss of the bike.*

Accessory Fuse and Terminal

A nice built-in feature of the XS1100 is the auxiliary-fused DC terminal (**Figure 86**) located under the right-hand side panel. It can be used for a radio, CB, or any accessory that does not exceed 50 watts. The maximum rating is 12 V, 50 W and is to be used with a 12 V, 10A slo-blo fuse.

> CAUTION
> *Do not exceed any of these maximum ratings as it will overload the circuit. This could result in a fire and complete loss of the bike.*

Connect any accessory in accordance with the manufacturer's instructions in regard to wire type, size, and terminal configuration. Be sure to connect the accessory correctly in regard to the positive (+) and negative (−) marks on the terminal backing just below the wire attachment screws.

WIRING DIAGRAMS

Full color wiring diagrams are located at the end of this book.

NOTE: If you own a 1980 or 1981 model, first check the Supplement at the back of the book for any new service information.

CHAPTER EIGHT

FRONT SUSPENSION AND STEERING

This chapter describes repair and maintenance of the front wheel, forks, and steering components.

FRONT WHEEL

Refer to **Figure 1** for this procedure.

Removal

1. Place a wooden block under the crankcase to lift the front of the bike off the ground.
2. On models except special, unscrew the speedometer cable (A, **Figure 2**) and pull it out.
3. On special models, remove the setscrew securing the speedometer cable (**Figure 3**) and pull it out.
4. Remove the axle nut cotter pin and nut (**Figure 4**). Discard the cotter pin.

> *NOTE*
> *Never reuse a cotter pin.*

5. On models except special, remove the 2 nuts securing the front axle holder (B, **Figure 2**) and remove it.
6. On models except special, remove the 2 bolts (**Figure 5**) securing the left-hand caliper assembly. On special models remove the caliper mounting bolt assembly (**Figure 6**) on the left-hand caliper assembly. Remove the caliper from the disc – *do not* remove the brake hose. Tie up the caliper with a piece of wire to the brake hose support bracket (**Figure 7**) to keep tension off the brake hose.
7. On special models, loosen the axle pinch bolt (**Figure 8**).
8. Push the axle out with a drift or screwdriver and remove it.
9. Remove the wheel; pull the wheel forward to disengage the disc from the right-hand caliper.

> *CAUTION*
> *Do not set the wheel down on the disc surface as it may get scratched or warped. Place it on a couple of wood blocks (Figure 9).*

> NOTE: *Insert a piece of wood in both calipers in place of the discs. That way, if the brake lever is inadvertently squeezed, the piston will not be forced out of the cylinder. If this does happen, the caliper might have to be disassembled to reseat the piston and the system will have to be bled. By using the wood, bleeding the brake is not necessary when installing the wheel.*

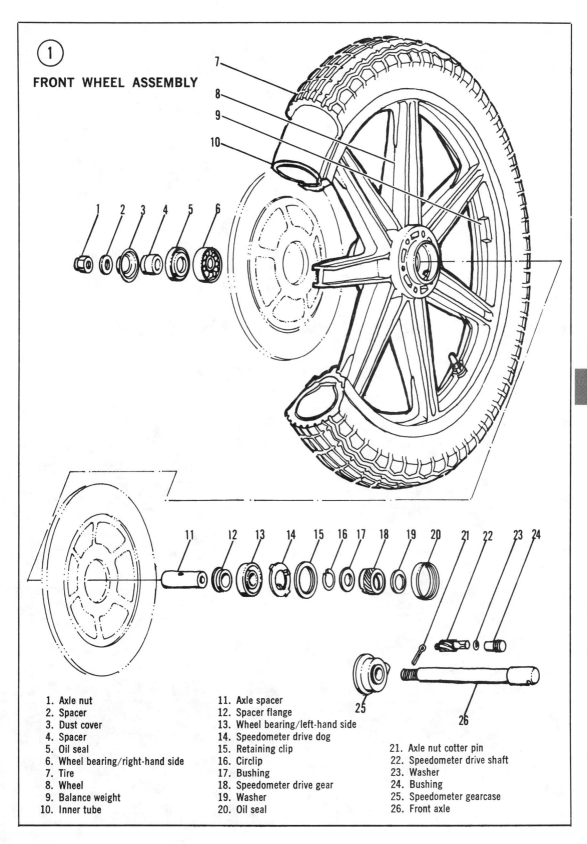

① FRONT WHEEL ASSEMBLY

1. Axle nut
2. Spacer
3. Dust cover
4. Spacer
5. Oil seal
6. Wheel bearing/right-hand side
7. Tire
8. Wheel
9. Balance weight
10. Inner tube

11. Axle spacer
12. Spacer flange
13. Wheel bearing/left-hand side
14. Speedometer drive dog
15. Retaining clip
16. Circlip
17. Bushing
18. Speedometer drive gear
19. Washer
20. Oil seal

21. Axle nut cotter pin
22. Speedometer drive shaft
23. Washer
24. Bushing
25. Speedometer gearcase
26. Front axle

8

Inspection

Measure the lateral and vertical runout of the wheel rim with a dial indicator as shown in **Figure 10**. The maximum lateral runout is 0.04 in. (1mm) and the maximum vertical runout is 0.08 in. (2mm). If the runout exceeds these dimensions, check the wheel bearing condition and/or replace the wheel. The stock Yamaha aluminum wheel cannot be serviced, but must be replaced.

Installation

1. *Carefully* insert the disc between the pads when installing the wheel.

2. Make sure the locating slot in the speedometer gear case is aligned with the boss on the fork tube (**Figure 11**).

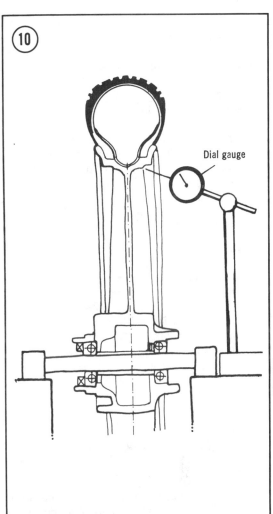

Dial gauge

8

3. Insert the axle and install it. Then install the axle nut; do not tighten at this time.

4. Install the left-hand caliper assembly. On models except special, tighten the caliper mounting bolts to 32.5 ft.-lb. (45 N•m). On special models install the caliper mounting bolt assembly in the order shown in **Figure 12**. Torque the bolt to 18 ft.-lb. (24 N•m).

5. On models except special, install the axle holder, washers, and self-locking nuts; do not tighten the nuts at this time. Tighten the axle nut to 77 ft.-lb. (107 N•m). Install a new cotter pin. Move the left-hand fork leg in and out sideways until the left-hand disc is centered within the caliper assembly. See **Figure 13** for details. Tighten the front axle holder nut first and then the rear nut to 14.5 ft.-lb. (20 N•m).

> *WARNING*
> *The clamp nuts must be tightened in this manner and to this torque value. After installation is complete, there will be a slight gap (**Figure 14**) at the rear, with no gap at the front. If done incorrectly, the studs could fail, resulting in the loss of control of the bike when riding. Be sure to install the axle holder with the arrow facing forward.*

> *NOTE*
> *Never reuse a cotter pin on the axle nut; always install a new one.*

6. On special models, tighten the axle nut to 76 ft.-lb. (103 N•m) and install a new cotter pin. Move the front forks up and down several times. Move the right-hand fork sideways until the left-hand disc is centered within the caliper assembly (**Figure 13**). Tighten the axle pinch bolt to 14.5 ft.-lb. (20 N•m).

> *NOTE*
> *Never reuse a cotter pin on the axle nut; always install a new one.*

7. Insert the speedometer cable and on special models, install the setscrew.

> *NOTE*
> *Rotate the wheel slowly when inserting the cable so that it will engage properly.*

8. After the wheel is installed, completely rotate it and apply the brake several times to make sure it rotates freely.

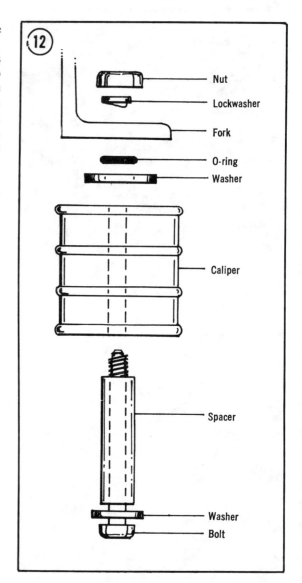

Nut
Lockwasher
Fork
O-ring
Washer
Caliper
Spacer
Washer
Bolt

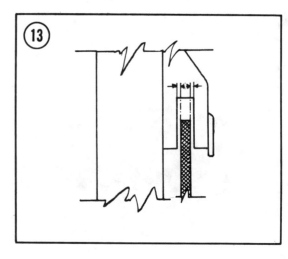

FRONT HUB

Disassembly

1. Remove the front wheel as described under *Front Wheel Removal/Installation* in this chapter.

2. Remove the dust seal (**Figure 15**) and oil seal (**Figure 16**) on the right-hand side.

3. Remove the oil seal (A, **Figure 17**) and speedometer drive dog (B, **Figure 17**) on the left-hand side.

4. Remove the wheel bearings and spacer. Tap the bearings out with a soft aluminum or brass drift.

CAUTION
Tap only on the outer bearing race. The bearing will be damaged if struck on the inner race.

Inspection

1. Clean bearings thoroughly in solvent and dry with compressed air. Do not let the bearing spin while drying.

2. Clean the inside and outside of the hub with solvent. Dry with compressed air.

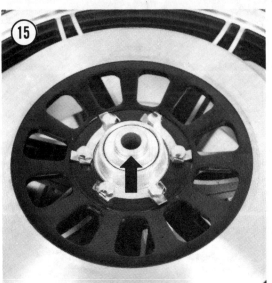

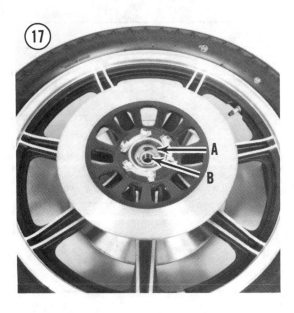

3. Turn each bearing by hand (**Figure 18**). Make sure bearings turn smoothly. Check balls for evidence of wear, pitting or excessive heat (bluish tint). Replace bearings if necessary; always replace as a complete set.

4. Check the axle for wear and straightness. Use V-blocks and a dial indicator as shown in **Figure 19**. If the runout is 0.008 in. (0.2mm) or greater, the axle must be replaced.

Assembly

1. Pack the bearings thoroughly with multipurpose grease. Work the grease in between the balls thoroughly.

2. Pack the wheel hub and axle spacer with multipurpose grease.

3. Install the right-hand wheel bearing.

4. Press in the bearing spacer.

5. Install the left-hand wheel bearing.

> NOTE: *Install the wheel bearings with the sealed side facing outward.*

CAUTION
Tap the bearings squarely into place and tap on the outer race only. Use a socket that matches the outer race diameter. Do not tap on the inner race or the bearing might be damaged. Be sure that the bearings are completely seated.

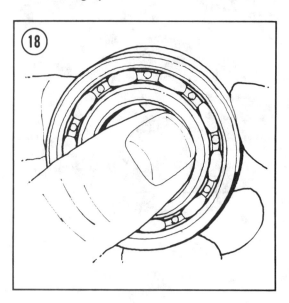

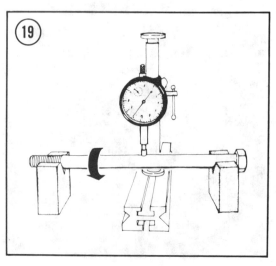

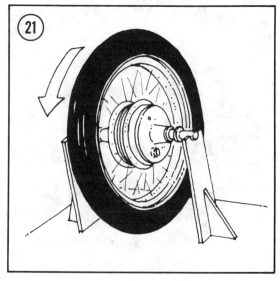

6. Lubricate the dust seal with grease.

7. Install the dust seal and the oil seal in the right-hand side.

8. Install the speedometer drive dog and oil seal in the hub on the left-hand side.

9. Lubricate the oil seals.

10. Disassemble the speedometer gear box and lubricate the gears and sliding faces with a lightweight lithium soap base grease. Reassemble it.

11. Install the speedometer gear into the hub. Align the tangs of the gear with the notches in the wheel retainer.

12. Install the front wheel as described under *Front Wheel Removal/Installation* in this chapter.

WHEEL BALANCING

An unbalanced wheel results in unsafe riding conditions. Depending on the degree of unbalance and the speed of the motorcycle, the rider may experience anything from a mild vibration to a violent shimmy which may even result in loss of control.

On the stock aluminum wheel, weights are attached to the rim. A kit of Tape-A-Weight, or clamp-on type, may be purchased from most motorcycle supply stores. This kit contains test weights and strips of adhesive-backed weights that can be cut to desired weight and attached directly to the rim.

Weights should not be placed any closer to the spokes than shown in **Figure 20**.

NOTE: *Be sure to balance the wheel with the brake discs in place as they also affect the balance.*

Before you attempt to balance the wheel, check to be sure that the wheel bearings are in good condition and properly lubricated. The wheel *must rotate freely*.

1. Remove the wheel as described under *Front Wheel Removal* in this chapter.

2. Mount the wheel on a fixture such as the one in **Figure 21** so it can rotate freely.

3. Give the wheel a spin and let it coast to a stop. Mark the tire at the lowest point.

4. Spin the wheel several more times. If the wheel keeps coming to rest at the same point, it is out of balance.

5. Tape a test weight to the upper (or light) side of the wheel.

6. Experiment with different weights until the wheel, when spun, comes to rest at a different position each time.

7. Remove the test weight and install the correct size adhesive-backed weight.

TIRE CHANGING

The stock Yamaha wheel is aluminum and the exterior appearance can easily be damaged. Special care must be taken with tire irons when changing a tire to avoid scratches and gouges to the outer rim surface.

Some models are factory equipped with tubeless type tires and *aluminum wheels designed specifically for use with tubeless tires.* The wheels are labeled "Suitable for Tubeless Tires" on one of the spokes.

WARNING
Do not install tubeless tires on wheels designed for use only with tube-type tires. Personal injury and tire failure may result from rapid tire deflation while riding.

Tire removal/installation is basically the same for tube and tubeless tires, where differences occur they are noted. Tire repair is different and is covered in separate procedures.

Removal

1. Remove the valve core to deflate the tire.

2. Press the entire bead on both sides of the tire into the center of the rim.

3. Lubricate the beads with soapy water.

4. Insert the tire iron under the bead next to the valve (**Figure 22**). Force the bead on the opposite side of the tire into the center of the rim and pry the bead over the rim with the tire iron.

NOTE: *Insert scraps of leather between the tire irons and the rim to protect the rim from damage.*

5. Insert a second tire iron next to the first to hold the bead over the rim. Then work around

the tire with the first tire iron, prying the bead over the rim (**Figure 23**). Be careful not to pinch the inner tube with the tire irons.

6. Remove the valve from the hole in the rim and remove the tube from the tire (tube-type tires only).

> NOTE: *Step 7 is required only if it is necessary to completely remove the tire from the rim, such as for tire replacement.*

7. Stand the tire upright. Insert the tire iron between the second bead and the side of the rim that the first bead was pried over (**Figure 24**). Force the bead on the opposite side from the tire iron into the center of the rim. Pry the second bead off the rim, working around as with the first.

8. On tubeless tires, inspect the condition of the rubber O-ring seal where the valve stem seats against the inner surface of the wheel. Replace it if it's starting to deteriorate or has lost its resiliency. This is a common location of air loss.

Installation

1. Carefully inspect the tire for any damage, especially inside.

2. A new tire may have balancing rubbers inside. These are not patches and should not be disturbed. A colored spot near the bead indicates a lighter point on the tire. This spot should be placed next to the valve stem.

3. On tube-type tires, inflate the tube just enough to round it out. Too much air will make installation difficult. Place the inner tube inside the tire.

4. Lubricate both beads of the tire with soapy water.

5. Place the backside of the tire into the center of the rim and insert the valve stem through the stem hole in the wheel. The lower bead should go into the center of the rim and the upper bead outside. Work around the tire in both directions (**Figure 25**). Use a tire iron for the last few inches of bead (**Figure 26**).

6. Press the upper bead into the rim opposite the valve (**Figure 27**). Pry the bead into the rim on both sides of the initial point with a tire iron, working around the rim to valve (**Figure 28**).

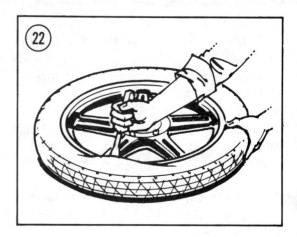

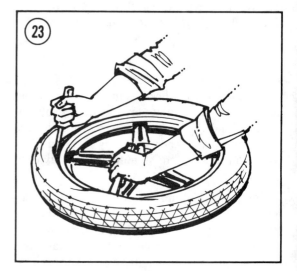

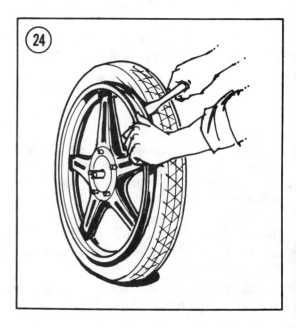

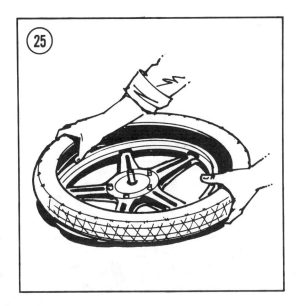

7. On tube-type tires, wiggle the valve to be sure the tube is not under the bead. Set the valve squarely in its hole before screwing in the valve nut to hold it against the rim.

8. Check the bead on both sides of the tire for an even fit around the rim.

9. On tube-type tires, inflate the tire slowly to seat the beads in the rim. It may be necessary to bounce the tire to complete the seating. Inflate to the required pressure. Balance the wheel as described previously.

10. On tubeless tires place an inflatable band around the circumference of the tire. Slowly inflate the band until the tire beads are pressed against the rim. Inflate the tire enough to seat it, deflate the band and remove it. Inflate the tire to the required pressure. Balance the tire as described previously.

TIRE REPAIRS
(TUBE-TYPE TIRES)

Every rider eventually experiences trouble with a tire or tube. Repairs and replacement are fairly simple, and every rider should know the techniques.

Patching a motorcycle tube is only a temporary fix. A motorcycle tire flexes too much and could rub a patch right off. However, a patched tire will get you far enough to buy a new tube.

8

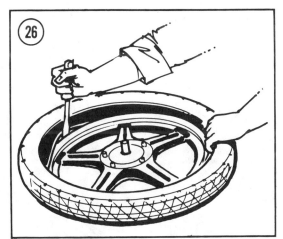

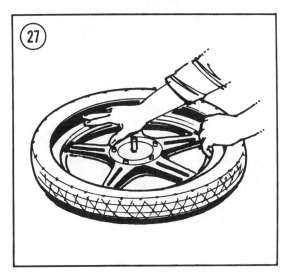

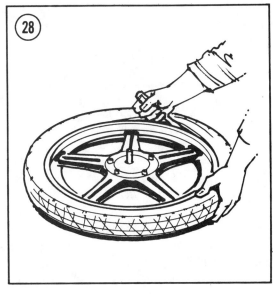

Tire Repair Kits

Tire repair kits can be purchased from motorcycle dealers and some auto supply stores. When buying, specify that the kit you want is for motorcycles.

There are two types of tire repair kits:

a. Hot patch
b. Cold patch

Hot patches are stronger because they actually vulcanize to the tube, becoming part of it. However, they are far too bulky to carry for roadside repairs, and the strength is unnecessary for a temporary repair.

Cold patches are not vulcanized to the tube; they are simply glued to it. Though not as strong as hot patches, cold patches are still very durable. Cold patch kits are less bulky than hot and more easily applied under adverse conditions. A cold patch kit containing everything necessary tucks in easily with your emergency tool kit.

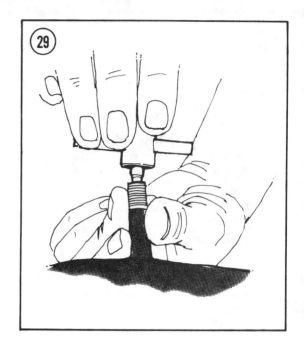

Tube Inspection

1. Install the valve core into the valve stem (**Figure 29**) and inflate the tube slightly. Do not overinflate.

2. Immerse the tube in water a section at a time. See **Figure 30**. Look carefully for bubbles indicating a hole. Mark each hole and continue checking until you are certain that all holes are discovered and marked. Also make sure that the valve core is not leaking; tighten it if necessary.

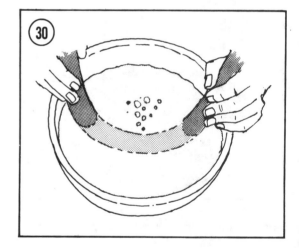

> NOTE: *If you do not have enough water to immerse sections of the tube, try running your hand over the tube slowly and very close to the surface. If your hand is damp, it works even better. If you suspect a hole anywhere, apply some saliva to the area to verify it (**Figure 31**).*

3. Apply a cold patch using the techniques described under *Cold Patch Repair*, following.

4. Dust the patch area with talcum powder to prevent it from sticking to the tire.

5. Carefully check inside the tire casing for glass particles, nails or other objects which may have damaged the tube. If inside of tire is split,

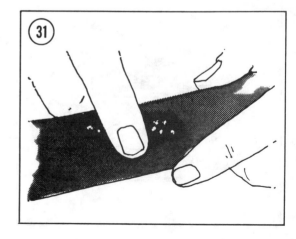

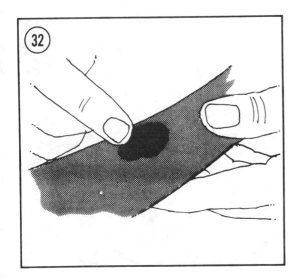

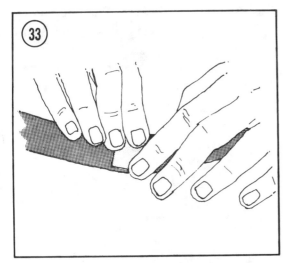

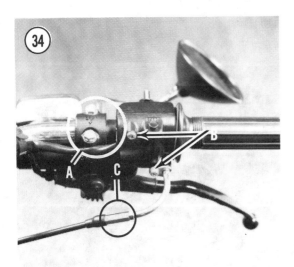

apply a patch to the area to prevent it from pinching and damaging the tube again.

6. Deflate tube prior to installation in the tire.

Cold Patch Repair

1. Remove the tube from tire as described under *Tire Removal* in this chapter.

2. Roughen area around hole slightly larger than the patch; use a cap from tire repair kit or pocket knife. Do not scrape too vigorously or you may cause additional damage.

3. Apply a small quantity of special cement to the puncture and spread it evenly with a finger (**Figure 32**).

4. Allow cement to dry until tacky — usually thirty seconds or so is sufficient.

5. Remove the backing from the patch.

> CAUTION
> *Do not touch the newly exposed rubber with your fingers or the patch will not stick firmly.*

6. Center patch over hole. Hold patch firmly in place for about 30 seconds to allow the cement to set (**Figure 33**).

7. Dust the patched area with talcum powder to prevent sticking.

TIRE REPAIRS
(TUBELESS TIRES)

Patching a tubeless tire on the road is very difficult. If both beads are still in place against the rim a can of pressurized tire sealant *may* inflate the tire and seal the hole. The beads must be against the wheel for this method to work.

Another solution is to carry a spare inner tube that could be temporarily installed and inflated. This will enable you to get to a service station where the tire can be correctly repaired. Be sure that the tube is designed for use with a tubeless tire.

HANDLEBAR

Removal/Installation

1. Remove the 2 bolts (A, **Figure 34**) securing the master cylinder and lay it on the fuel tank. It is not necessary to remove the hydraulic brake line.

> **CAUTION**
> *Cover the fuel tank with a heavy cloth or plastic tarp to protect it from accidental spilling of brake fluid. Wash any brake fluid off of any painted or plated surface immediately, as it will destroy the finish. Use soapy water and rinse thoroughly.*

2. Slacken the clutch cable (**Figure 35**) and disconnect it from the hand lever.

3. Separate the 2 halves of the start switch assembly (B, **Figure 34**). Disconnect the throttle cable from the twist grip (C, **Figure 34**). Separate the 2 halves (**Figure 36**) of the directional signal switch assembly.

4. Remove the rear view mirrors and clamps securing electrical cables to the handlebar.

5. Remove the 4 rubber plugs (A, **Figure 37**) and 4 Allen bolts (B, **Figure 37**) securing the handlebar holder(s) and remove it (or them).

> **NOTE**
> *Figure 37 shows a model except special; special models have 2 small handlebar holders.*

6. Lift off the handlebars.

7. Install by reversing these steps. Align the punch marks on the handlebar with the line that separates the upper and lower handlebar holder.

8. Tighten the 4 Allen screws of the handlebar holder. Tighten to a torque of 13 ft.-lb. (18 N•m). Install the rubber plugs.

9. Make sure the UP mark (A, **Figure 34**) on the master cylinder clamp is pointing up.

STEERING HEAD

Disassembly

Refer to **Figure 38** for this procedure.

1. Remove the front wheel as described under *Front Wheel Removal/Installation*, this chapter.

2. Remove both front caliper assemblies as described under *Caliper Removal/Installation* in Chapter Ten.

3. Remove the union bolt (**Figure 39**) securing the hose from the master cylinder to the fitting.

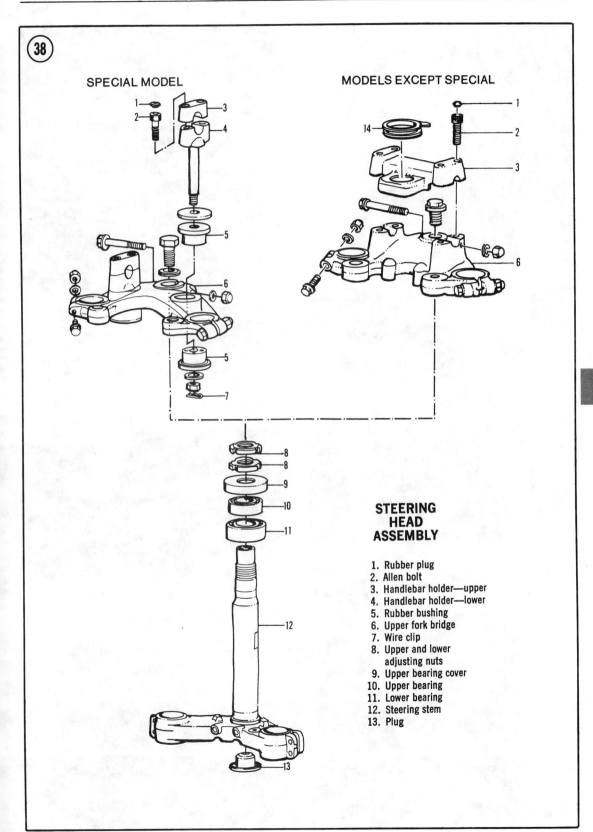

(38)

SPECIAL MODEL

MODELS EXCEPT SPECIAL

8

**STEERING
HEAD
ASSEMBLY**

1. Rubber plug
2. Allen bolt
3. Handlebar holder—upper
4. Handlebar holder—lower
5. Rubber bushing
6. Upper fork bridge
7. Wire clip
8. Upper and lower
   adjusting nuts
9. Upper bearing cover
10. Upper bearing
11. Lower bearing
12. Steering stem
13. Plug

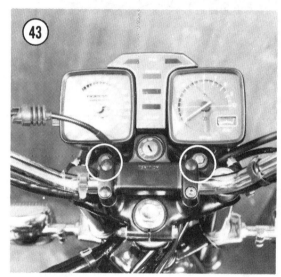

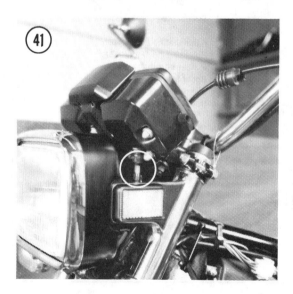

Remove the union bolt (**Figure 40**) securing the caliper hoses to the fitting and remove them.

4. Remove the handlebar as described under *Handlebar Removal/Installation*, this chapter.

5. Remove the speedometer cable (**Figure 41 or 42**) from the instrument pod.

6. Remove the 2 bolts (**Figure 43 or 44**) securing the instrument pod and lay it over the fuel tank.

7. Remove the headlight and front turn indicators.

8. Loosen the pinch bolts (**Figure 45**) on the upper fork bridge.

9. Loosen lower fork bridge bolts (**Figure 46 or 47**).

10. Slide entire fork and fender assembly out.

11. Loosen crown pinch bolt (A, **Figure 48**).

12. Loosen steering stem bolt (B, **Figure 48**) and remove the upper fork bridge.

13. Remove the upper and lower adjusting nuts with the pin spanner, provided in the XS1100 tool kit, or use an easily improvised unit (**Figure 49**).

8

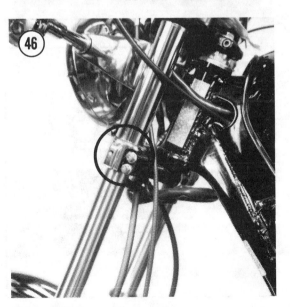

14. Remove the upper bearing cover.

15. Pull the steering stem out of the frame. The upper and lower bearings are assembled roller bearings — don't worry about catching any loose ball bearings.

Inspection

1. Clean the bearing races in the steering head and both roller bearings with solvent.

2. Check for broken welds on the frame around the steering head.

3. Check the bearings for pitting, scratches, or discoloration, indicating wear or corrosion. Replace them *in sets* if any are bad.

4. Check upper and lower races in the steering head. See *Bearing Race Replacement* if races are pitted, scratched, or badly worn.

5. Check steering stem for cracks.

Bearing Race Replacement

The headset and steering stem bearing races are pressed into place. Because they are easily bent, do not remove them unless they are worn and require replacement. Take old races to the dealer to ensure exact replacement.

To remove a headset race, insert a hardwood stick into the head tube and carefully tap the race out from the inside (**Figure 50**). Tap all around the race so that neither the race nor the head tube are bent. To install a race, fit it into the end of the head tube. Tap it slowly and squarely with a block of wood (**Figure 51**).

Assembly

Refer to **Figure 38** for this procedure.

1. Make sure the steering head bearing races are properly seated. Coat them with wheel bearing grease.

2. Thoroughly pack the bearings with wheel bearing grease.

3. Install the lower bearing onto the steering stem.

4. Insert the steering stem into the head tube. Hold it firmly in place.

5. Install the upper bearing and upper bearing cover.

6. Install the lower adjusting nut and tighten it (**Figure 52**) to approximately 7-9 ft.-lb. (9-12 N•m). *Do not* overtighten it. Install the upper adjusting nut tight up against the lower nut.

> NOTE: *The adjusting nuts should be just tight enough to remove play, both horizontal and vertical (Figure 53), yet loose enough so that the assembly will turn to both lock positions under its own weight after an initial assist.*

7. Continue assembling by reversing *Removal* Steps 12-1. Torque the bolts as follows (all models except as noted):

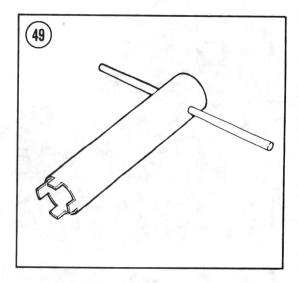

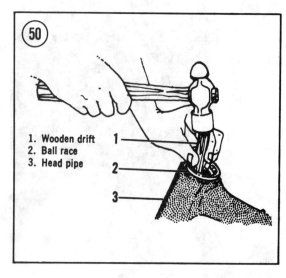

1. Wooden drift
2. Ball race
3. Head pipe

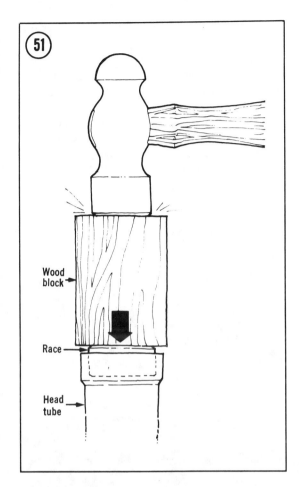

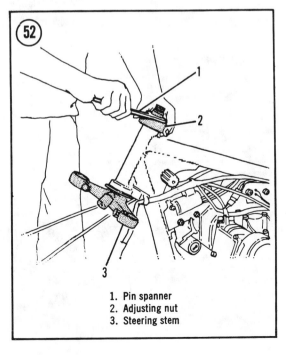

1. Pin spanner
2. Adjusting nut
3. Steering stem

a. Crown pinch bolt to 14.5 ft.-lb. (20 N•m)
b. Steering stem bolt to 61.5 ft.-lb. (85 N•m)
c. Upper fork bridge bolts 14.5 ft.-lb. (20 N•m)
d. Lower fork bridge bolts-models except special to 12.5 ft.-lb. (17 N•m). Special models to 14.5 ft.-lb. (20 N•m)

8. After the total assembly is completed, check the stem for looseness or binding—readjust if necessary.

9. On special models, install instrument pod with the attachment bracket *below* top fork bridge (**Figure 54**). If it is mounted above, the speedometer cables will be stretched and damaged when the steering is turned to its limits.

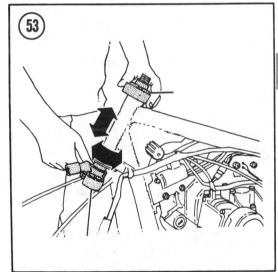

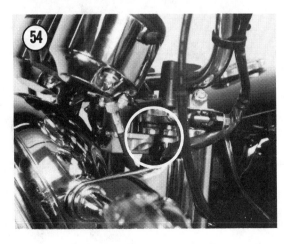

Steering Stem Adjustment

If play develops in the steering system, it may only require adjustment. However, don't take a chance on it. Disassemble the stem in Step 6, *Steering Head Assembly* in this chapter.

FRONT FORKS

The Yahama front suspension consists of a spring-controlled, hydraulically dampened telescopic fork. Before suspecting major trouble, drain the fork oil and refill with the proper type and quantity; refer to Chapter Three. On air/oil type, also check the fork air pressure. If you still have trouble, such as poor dampening, tendency to bottom out or top out, or leakage around rubber seals, then follow the service procedures in this section.

To simplify fork service and to prevent the mixing of parts, the legs should be removed, serviced, and reinstalled individually.

Removal/Installation

1. Remove the front wheel as described under *Front Wheel Removal* in this chapter.

2. Remove the bolts (**Figure 55**) securing the front fender and remove it.

3. Remove the remaining caliper(s). Tie them up with wire to the frame to keep tension off the brake hoses.

> NOTE: *Insert a piece of wood in the calipers in place of the discs. That way,*

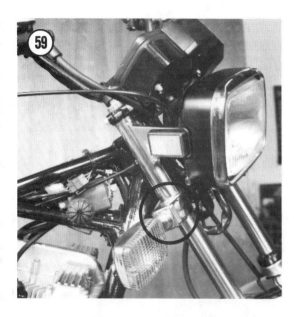

if the brake lever is inadvertently squeezed, the piston will not be forced out of the cylinder. If it does happen, the caliper might have to be disassembled to reseat the piston, and the system will have to be bled. By using the wood, bleeding the brake is not necessary when installing the wheel.

4. On regular forks, remove the top rubber cap (A, **Figure 56**).

5. On air/oil forks, remove the air cap (A, **Figure 57**) and *bleed off all air pressure* by depressing the valve stem (**Figure 58**).

> *WARNING*
> *Always bleed off all air pressure, failure to do so may cause personal injury when disassembling the fork assembly.*

6. Loosen the pinch bolts (B, **Figure 56**) or (B, **Figure 57**) on the upper fork bridge.

7. Loosen the lower fork bridge bolts (**Figure 59 or 60**).

8. Withdraw the fork tube. It may be necessary to slightly rotate the tube while removing it.

9. Install by reversing these removal steps. Torque the bolts as follows (all models except as noted):

    a. Upper fork pinch bolts 14.5 (20 N•m)

    b. Lower fork bridge bolts — regular forks to 12.5 ft.-lb. (17 N•m), air/oil forks to 14.5 ft.-lb. (20 N•m)

Disassembly

Refer to **Figure 61** for this procedure.

1. Hold the upper fork tube in a vise with soft jaws.

2. On regular forks remove the cap bolt, cap bolt ring, and washer.

3. On air/oil forks remove the air cap bolt, cap bolt ring, and washer.

4. Remove the fork spring.

5. Remove the fork from vise and pour the oil out and discard it. Pump the fork several times by hand to expel most of the remaining oil.

6. Remove the rubber boot out of the notch in the slider and slide it off of the fork tube.

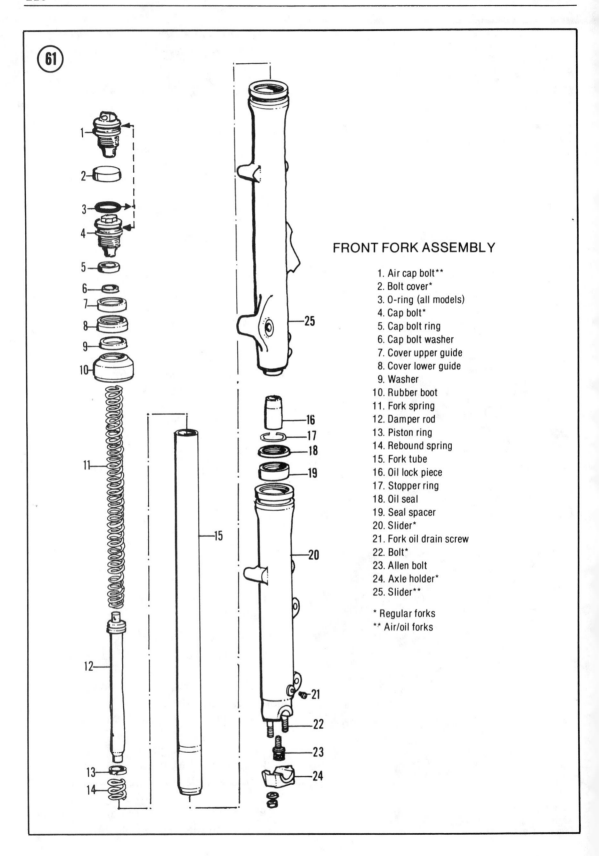

FRONT FORK ASSEMBLY

1. Air cap bolt**
2. Bolt cover*
3. O-ring (all models)
4. Cap bolt*
5. Cap bolt ring
6. Cap bolt washer
7. Cover upper guide
8. Cover lower guide
9. Washer
10. Rubber boot
11. Fork spring
12. Damper rod
13. Piston ring
14. Rebound spring
15. Fork tube
16. Oil lock piece
17. Stopper ring
18. Oil seal
19. Seal spacer
20. Slider*
21. Fork oil drain screw
22. Bolt*
23. Allen bolt
24. Axle holder*
25. Slider**

* Regular forks
** Air/oil forks

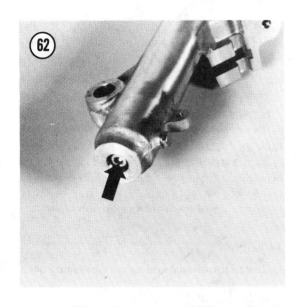

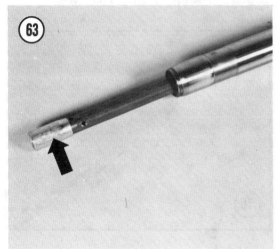

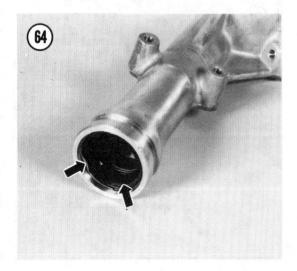

7. Clamp the slider in a vise with soft jaws.

8. Remove the Allen bolt (**Figure 62**) at the bottom of the slider and pull the fork tube out of the slider.

9. Remove the oil lock piece (**Figure 63**), the damper rod, and rebound spring.

10. Remove snap ring and oil seal (**Figure 64**).

CAUTION
Use a dull screwdriver blade to remove oil seal. Do not damage the outer or inner surface of the slider.

Inspection

1. Thoroughly clean all parts in solvent and dry. Check the fork tube for signs of wear or galling.

2. Check the damper rod for straightness. **Figure 65** shows one method. The rod should be replaced if the runout is 0.008 in. (0.2mm) or greater.

3. Carefully check the damper valve and the piston ring (**Figure 66**) for wear or damage.

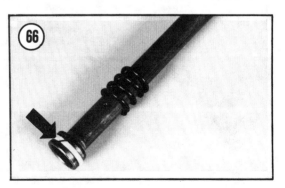

4. Inspect the oil seals for scoring and nicks and loss of resiliency. Replace if its condition is questionable.

5. Check upper fork tube exterior for scratches and straightness. If bent or scratched, it should be replaced.

6. Check the lower slider for dents or exterior damage that may cause the upper fork tube to hang up during riding conditions. Replace if necessary.

7. Measure the uncompressed length of the fork spring with a square as shown in **Figure 67**. Replace either spring if it is shorter than the following dimension:

   a. Regular fork—19.82 in. (503.5mm)
   b. Air/oil—24.10 in. (612.2mm)

8. Inspect the condition of the O-ring seal on the cap bolt (all models); replace if necessary.

9. Any parts that are worn or damaged should be replaced. Simply cleaning and reinstalling unserviceable conponents will not improve performance of the front suspension.

Assembly

1. Install the oil seal and snap ring **(Figure 64)**.

> NOTE: *Make sure the seal seats squarely and fully in the bores of the slider.*

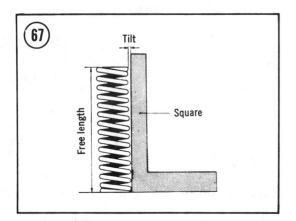

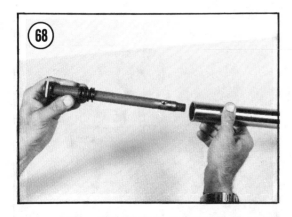

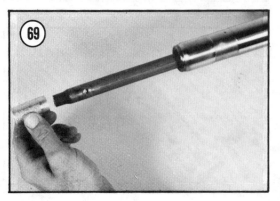

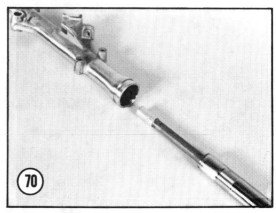

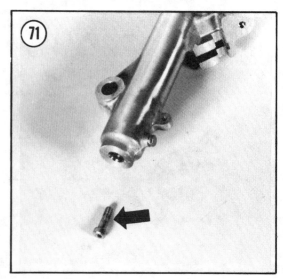

2. Insert the damper rod into the fork tube **(Figure 68)** and install oil lock piece **(Figure 69)**.

3. Apply a light coat of oil to the outside of the fork tube and install it into slider **(Figure 70)**. Apply Loctite Lock 'N' Seal to the threads of the Allen bolt and install it **(Figure 71)**.

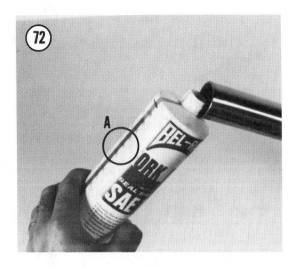

4. Slide rubber boot into place on the slider.

5. Fill fork tube with fresh fork oil **(Figure 72)**. Capacity per each fork tube is as follows:
   a. Regular fork—7.12 oz. (212cc)
   b. Air/oil—7.61 oz. (225cc)

> NOTE: *In order to measure the correct amount of fluid, use a plastic baby bottle. These have measurements in fluid ounces (oz.) and cubic centimeters (cc) on the side (**Figure 73**). Many fork oil containers have a semi-transparent strip on the side of the bottle (A, **Figure 72**) to aid in the measuring.*

6. Insert the spring with the tapered end down toward the axle.

7. Install the washer, cap bolt ring, and (air) cap bolt.

> NOTE: *Make sure the O-ring is in place and in good condition (**Figure 74**).*

8. Install the fork as described under *Front Fork Removal/Installation* in this chapter.

8

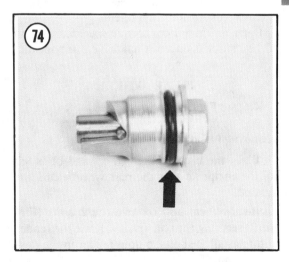

NOTE: If you own a 1980 or 1981 model, first check the Supplement at the back of the book for any new service information.

CHAPTER NINE

REAR SUSPENSION AND FINAL DRIVE

This chapter includes repair and replacement procedures for the rear wheel, final drive unit, and rear suspension components.

Refer to **Table 1** for torque specifications on all rear suspension and final drive components.

REAR WHEEL

Refer to **Figure 1** for this procedure.

Removal/Installation

1. Place the bike on the centerstand or block up the engine so that the rear wheel clears the ground.

2. Remove seat and remove the 2 bolts (**Figure 2**) securing the rear fender. Raise the fender and reinstall the bolts to hold fender in the raised position.

3. Remove cotter pin and axle nut (**Figure 3**). Discard the cotter pin.

4. Loosen rear axle pinch bolt (A, **Figure 4**).

5. Hold onto the caliper assembly and withdraw the rear axle (B, **Figure 4**). Do not lose the axle spacer (**Figure 5**).

6. Remove the bolt (**Figure 6**) securing the caliper assembly and tie it up to the frame (**Figure 7**).

NOTE: *Insert a piece of wood in the caliper in place of the disc. This way, if brake lever is inadvertently depressed, the piston will not be forced out of the cylinder. If this does happen the caliper might have to be disassembled to reseat the piston, and the system will have to be bled. By using the wood, bleeding the brake is not necessary when installing the wheel.*

7. Slide the wheel to the right to disengage it from the hub drive splines and remove the wheel.

CAUTION
Do not set the wheel down on the disc surface as it may get scratched or warped. Place it on a couple of wood blocks (Figure 8).

8. Install by reversing these removal steps. Apply molybdenum disulfide grease to the final drive flange splines on the wheel and the ring gear. Lightly grease the grease seals on each side of the wheel.

9. Make sure that the wheel hub splines engage with the final drive.

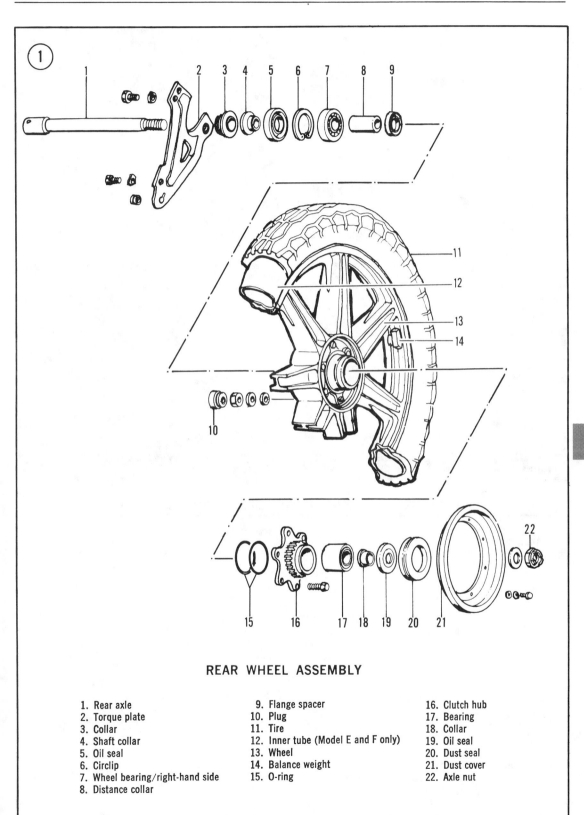

REAR WHEEL ASSEMBLY

1. Rear axle
2. Torque plate
3. Collar
4. Shaft collar
5. Oil seal
6. Circlip
7. Wheel bearing/right-hand side
8. Distance collar

9. Flange spacer
10. Plug
11. Tire
12. Inner tube (Model E and F only)
13. Wheel
14. Balance weight
15. O-ring

16. Clutch hub
17. Bearing
18. Collar
19. Oil seal
20. Dust seal
21. Dust cover
22. Axle nut

Table 1   REAR SUSPENSION AND FINAL DRIVE TORQUE SPECIFICATIONS

Item	Foot-Pounds (Ft.-lb.)	Newton Meters (N•m)
Rear axle nut		
Except special models	108	150
Special model	76	105
Pinch bolt		
Except special models	4.5	6
Special models	14.5	20
Final drive to rear swing arm	30	42
Rear swing arm pivot shaft locknuts	72	100
Rear shock absorbers acorn nuts		
Upper — Except special models	23	32
— Special models	28	39
Lower — Except special models		
(right-hand side)	30	42
(left-hand side)	23	32
—Special model		
(both sides)	28	39

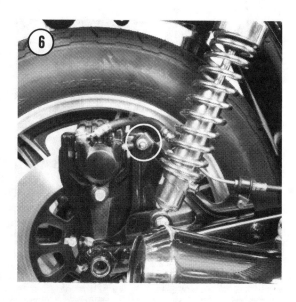

10. Torque the axle nut and pinch bolt as follows:

   a. Except special models—Axle nut to 108 ft.-lb. (150 N•m). Pinch bolt to 4.5 ft.-lb. (6 N•m).

   b. Special models—Axle nut to 76 ft.-lb. (105 N•m). Pinch bolt to 14.5 ft.-lb. (20 N•m).

NOTE: *Always install a new cotter pin, never reuse an old one.*

Inspection

Measure the lateral and vertical runout of the wheel rim with a dial indicator as shown in **Figure 9**. The maximum lateral runout is 0.08 in. (2mm) and the maximum vertical runout is 0.08 in. (2mm). If the runout exceeds these dimensions, check the wheel bearings' condition and/or replace the wheel. The stock Yamaha aluminum wheel cannot be serviced; it must be replaced.

9

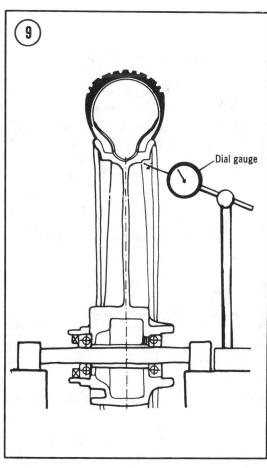

Dial gauge

REAR HUB

Disassembly

Refer to **Figure 1** for this procedure.

1. Remove the rear wheel as described under *Rear Wheel Removal/Installation* in this chapter.

2. Remove the collar and shaft collar from the right-hand side (**Figure 10**).

3. Remove the oil seal (**Figure 11**) and circlip on the right-hand side.

4. Remove the oil seal and collar (**Figure 12**) on the left-hand side.

5. Remove the wheel bearings and spacer. Tap the bearings out with a soft aluminum or brass drift.

> CAUTION
> *Tap only on the outer bearing race. The bearing will be damaged if struck on the inner race.*

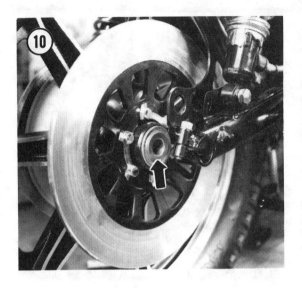

Inspection

1. Clean bearings thoroughly in solvent and dry with compressed air. Do not let the bearing spin while drying.

2. Clean the inside and outside of the hub with solvent. Dry with compressed air.

3. Turn each bearing by hand (**Figure 13**). Make sure bearings turn smoothly. Check the balls for evidence of wear, pitting, or excessive heat (bluish tint). Replace if necessary; always replace as a complete set.

4. Check the axle for wear and straightness. Use V-blocks and a dial indicator as shown in **Figure 14**. If the runout is 0.008 in. (0.2mm) or greater, the axle must be replaced.

Assembly

1. Pack the bearings thoroughly with multipurpose grease. Work grease in between the balls completely.

2. Install the left-hand wheel bearing.

3. Press in the bearing spacer.

4. Install the right-hand wheel bearing and circlip.

> NOTE: *Install bearings with the sealed side facing outward.*

CAUTION
Tap the bearings squarely into place and tap on the outer race only. Do not tap on the inner race or the bearings might be damaged. Be sure that the bearings are completely seated.

5. Lubricate the oil and dust seals with grease.

6. Install the collar and the oil and dust seal on the left-hand side.

7. Install the oil seal and collars on the right-hand side.

8. Install the rear wheel as described under *Rear Wheel Removal/Installation*, this chapter.

WHEEL BALANCING

For complete information refer to *Wheel Balancing* in Chapter Eight.

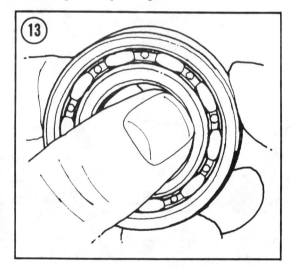

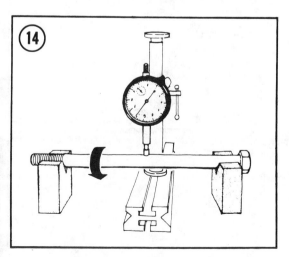

TIRE CHANGING

Refer to *Tire Changing* in Chapter Eight.

FINAL DRIVE

Removal/Installation

1. Remove the rear wheel as described under *Rear Wheel Removal/Installation*, this chapter.

2. Remove 4 nuts and washers (A, **Figure 15**) securing the final drive unit to the swing arm.

3. Remove the left-hand lower shock absorber acorn nut (B, **Figure 15**).

4. Pull the final drive unit straight back until it is free.

5. Wipe the grease from the splines on the end of the drive shaft and final drive unit.

6. Check the splines (**Figure 16**) of both units

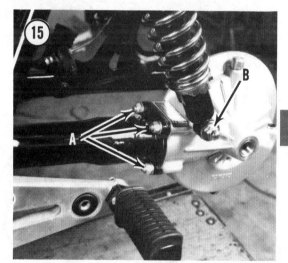

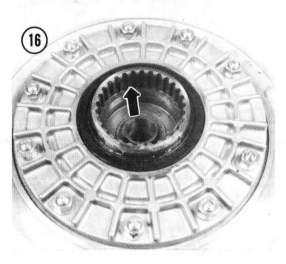

carefully for signs of wear. Also inspect the splines in the clutch hub (**Figure 17**) in the rear wheel.

7. Pack the splines with multipurpose molybdenum disulfide grease.

8. Install the final drive unit onto the swing arm. Make sure that the splines of the drive shaft engage properly with the final drive unit.

9. Install 4 nuts and washers and tighten to 30 ft.-lb. (42 N•m) and the shock absorber acorn nut to 23 ft.-lb. (32 N•m).

10. Install the rear wheel as described under *Rear Wheel Removal/Installation*, this chapter.

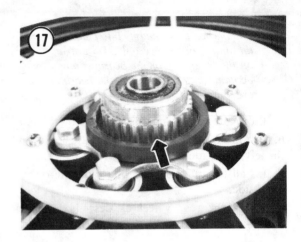

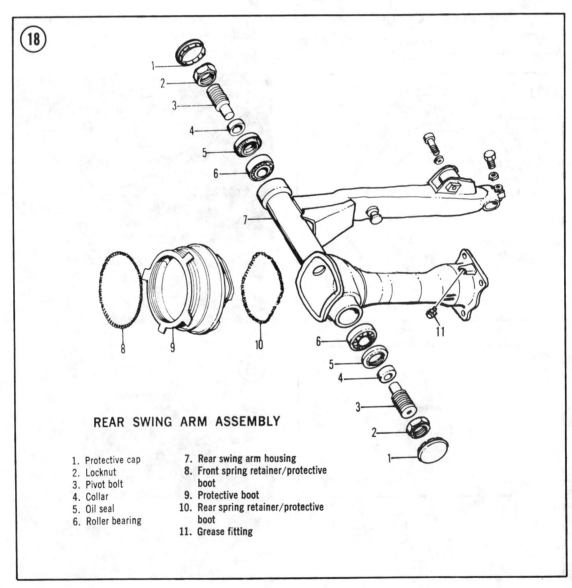

REAR SWING ARM ASSEMBLY

1. Protective cap
2. Locknut
3. Pivot bolt
4. Collar
5. Oil seal
6. Roller bearing
7. Rear swing arm housing
8. Front spring retainer/protective boot
9. Protective boot
10. Rear spring retainer/protective boot
11. Grease fitting

Disassembly and Inspection

Although it may be practical for you to disassemble the final drive for inspection, you cannot replace the bearings or seals (which require bearing removal) without special tools. If there is trouble in the final drive unit, it may be best to remove the unit, and take it to your Yamaha dealer and let them overhaul it. They are also better equipped to check and adjust gear lash.

Inspect the exterior of the unit for signs of wear, cracks, damage, or oil leakage. If any damage is present or there are signs of oil leakage, take the unit to your Yamaha dealer for service.

REAR SWING ARM

Refer to **Figure 18** for this procedure.

Removal/Installation

1. Remove the rear wheel as described under *Rear Wheel Removal/Installation*, this chapter.
2. Remove the final drive unit as described under *Final Drive Removal/Installation* in this chapter.
3. Slide back the rubber protective boot and remove the 4 bolts (A, **Figure 19**) securing the drive shaft to the middle gear housing.

4. Disengage the drive shaft and remove it through the rear.
5. Remove the right-hand lower shock absorber acorn nut.
6. Remove the caliper assembly from the swing arm. Tie it up to the frame with wire to relieve tension on the brake hose.
7. Remove the protective caps (B, **Figure 19**) and remove the locknut from the pivot bolt on both sides.
8. Remove both pivot bolts and the swing arm.
9. Install by reversing these removal steps, noting the following.
10. After the rear swing arm is installed, adjust side clearance as described under *Rear Swing Arm Adjustment* in this chapter.
11. Make sure that the swing arm moves up and down smoothly without tightness, binding or rough spots. If the movement is rough, the bearings should be replaced.

Inspection

1. Remove the rubber boot from the swing arm and inspect it for tears or deterioration; replace if necessary.
2. Remove the oil seals and bearings.
3. Thoroughly clean the bearings in solvent and dry with compressed air.
4. Turn each bearing by hand (**Figure 13**). Make sure bearings turn smoothly. Check the balls for evidence of wear or pitting. Replace if necessary. Always replace both bearings and inner and outer races at the same time.
5. If bearings have been replaced, the grease seals should be replaced also.
6. Pack the bearings with a lithium base, waterproof wheel bearing grease.
7. Install the bearings into the swing arm.

> CAUTION
> *Tap the bearings squarely into place and tap on the outer race only. Do not tap on the inner race or the bearings might be damaged. Be sure that the bearings are completely seated.*

Adjustment

1. Measure the distance between the frame and

9

the swing arm on both right- and left-hand sides (**Figure 20**).

2. The difference between the two measurements should not be more than 0.062 in. (1.6mm).

3. If these measurements differ by more than that specified, adjustment should be made.

4. Remove the protective caps (**Figure 21**).

5. Loosen the pivot shaft locknuts (**Figure 22**) on both sides.

6. Loosen the pivot shaft bolt on the side with the greatest dimension.

> NOTE: *Loosen only slightly, approximately ½ turn.*

7. Tighten the opposite pivot shaft bolt to approximately 47 ft.-lb. (64 N•m).

8. Measure the gap again, if the dimension is still not within that specified, repeat Steps 6-8 until correct.

9. When correct, tighten the pivot shaft locknuts to 72 ft.-lb. (100 N•m).

> NOTE: *Do not allow the pivot shaft bolts to rotate while tightening the locknuts.*

After tightening, recheck to make sure the dimensions are still correct.

REAR SHOCKS

The rear shocks are spring controlled and hydraulically dampened. Spring preload can be adjusted by rotating the cam ring at the base of the spring (**Figure 23**) — *clockwise to increase* preload and *counterclockwise to decrease it.*

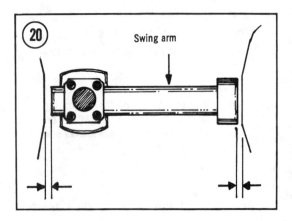

Swing arm

NOTE: *Use the spanner wrench furnished in the XS1100 tool kit for this adjustment.*

Both cams must be indexed on the same detent. The shocks are sealed and cannot be rebuilt. Service is limited to removal and replacement of the hydraulic unit.

NOTE

*On models with air/oil front forks there is an additional adjustment located on the top of the shock (**Figure 24**). On this model the upper and lower shock adjustments must correspond to the air pressure in the front forks for various load conditions. Refer to **Front Forks and Rear Shocks—Air/Oil Front Fork Models**, in Chapter Three.*

Removal/Installation

Removal and installation of the rear shocks is easier if they are done separately. The remaining unit will support the rear of the bike and maintain the correct relationship between the top and bottom mounts.

1. Block up the engine or support it on the centerstand.

2. Adjust both shocks to their softest setting, *completely counterclockwise*.

3. Remove the upper and lower acorn nuts **(Figure 25)**.

4. Pull the shock off.

5. Install by reversing removal steps. Torque the nuts as follows:

    a. Regular fork models—Upper to 23 ft.-lb. (32 N•m); lower (left-hand side) to 23 ft.-lb. (32 N•m); lower (right-hand side) to 30 ft.-lb. (42 N•m).

    b. Air/oil front fork models—upper and lower (both sides) to 28 ft.-lb. (39 N•m).

NOTE: If you own a 1980 or 1981 model, first check the Supplement at the back of the book for any new service information.

CHAPTER TEN

BRAKES

The XS1100 has dual disc front brakes operated by the right-hand lever and a single disc rear brake operated by a foot lever. This chapter describes repair and replacement procedures for all brake components.

Refer to **Table 1** for torque specifications on all brake components.

FRONT DISC BRAKES

The front disc brakes are actuated by hydraulic fluid and are controlled by a hand lever. As the brake pads wear, the brake fluid level drops in the reservoir and automatically adjusts for wear. However, brake lever free play must be maintained. Refer to *Front Brake Lever Adjustment* in Chapter Three.

When working on hydraulic brake systems, it is necessary that the work area and all tools be absolutely clean. Any tiny particles of foreign matter and grit in the caliper assembly or the master cylinder can damage the components. Also, sharp tools must not be used inside the caliper or on the piston. If there is any doubt about your ability to correctly and safely carry out major service on the brake components, take the job to a Yamaha dealer or brake specialist.

FRONT MASTER CYLINDER

Removal/Installation

1. Remove the rear view mirror (A, **Figure 1**).

> ### CAUTION
> *Cover the fuel tank and instrument cluster with a heavy cloth or plastic tarp to protect them from accidental spilling of brake fluid. Wash any brake fluid off of any painted or plated surface immediately, as it will destroy the finish. Use soapy water and rinse completely.*

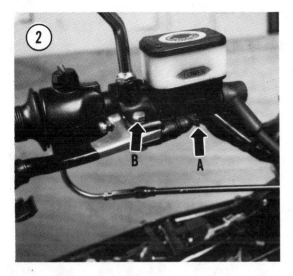

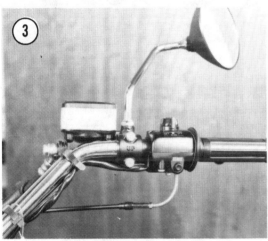

Table 1   BRAKE COMPONENT TORQUE SPECIFICATIONS

Item	Foot-Pounds (Ft.-lb.)	Newton Meters (N•m)
Brake hose union bolts (all)	18	24
Caliper mounting bolts		
Except special models		
Upper	32	45
Lower	13	18
Special models	18	24
Master cylinder cap screws	1.5	2.0
Rear axle		
Pinch bolt	4	6
Axle nut	108	150
Rear master cylinder mounting bolt	16	23

2. Pull back the rubber boot and remove the union bolt (B, **Figure 1**) securing the brake hose to the master cylinder and remove it.

3. Remove the electrical leads from the brakelight switch (A, **Figure 2**).

4. Remove the bolt and nut (B, **Figure 2**) securing the brake lever and remove it.

5. Remove the 2 clamping bolts (**Figure 3**) securing the master cylinder to the handlebar, and remove it.

6. Install by reversing the removal steps. Be sure to install the clamp with the UP arrow pointing up (**Figure 3**).

7. Bleed the brake as described under *Bleeding the System* at the end of this chapter.

Disassembly

Refer to **Figure 4** for the front and **Figure 5** for the rear master cylinder, for this procedure.

1. Remove the master cylinder as described under *Front Master Cylinder Removal/ Installation* in this chapter.

2. Remove the top cap, diaphragm, and gasket; pour out the brake fluid and discard it — *never* reuse brake fluid.

3. Remove the boot and snap ring.

4. Remove the piston cap assembly.

Inspection

1. Clean all parts in denatured alcohol or fresh brake fluid. Inspect the cylinder bore and piston contact surfaces for signs of wear and damage. If either part is less than perfect, replace it.

2. Check the end of the piston for wear caused by the hand lever or brake actuating rod and check the pivot bore in the front hand lever. Discard the caps.

3. Make sure the passages in the bottom of the brake fluid reservoir are clear. Check the reservoir cap and diaphragm for damage and deterioration and replace as necessary.

4. Inspect the condition of the threads in the bores for the brake line and the switch.

5. Check the front hand lever pivot lug for cracks.

6. Replace all internal seals every 2 years.

10

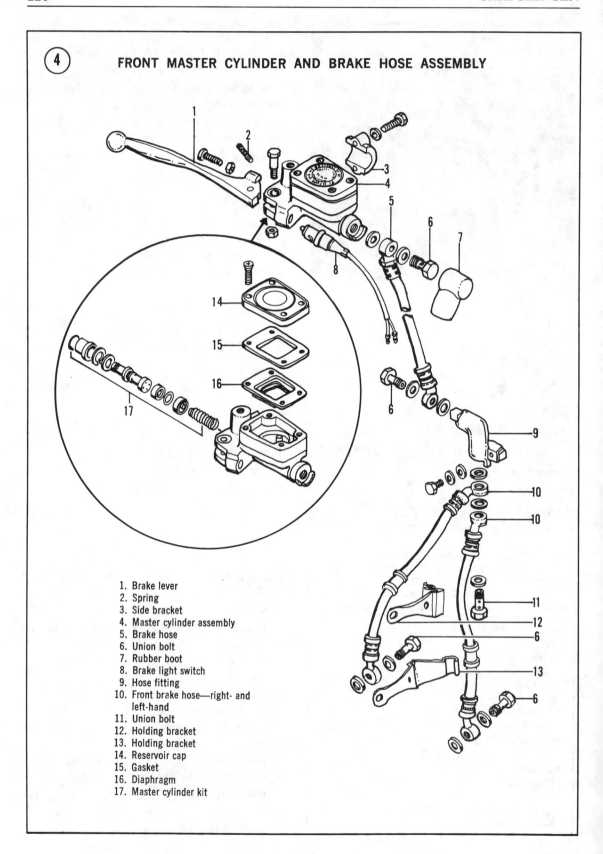

④ FRONT MASTER CYLINDER AND BRAKE HOSE ASSEMBLY

1. Brake lever
2. Spring
3. Side bracket
4. Master cylinder assembly
5. Brake hose
6. Union bolt
7. Rubber boot
8. Brake light switch
9. Hose fitting
10. Front brake hose—right- and
    left-hand
11. Union bolt
12. Holding bracket
13. Holding bracket
14. Reservoir cap
15. Gasket
16. Diaphragm
17. Master cylinder kit

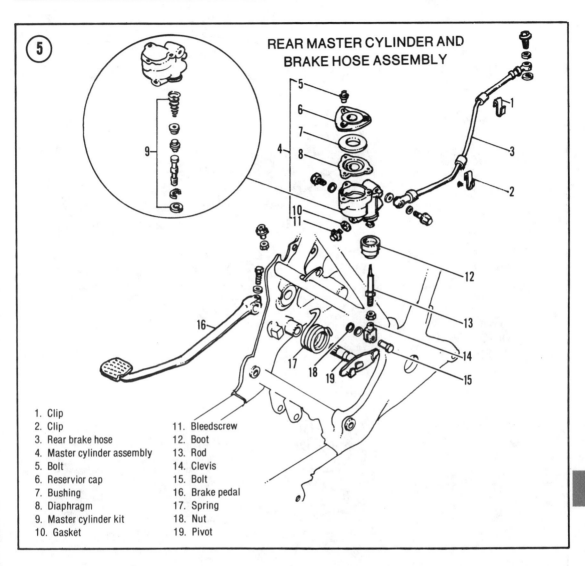

⑤

REAR MASTER CYLINDER AND BRAKE HOSE ASSEMBLY

1. Clip
2. Clip
3. Rear brake hose
4. Master cylinder assembly
5. Bolt
6. Reservior cap
7. Bushing
8. Diaphragm
9. Master cylinder kit
10. Gasket
11. Bleedscrew
12. Boot
13. Rod
14. Clevis
15. Bolt
16. Brake pedal
17. Spring
18. Nut
19. Pivot

10

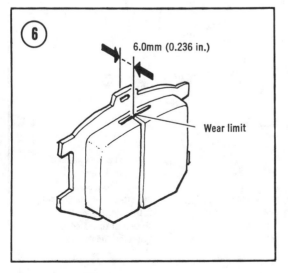

⑥

6.0mm (0.236 in.)

Wear limit

Assembly

1. Soak the new caps in fresh brake fluid for at least 15 minutes to make them pliable.

2. Install the spring.

3. Install the primary and secondary caps into the cylinder.

4. Install the piston and washer and install the snap ring and boot.

5. Install the diaphragm, gasket, and top cap.

6. Install the front master cylinder on the handlebar and connect the brake hose and brakelight switch electrical leads.

7. Install the rear master cylinder to the frame and connect the brake hose. Tighten the brake hose union bolts to 18 ft.-lb. (24 N•m).

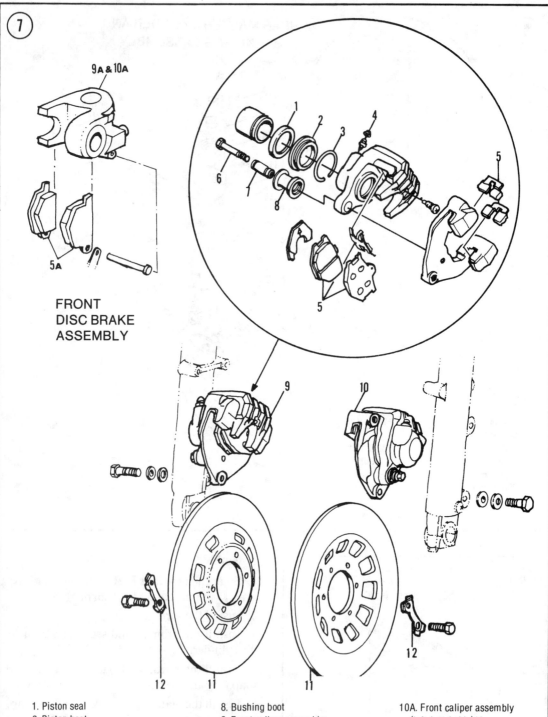

FRONT
DISC BRAKE
ASSEMBLY

1. Piston seal
2. Piston boot
3. Dust cover clip
4. Bleeder cap and screw
5. Brake pads and spring*
5A. Brake pads, spring clip, and rod**
6. Support bolt
7. Sleeve

8. Bushing boot
9. Front caliper assembly
   (right-hand side)*
9A. Front caliper assembly
   (right-hand side)**
10. Front caliper assembly
   (left-hand side)*

10A. Front caliper assembly
   (left-hand side)**
11. Front brake disc
   (right-and left-hand side)
12. Disc lockwasher
* Except Special Models
** Special Models

FRONT BRAKE PAD REPLACEMENT

There is no recommended mileage interval for changing the friction pads in the disc brake. Pad wear depends greatly on riding habits and conditions. The pads should be checked for wear every 2,500 miles (4,000km) and replaced when the wear indicator (**Figure 6**) reaches the edge of the brake disc. Always replace all four pads (two per disc) at the same time.

It is not necessary to remove the front wheel to replace the pads.

Refer to **Figure 7** for this procedure.

1. On models except special, remove the upper mounting bolt (A, **Figure 8**) and the lower support bolt (B, **Figure 8**). Support the caliper assembly with a piece of wire to the brake hose clamp (**Figure 9**). Remove the screw (**Figure 10**) securing the pads in place and remove them.

2. On special models, remove the caliper mounting bolt assembly (**Figure 11**). Pull the caliper assembly off the disc. Pinch the spring retainer (A, **Figure 12**) together and slide the pad locating pin out (B, **Figure 12**) and remove the old pads.

10

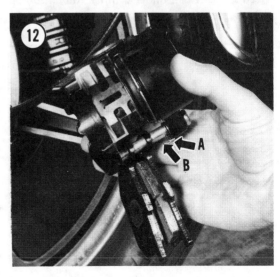

3. Clean the pad recess and end of the piston with a soft brush. Do not use solvent, a wire brush, or any hard tool which would damage the cylinder or the piston.

4. Lightly coat the end of the piston and the backs of the new pads (not the friction material) with disc brake lubricant.

WARNING
*On models except special, the brake pads for the front and rear appear to be the same. Their shape is identical **but the friction material is different**. The pads designed specifically for the rear are marked REAR on the base plate of the pads. **Do not** interchange the front and rear pads as brake effectiveness, especially in wet weather, will be dangerously reduced.*

NOTE: *Check with your dealer to make sure the friction compound of the new pads is compatible with the disc material. Remove any roughness from the backs of new pads with a fine cut file and blow clean with compressed air.*

5. Remove the cap from the master cylinder (**Figure 13**) and slowly push the piston into the caliper while checking the reservoir to make sure the brake fluid does not overflow. Remove fluid if necessary prior to overflowing. The piston should move freely. If it does not and there is any evidence of it sticking in the cylinder, the caliper should be removed and serviced as described under *Caliper Rebuilding* in this chapter.

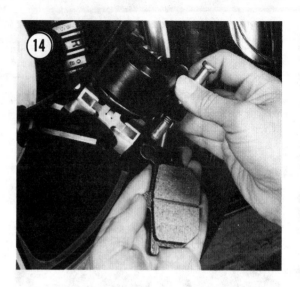

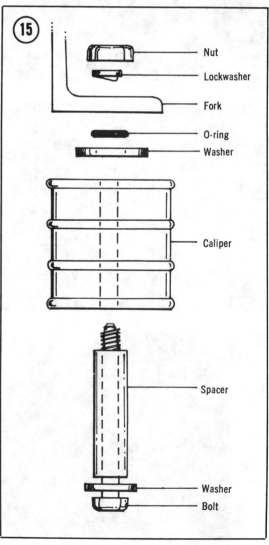

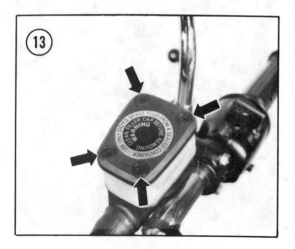

6. Push the caliper to the right and push the piston in to allow the new pads to be installed.

7. Install the new pads (**Figure 14**). On models except special, replace the 3 shims and the pad retaining screw. On special models install the caliper mounting bolt assembly in the order shown in **Figure 15**.

NOTE: *Do not forget to install the O-ring.*

8. Carefully remove any rust or corrosion from the disc.

9. Block the motorcycle up so that the front wheel is off the ground. Spin the front wheel and activate the brake lever for as many times as it takes to refill the cylinder in the caliper and correctly locate the pads.

10. Refill the fluid in the reservoir if necessary and replace the top cap.

WARNING
Use brake fluid clearly marked DOT-3 only. Others may vaporize and cause brake failure. Always use the same brand name; do not intermix as many brands are not compatible.

WARNING
*Do not ride the motorcycle until you are sure that the brake is operating correctly with full hydraulic advantage. If necessary, bleed the brakes as described under **Bleeding the System** at the end of this chapter.*

11. Bed the pads in gradually for the first 50 miles by using only light pressure as much as possible. Immediate hard applications will glaze the new friction pads and greatly reduce the effectiveness of the brakes.

FRONT CALIPER

Removal/Installation

It is not necessary to remove the front wheel to remove either or both caliper assemblies.
Refer to **Figure 7** for this procedure.
1. On models except special, remove the upper and lower bolts (**Figure 8**). Pull the caliper assembly off the disc.
2. On special models, remove the caliper mounting bolt assembly (**Figure 11**). Slide the caliper assembly off the disc.
3. Remove the union bolt (**Figure 16**) securing the brake hose to the caliper and remove it. Drain the brake fluid from the hose and discard it; *never* reuse brake fluid.
4. Repeat Steps 1-3 for the other caliper.
5. Install by reversing these removal steps. Carefully insert the caliper onto the disc. Avoid damage to the pads.
6. Torque the brake hose union bolts to 18 ft.-lb. (24 N•m).
7. On models except special, torque the upper mounting bolt to 32 ft.-lb. (45 N•m) and the lower support bolt to 13 ft.-lb. (18 N•m).
8. On special models, torque the mounting assembly bolt to 18 ft.-lb. (24 N•m).

NOTE: *Install caliper mounting bolt assembly in the order shown in Figure 15.*

9. Bleed the brakes as described under *Bleeding the System* at the end of this chapter.

WARNING
Don't ride the motorcycle until you are sure that brakes are operating properly.

Caliper Rebuilding

If the caliper leaks, it should be rebuilt. If the piston sticks in the cylinder, indicating severe wear or galling, the entire unit should be re-

10

placed. Rebuilding a leaky caliper requires special tools and experience.

Caliper service should be entrusted to your Yamaha dealer or brake specialist. Considerable money can be saved by removing the caliper yourself and taking it in for repair.

The factory recommends that the internal seals of the calipers be replaced every two years.

FRONT BRAKE HOSE REPLACEMENT

The factory recommends that all brake hoses be replaced every four years or when they show signs of cracking or damage.

Refer to **Figure 4** for this procedure.

CAUTION
Cover the front wheel, fender, and fuel tank with a heavy cloth or plastic tarp to protect it from accidental spilling of brake fluid. Wash any brake fluid off of any painted or plated surface immediately, as it will destroy the finish. Use soapy water and rinse completely.

1. Remove the union bolt **(Figure 17)** securing the brake hose to the caliper and remove it. Drain the brake fluid from the hose and discard it—*never* reuse brake fluid. Repeat for the other caliper.
2. Remove the union bolt securing both hoses to the fitting. On models except special, remove the 2 screws **(Figure 18)** securing the bracket and remove it. Move the 3 electrical wiring harnesses to the side to gain access to the hose fittings.

NOTE
*Refer to **Figure 19** for models except special and **Figure 20** for special models.*

3. Remove union bolt **(Figure 21)** securing the upper hose to the fitting.
4. Remove the union bolt **(Figure 22)** securing the upper hose to the master cylinder and remove the hose.
5. Install new hoses, washers, and union bolts in the reverse order of removal. Be sure to install all washers in the correct position; refer to **Figure 4**. Torque all union bolts to 18 ft.-lb. (24 N•m).
6. Refill the master cylinder with brake fluid clearly marked DOT-3 only. Bleed the brakes as described under *Bleeding the System* at the end of this chapter.

REAR DISC BRAKE

The rear disc brake is actuated by hydraulic brake fluid and is controlled by the foot operated brake lever. As the brake pads wear, the brake fluid drops in the reservoir and automatically adjusts for wear. However, brake lever free play must be maintained; refer to *Rear Brake Height and Free Play Adjustment* in Chapter Three.

Refer to the note regarding hydraulic brake work habits in *Front Disc Brakes* at the beginning of this chapter.

REAR MASTER CYLINDER

Removal/Installation

CAUTION
Cover the surrounding frame with a heavy cloth or plastic tarp to protect it from accidental spilling of brake fluid. Wash any brake fluid off of any painted or plated surface immediately, as it will destroy the finish. Use soapy water and rinse completely.

Refer to **Figure 5** for this procedure.

1. Remove the union bolt (**Figure 23**) securing the brake hose to the master cylinder and remove the hose.

10

2. Remove the 2 bolts and lockwashers (**Figure 24**) securing the master cylinder to the frame and remove it. Pull the master cylinder straight up and off the brake actuating rod.

3. Install by reversing these removal steps. Inspect the brake actuating rod boot (**Figure 25**) on the bottom of master cylinder. Replace it if cracked or deteriorated.

4. Torque master cylinder to frame bolts to 16 ft.-lb. (23 N•m).

5. Torque the union bolts to 18 ft.-lb. (24 N•m).

6. Bleed the brake as described under *Bleeding the System* at the end of this chapter.

Disassembly/Inspection/Assembly

These procedures are identical for front and rear master cylinders. Refer to *Master Cylinder Disassembly/Inspection/Assembly* procedures under *Front Disc Brake*.

REAR BRAKE PAD REPLACEMENT

There is no recommended mileage interval for changing the friction pads in the disc brake. Pad wear depends greatly on riding habits and conditions. The pads should be checked for wear every 2,500 miles (4,000km) and replaced when the wear indicator (**Figure 26**) reaches the edge of the brake disc. Always replace both pads at the same time.

It is not necessary to remove the rear wheel to replace the pads.

Refer to **Figure 27** for this procedure.

1. Place the bike on the centerstand. Remove the seat, remove the 2 bolts and hinge up the rear fender.

2. Remove the cotter pin and rear axle nut (**Figure 28**).

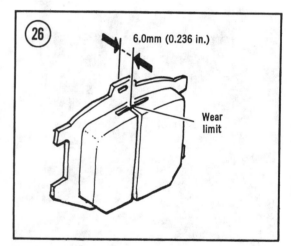

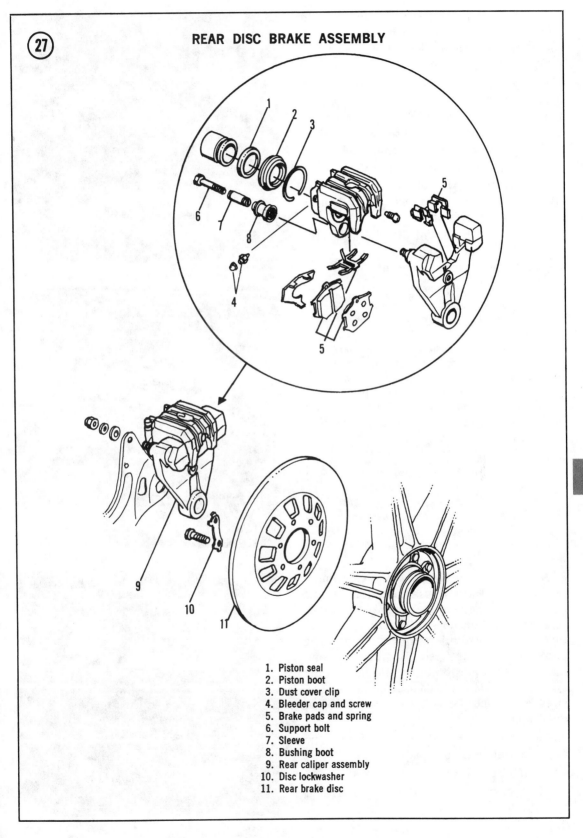

REAR DISC BRAKE ASSEMBLY

1. Piston seal
2. Piston boot
3. Dust cover clip
4. Bleeder cap and screw
5. Brake pads and spring
6. Support bolt
7. Sleeve
8. Bushing boot
9. Rear caliper assembly
10. Disc lockwasher
11. Rear brake disc

10

3. Loosen the axle pinch bolt (**Figure 29**) and withdraw the axle from the right-hand side. Do not lose the axle spacer (**Figure 30**).

4. Remove the acorn nut and lockwasher (**Figure 31**) and pivot the caliper assembly up (**Figure 32**) and off the disc.

5. From the backside of the caliper assembly, remove the screw (**Figure 33**) securing the pads in place. Remove the pads and shims.

6. Clean the pad recess and end of the piston with a soft brush. Do not use solvent, a wire brush, or any hard tool which would damage the cylinder or the piston.

7. Lightly coat the end of the piston and the backs of the new pads (not the friction material) with disc brake lubricant.

> *WARNING*
> *On models except special, the brake pads for the front and rear appear to be the same. Their shape is identical **but the friction material is different**. The pads designed specifically for the rear are marked REAR on the base plate of the pads. Do not interchange the front and rear pads as brake effectiveness, especially in wet weather, will be dangerously reduced.*

> NOTE: *Check with your dealer to make sure the friction compound of the new pads is compatible with the disc material. Remove any roughness from backs of the new pads with a fine cut file and blow clean with compressed air.*

8. Remove the cap from the master cylinder (**Figure 34**) and slowly push the piston into the caliper while checking the reservoir to make sure the brake fluid does not overflow. Remove fluid if necessary, prior to overflowing. The piston should move freely. If it does not and there is any evidence of it sticking in the cylinder, the caliper should be removed and serviced as described under *Caliper Rebuilding* in this chapter.

9. Push the caliper to the right and push the piston in to allow the new pads to be installed.

10. Install the new pads and new shims.

11. Carefully remove any rust or corrosion from the disc.

12. Block the motorcycle up so that the front wheel is off the ground. Spin the front wheel and activate the brake lever for as many times as it takes to refill the cylinder in the caliper and correctly locate the pads.

13. Refill the fluid in the reservoir if necessary and replace the top cap.

> WARNING
> *Use brake fluid clearly marked DOT-3 only. Others may vaporize and cause brake failure. Always use the same brand name; do not intermix as many brands are not compatible.*

> WARNING
> *Do not ride the motorcycle until you are sure that the brake is operating correctly with full hydraulic advantage. If necessary, bleed the brakes as described under Bleeding the System in this chapter.*

14. Bed the pads in gradually for the first 50 miles by using only light pressure as much as possible. Immediate hard application will glaze the new friction pads and greatly reduce the effectiveness of the brake.

15. Torque the rear axle pinch bolt to 4 ft.-lb. (6 N•m) and the axle bolt to 108 ft.-lb. (150 N•m).

REAR CALIPER

Removal/Installation

It is not necessary to remove the rear wheel to remove the caliper assembly.

Refer to **Figure 27** for this procedure.

1. Remove the union bolt (**Figure 35**) securing the brake hose to the caliper and remove the hose. Drain the brake fluid from the hose and discard it; *never* reuse brake fluid.

10

2. Perform Steps 1-4, *Rear Brake Pad Replacement* in this chapter.

3. Install by reversing these removal steps. Torque the rear axle pinch bolt to 4 ft.-lb. (6 N•m), and the axle bolt to 108 ft.-lb. (150 N•m).

4. Bleed the brake as described under *Bleeding the System* at the end of this chapter.

> **WARNING**
> *Do not ride the motorcycle until you are sure the brakes are operating properly.*

Caliper Rebuilding

If the caliper leaks, it should be rebuilt. If the piston sticks in the cylinder, indicating severe wear or galling, the entire unit should be replaced. Rebuilding a leaky caliper requires special tools and experience.

Caliper service should be entrusted to your Yamaha dealer or brake specialist. Considerable money can be saved by removing the caliper yourself and taking it in for repair.

The factory recommends that the internal caliper seals be replaced every two years.

REAR BRAKE HOSE REPLACEMENT

The factory recommends that the brake hose be replaced every four years or when it shows signs of cracking or damage.

Refer to **Figure 5** for this procedure.

> **CAUTION**
> *Cover the surrounding frame area with a heavy cloth or plastic tarp to protect it from the accidental spilling of brake fluid. Wash any brake fluid off of any painted or plated surface immediately, as it will destroy the finish. Use soapy water and rinse completely.*

1. Remove the union bolt (A, **Figure 36**) securing the brake hose to the master cylinder. Drain the brake fluid from the hose and discard it — *never* reuse brake fluid.

2. Remove the union bolt (A, **Figure 37**) securing the brake hose to the caliper. Remove the hose brackets (B, **Figure 36** and B, **Figure 37**) and remove the hose assembly.

3. Install the new hose, washers, and union bolts in the reverse order of removal. Be sure to install all washers in the correct positions; refer to **Figure 5**.

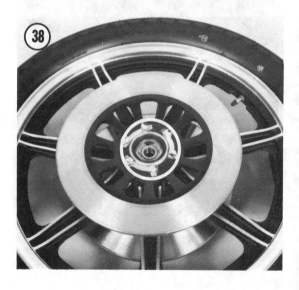

4. Make sure the brake hose is positioned correctly in the holding brackets (B, **Figure 36** and B, **Figure 37**) so it will not come in contact with any moving parts (shock absorber, wheel, etc.). Tighten all union bolts to 18 ft.-lb. (24 N•m).

5. Refill the master cylinder with brake fluid clearly marked DOT-3. Bleed the brake as described under *Bleeding the System* at the end of this chapter.

BRAKE DISC (FRONT AND REAR)

Removal/Installation

This procedure applies to both front and rear discs.

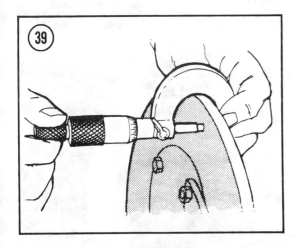

1. Remove the wheel as described under *Front* or *Rear Wheel Removal/Installation* in Chapters Eight or Nine respectively.

> NOTE: *Insert a piece of wood in the caliper(s) in place of the disc. This way, if the brake lever is inadvertently squeezed or depressed the piston will not be forced out of the cylinder. If this does happen, the caliper might have to be disassembled to reseat the piston, and the system will have to be bled. By using the wood, bleeding the brake is not necessary when installing the wheel.*

2. Straighten the locking tabs and remove the 6 bolts (**Figure 38**) securing the disc to the wheel.

3. Install by reversing these steps. Torque the bolts to 15 ft.-lb. (20 N•m). Always install new locking tabs and make sure to bend up one tab against a flat side of each bolt.

Inspection

It is not necessary to remove the disc from the wheel to inspect it. Small marks on the disc are not important, but deep radial scratches, deep enough to snag a fingernail, reduce braking effectiveness and increase pad wear. The disc should be replaced.

1. Measure the thickness at several points around the disc with vernier caliper or micrometer (**Figure 39**). The disc must be replaced if the thickness, at any point, is less than 0.26 in. (6.5mm).

2. Check the disc runout with a dial indicator. Raise the wheel being checked and set the arm of a dial indicator against the surface of the disc (**Figure 40**) and slowly rotate the wheel while watching the indicator. If the runout is greater than 0.006 in. (0.15mm), the disc must be replaced.

3. Clean the disc of any rust or corrosion with a non-petroleum solvent such as trichloroethylene.

BLEEDING THE SYSTEM

This procedure is not necessary unless the brakes feel spongy, there has been a leak in the

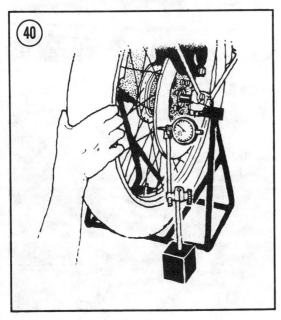

10

system, a component has been replaced, or the brake fluid has been replaced.

This procedure pertains to both the front and rear brake systems. When bleeding the front system, do one caliper at a time.

1. Remove the dust cap from the brake bleed valve.

2. Connect a length of ³⁄₁₆ in. (4.5mm) clear plastic tubing tightly to the bleed valve on the caliper. See **Figure 41** for the front and **Figure 42** for the rear. Place the other end of the tube into a clean container. Fill the container with enough fresh brake fluid to keep the end submerged. The tube should be long enough so that a loop can be made higher than the bleed valve to prevent air from being drawn into the caliper during bleeding.

> CAUTION
> *Cover the fuel tank and instrument cluster or the rear frame area with a heavy cloth or plastic tarp to protect it from the accidental spilling of brake fluid. Wash any brake fluid off of any painted or plated surface immediately, as it will destroy the finish. Use soapy water and rinse completely.*

3. Clean the top of the master cylinder of all dirt and foreign matter. Remove the screws (**Figure 43** and **Figure 44**) securing the cap and remove the cap, diaphragm, and gasket. Fill the reservoir almost to the top lip, insert the diaphragm and gasket, and reinstall the cap loosely. Leave the cap in place during this procedure to prevent the entry of dirt.

> WARNING
> *Use brake fluid clearly marked DOT-3 only. Others may vaporize and cause brake failure. Always use the same brand name; do not intermix as many brands are not compatible.*

4. Slowly apply the brake lever or pedal several times. Pull the lever in or push the pedal down. Hold the lever or pedal in the ON position. Open the bleed valve about one-half turn. Allow the lever or pedal to travel to its limit. When this limit is reached, tighten the bleed screw. As the fluid enters the system, the level will drop in the reservoir. Maintain the level at about ³⁄₈ inch from the top of the reservoir to prevent air from being drawn into the system.

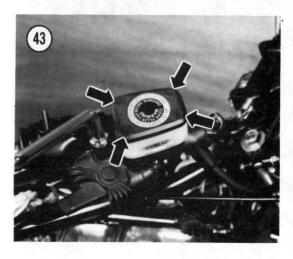

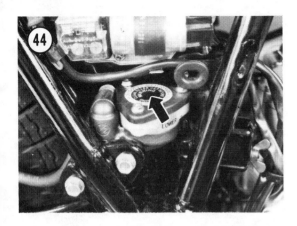

5. Continue to pump the lever or pedal and fill the reservoir until the fluid emerging from the hose is completely free of bubbles.

> NOTE: *Do not allow the reservoir to empty during the bleeding operation or more air will enter the system. If this occurs, the entire procedure must be repeated.*

6. Hold the lever or pedal down, tighten the bleed valve, remove the bleed tube, and install the bleed valve dust cap.

7. If necessary, add fluid to correct the level in the reservoir. It should be to the *upper* level line.

8. Install the reservoir cap tightly.

9. Test the feel of the brake lever and pedal. It should be firm and should offer the same resistance each time that it's operated. If it feels spongy, it is likely that there is still air in the system and it must be bled again. When all air has been bled from the system and the fluid level is correct in the reservoir, double check for leaks and tighten all the fittings and connections.

WARNING

Before riding the motorcycle, make certain that the brakes are operating correctly by operating the lever and pedal several times.

10

NOTE: If you own a 1980 or 1981 model, first check the Supplement at the back of the book for any new service information.

CHAPTER ELEVEN

FRAME AND REPAINTING

This chapter describes procedures for completely stripping the frame. In addition, recommendations are provided for repainting the stripped frame.

This chapter also includes procedures for the kickstand, centerstand, and footpegs.

KICKSTAND (SIDE STAND)

Removal/Installation

1. Place the bike on the centerstand.

2. Raise the kickstand and disconnect the return spring (**Figure 1**) from the frame with Vise Grips.

3. Unbolt the kickstand from the frame (**Figure 2**).

4. Install by reversing these removal steps. Apply a light coat of multipurpose grease to the pivot surfaces of the frame tab and the kickstand yoke prior to installation.

CENTERSTAND

Removal/Installation

1. Block up the engine or support the bike on the kickstand.

2. Place the centerstand in the raised position and disconnect the return spring (**Figure 3**) from the frame pin with Vise Grips.

3. Loosen the self-locking nuts on the frame brackets (**Figure 4**). Remove the bolts and the centerstand.

4. Install by reversing these removal steps. Apply a light coat of multipurpose grease to all pivoting points prior to installation.

FOOTPEGS

Replacement

The front footpegs are held in place with the rear engine mounting bolt.

1. Place the bike on the centerstand.

2. Place a suitable size jack with a piece of wood on it (to protect the crankcase) under the engine. Apply a *small amount* of jack pressure up on the engine.

3. Remove the self-locking nut (**Figure 5**) and withdraw the bolt from the right-hand side.

4. Remove and replace the footpeg(s).

5. Reinstall the rear engine mounting bolt and tighten to 72 ft.-lb. (100 N•m); remove the jack.

To replace the rear footpegs, remove the nuts securing the footpegs (**Figure 6**) to the frame. Tighten the nuts to 48 ft.-lb. (67 N•m).

FRAME

The frame does not require periodic maintenance. However, all welds should be examined immediately after any accident, even a slight one.

Component Removal/Installation

1. Disconnect the negative battery cable. Remove the fuel tank, seat, and battery.

2. Remove the engine as described in Chapter Four.

3. Remove the front wheel, steering, and suspension components as described in Chapter Eight.

4. Remove the rear wheel and suspension components. See Chapter Nine.

11

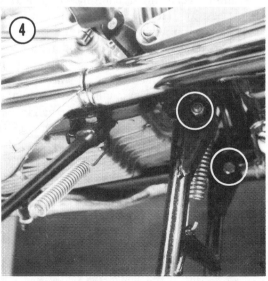

5. Remove the lighting and other electrical equipment. Remove the wiring harness. See Chapter Seven.

6. Remove the kickstand and centerstand as described in this chapter.

7. Remove the bearing races from the steering head tube as described in Chapter Eight.

8. Check the frame for bends, cracks, or other damage, especially around welded joints and areas which are rusted.

9. Assemble by reversing the removal steps.

Stripping and Painting

Remove all components from the frame. Thoroughly strip off all old paint. The best way is to have it sandblasted down to bare metal. If this is not possible, you can use a liquid paint remover like Strypeeze, or equivalent, and steel wool and a fine, hard wire brush.

> CAUTION
> *The side panels, part of the rear fender, and the instrument housing, are plastic (**Figure 7**). If you wish to change the color of these parts, consult an automotive paint supplier for the proper procedure.*
>
> *Do not use any liquid paint remover on these components as it will damage the surface. The color is an integral part of component and cannot be removed.*

When the frame is down to bare metal, have it inspected for hair line and internal cracks. Magnafluxing is the most common process.

Make sure that the primer is compatible with the type of paint you are going to use for the final coat. Spray one or two coats of primer as smoothly as possible. Let it dry thoroughly and use a fine grade of wet sandpaper (400-600 grit) to remove any flaws. Carefully wipe the surface clean and then spray the final coat. Use either lacquer or enamel and follow the manufacturer's instructions.

A shop specializing in painting will probably do the best job. However, you can do a surprisingly good job with a good grade of spray paint. Spend a few extra bucks and get a good grade of paint as it will make a difference in how well it hooks and how long it will stand up. One trick in using spray paints is to first shake the can thoroughly — make sure the ball inside the can is loose; if not, return it and get a good one. Shake the can as long as is stated on the can. Then immerse the can *upright* in a pot or bucket of *warm water (not hot — not over 120°F).*

> WARNING
> *Higher temperatures could cause the can to burst. **Do not** place the can in direct contact with any flame or heat source.*

Leave the can in for several minutes. When thoroughly warmed, shake the can again and spray the frame. Several light mist coats are better than one heavy coat. Spray painting is best done in temperatures of 70°-80°F; any temperature above or below this will give you problems.

After the final coat has dried completely, at least 48 hours, any overspray or orange peel may be removed with *a light application* of rubbing compound and finished with polishing compound. Be careful not to rub too hard and go through the finish.

Finish off with a couple of good coats of wax prior to reassembling all the components.

11

SUPPLEMENT

1980–1981 SERVICE INFORMATION

The following supplement provides procedures unique to models manufactured since 1980. All other service procedures are identical to earlier models.

The chapter headings in this supplement correspond to those in the main body of this book. If a change is not included in the supplement, there are no changes affecting models since 1980.

Since 1981 the Special has been called the Venturer 1100. It is a full-dressed touring bike complete with fairing, saddlebags and luggage rack. These items will have to be removed to gain access to some components. Removal and installation of these items is covered in Chapter Eleven of this supplement.

CHAPTER ONE

GENERAL INFORMATION

Refer to **Table 1** for General Specifications.

Table 1   GENERAL SPECIFICATIONS

Engine type	Air cooled, 4-stroke, DOHC, 4-cylinder
Bore and stroke	2.815 x 2.701 in. (71.5 x 68.6 mm)
Displacement	67.25 cu. in. (1,102 cc)
Compression ratio	9.0 to 1
Carburetion	4 Mikuni, constant velocity, 30 mm
Model G	BS34-111 3HS-00
Model SG, SH, LG, LH	BS34-111 3J6-00
Model H	BS34-111 3H5-01
Ignition	Battery, fully transistorized
Lubrication	Wet sump, filter, oil pump
Clutch	Wet, multi-plate
Transmission	5-speed, constant mesh
Transmission ratios	
1st	2.235
2nd	1.625
3rd	1.285
4th	1.032
5th	0.882
Starting	Electric only
Wheelbase	60.8 in. (1.545 mm)
Steering head angle	29.5 degrees
Trail	5.12 in. (130 mm)
Ground clearance	
Model G, H	5.9 in. (150 mm)
Model SG, SH, LG, LH	6.1 in. (155 mm)
Seat height	
Model G, H	31.5 in. (800 mm)
Model SG, SH, LG, LH	31.1 in. (790 mm)
Model G, H	46.3 in. (1.175 mm)
Model SG, SH, LG, LH	48.4 in. (1,230 mm)
Overall width	
Model G, H	36.2 in. (920 mm)
Model SG, SH, LG, LH	33.7 in. (855 mm)
Overall length	
Model G	89.0 in. (2,260 mm)
Model SG, SH, LG, LH	89.6 in. (2,275 mm)
Model H	95.7 in. (2,430 mm)
Front suspension	Telescopic fork, 6.9 in. (175 mm) travel
Rear suspension	Swing arm, adjustable shock absorbers, 4.3 in. (108 mm) travel
Front tire	
Models G, H, SG, SH, LG, LH	3.50 H-19 4PR (tubeless)
Rear tire	
Model G, H	4.50 H-17 4PR (tubeless)
Model SG, SH, LG, LH	130/90H-16 67H (tubeless)
Fuel capacity	
Model G	5.3 U.S. gal. (20 liter; 4.4 Imp. gal.)
Model SG, SH, LG, LH	4.0 U.S. gal. (15 liter; 3.1 Imp. gal.)
Model H	6.3 U.S. gal. (24 liter; 5.3 Imp. gal.)
Oil capacity	
Oil change	3.2 U.S. qt. (3.0 liter; 2.7 Imp. qt.)
Oil and filter change	3.7 U.S. qt. (3.5 liter; 3.1 Imp. qt.)
Weight (net)	
Model G	562 lb. (262 kg)
Model SG, SH, LG, LH	556 lb. (252 kg)
Model H	633 lb. (278 kg)

12

CHAPTER THREE

PERIODIC MAINTENANCE AND TUNE-UP

TIRES

Pressure

Tire pressure must be checked with tires cold. Correct tire pressure depends on the load you are carrying. See **Table 2**.

PERIODIC LUBRICATION

Changing Oil and Filter

Since 1981, the model XS11OOH has been equipped with an oil cooler. Factory information indicates that the oil capacity is the same with or without the cooler. After changing the oil and adding the specified oil, be sure to check the oil level through the oil level window. Adjust the level if necessary.

It is not necessary to remove the oil cooler to change the oil. If you do remove the oil lines from the oil cooler, tighten the fittings to 32.5 ft.-lb. (45 N•m) upon installation.

FRONT FORK OIL CHANGE

Refer to **Table 3** for specific capacity of each fork leg.

TUNE-UP

Valve Clearance

Intake valve clearance has been decreased from the 1979 specification of 0.16-0.20 mm to 0.11-0.15 mm. This cuts down on engine noise, but is recommended only on 1980 and later models.

Valve clearance measurement and adjustment are exactly the same as on previous models. Refer to *Valve Clearance Measurement* and *Valve Clearance Adjustment* in Chapter Three in the main body of this book.

Ignition Timing (1980 Models Only)

It is no longer necessary to check the ignition timing unless the ignition advance

Table 2   TIRE PRESSURES

Load	Pressure
Models G, SG, LG, H, LH	
Up to 198 lb. (90 kg)	
Front	26 psi (1.8 kg/cm^2)
Rear	28 psi (2.0 kg/cm^2)
198-337 lb. (90-153 kg)	
Front	28 psi (2.0 kg/cm^2)
Rear	36 psi (2.5 kg/cm^2)
Maximum load limit*	
Front — 420 lb. (190 kg)	36 psi (2.5 kg/cm^2)
Rear — 670 lb. (304 kg)	40 psi (2.8 kg/cm^2)
Model SH (all load conditions)	
Front	40 psi (2.8 kg/cm^2)
Rear	40 psi (2.8 kg/cm^2)
*Maximum load includes the total weight of motorcycle with accessories, rider(s) and luggage.	

Table 3   FRONT FORK OIL CAPACITY

Model	Type	Quantity—Each Fork
Models G, H	SAE 10W fork oil	8.15 oz. (241 cc)
Models SH, LH	SAE 10W fork oil	7.1 oz. (210 cc)

mechanism has been removed and replaced or the engine has been disassembled.

The ignition advance mechanism is held in place with special attachment bolts and washers and cannot be loosened and adjusted as on previous models.

If you think that the ignition timing is incorrect perform Steps 1-5 of *Ignition Timing* in Chapter Three in the main body of this book. If timing is incorrect, the ignition advance mechanism must be removed as described under *Ignition Advance Mechanism Removal/Installation* in Chapter Four of this supplement and inspected as described under *Ignition Advance Mechanism* in Chapter Seven in the main body of this book.

Ignition Timing
(1981 Models)

The ignition advance mechanism can be installed in one position only; there are no provisions for adjustment. The only reason to check ignition timing is if you think that the advance mechanism is not operating correctly or another component in the ignition system is operating incorrectly.

Check the timing with this procedure. If timing is incorrect, the ignition advance mechanism must be removed as described under *Ignition Advance Mechanism Removal/Installation* in Chapter Four and inspected as described under *Ignition Advance Mechanism* in Chapter Seven in the main body of this book. If the ignition advance mechanism is operating correctly, check other ignition components as described in Chapter Seven in the main body of this book.

1. Place the bike on the centerstand.

2. Connect a portable tachometer following the manufacturer's instructions. The bike's tachometer is not accurate enough in the low rpm range for this adjustment.

3. Connect a timing light to the No. 1 cylinder (left-hand side) following the manufacturer's instructions (**Figure 1**).

4. Start the engine and let it warm up to normal operating temperature. Let the engine idle (1,100 +/- 100 rpm) and aim the timing light toward the timing marks on the timing plate.

5. The stationary pointer should align within the inverted "U" mark on the timing plate (**Figure 2**).

6. Ignition timing is not adjustable. If the timing marks do not align or if they waver, check to make sure the timing plate is attached securely. If it is secure, check the ignition components as described in Chaper Seven in the main body of the book.

12

CHAPTER FOUR

ENGINE

ENGINE

Removal/Installation

The model XS1100H is factory-equipped with a fairing. Remove it prior to removing the engine; see *Fairing Removal/Installation* in Chapter Eleven of this supplement.

The model XS1100H since 1981 is also equipped with an oil cooler. Unscrew the fittings on the oil lines at the oil cooler. Remove the oil lines and oil filter cover assembly. When installing the hoses tighten the fittings to 32.5 ft.-lb. (45 N•m).

IGNITION ADVANCE MECHANISM (1980 ONLY)

Removal

NOTE

The ignition advance mechanism is attached to the crankcase with special bolts and washers only on 1980 models. Removal is only necessary if the engine is to be disassembled or the mechanism is to be removed or replaced. The procedures in the main body of the book apply to 1981 models.

1. Disconnect the negative battery lead from the battery.

2. Remove the bolts securing the ignition cover (**Figure 3**) and remove it.

3. Remove the Allen bolt (A, **Figure 4**) securing the timing plate and remove it.

4. Rotate the engine until the projection on the centrifugal advance mechanism aligns with the slot on the pickup coil plate. This is necessary for removal of the backing plate.

NOTE
When the mechanism was installed at the factory, special bolts were used. They have a head that shears off when the correct torque is achieved, thus leaving no bolt head for removal.

5. Flatten the remaining portion of the bolt (B, **Figure 4**) with a drift or flat punch.

6. Use a center punch and hammer (A, **Figure 5**) and make a deep enough impression in each bolt for a drill guide.

CAUTION
Make sure the punch mark is centered, otherwise the drilled hole will be offset and will damage the threads in the crankcase.

7. Drill a hole approximately 0.39 in. (10 mm) deep, using a 3 mm drill bit, in each bolt (B, **Figure 5**).

8. Tap a screw extractor into the hole with a hammer (C, **Figure 5**) and unscrew the bolt (D, **Figure 5**). Repeat for the other bolt.

9. Remove the advance mechanism assembly and carefully let it hang down.

10. Disconnect the electrical connector (**Figure 6**) to the ignition advance mechanism located under the right-hand side cover.

11. Remove the electrical cable clips (A, **Figure 7**) from the left-hand crankcase cover and remove the cable.

12. Disconnect the electrical wire to the neutral safety switch (B, **Figure 7**). Remove the advance mechanism assembly and electrical harness.

NOTE
Make a drawing of the routing of the electrical cable so it will be installed in the same position.

13. Remove the centrifugal advance mechanism (**Figure 8**).

14. Inspect the condition of all components as described under *Ignition Advance Mechanism* in Chapter Seven in the main body of this book.

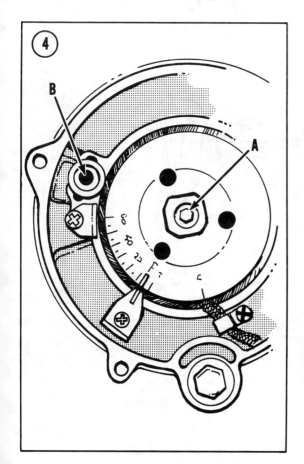

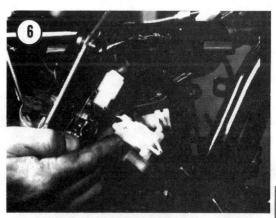

12

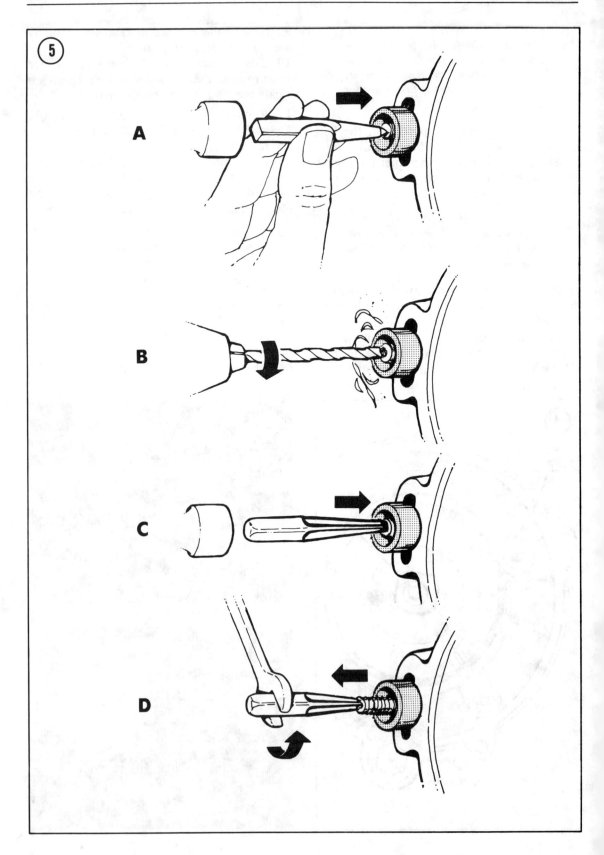

Installation

1. Install the centrifugal advance mechanism. Be sure to align the pin (A, **Figure 9**) on the crankshaft with the notch (B, **Figure 9**) on the centrifugal advance mechanism.

NOTE
*Rotate the engine so the projection on the centrifugal advance mechanism (**Figure 10**) is positioned at the 10 o'clock position so the pickup plate can be installed.*

2. Install the ignition advance mechanism and install the special washers and new special bolts. Tighten the bolts only lightly at this time, just tight enough to hold the mechanism in place but not tight enough to shear off their heads.

NOTE
A special tool is required for tightening these special bolts. It is a Torx bolt driver (Yamaha part No. 90890-01308-00).

3. Install the timing plate and tighten the Allen bolt to 14.5 ft.-lb. (20 N•m).
4. Check and adjust the ignition timing; refer to *Ignition Timing* in Chapter Three in the main body of this book. In Step 6 the 2 Phillips head screws have been replaced with these special Torx bolts.
5. Make sure the ignition timing is correct prior to tightening the special bolts—if it isn't, the bolts will have to be removed as previously described. *They cannot be loosened and retightened after the heads are sheared off.*
6. After ignition timing is correct, tighten the special bolts until the heads shear off.
7. Continue to install by reversing removal Steps 1, 2, 10, 11 and 12.
8. Be sure to route the electrical wires in the same location, especially in the clips shown in **Figure 7**.

KICKSTARTER

The kickstarter assembly has been eliminated on all models since 1980. Disregard any mention of it in the main body of this book when working on your bike.

12

CHAPTER SIX

FUEL AND EXHAUST SYSTEMS

CARBURETORS

Refer to **Table 4** for complete carburetor specifications.

You will notice that the main jets vary in size from the inner pair to the outer pair of carburetors. The inner carburetors (Nos. 2 and 3) have larger jets.

Float Adjustment (1980)

The float adjustment procedure is the same as on previous models but the correct height is changed to 0.906 +/- 0.020 in. (23.0 +/- 0.5 mm); refer to **Figure 11**. Refer to *Carburetor Float Adjustment* in Chapter Six in the main body in this book.

Fuel Level Measurement (1981)

The bike must be *exactly level* for this measurement to be accurate. Place pieces of wood or shims under either side of the centerstand or place a suitable size jack under the engine and position the bike so that the carburetor assembly is level from side to side.

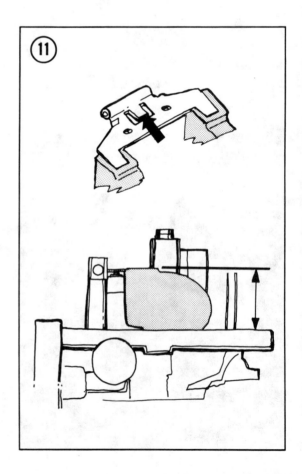

Table 4   CARBURETOR SPECIFICATIONS

	XS1100G	XS1100SG, LG
Manufacturer	Mikuni	Mikuni
Model No.	BS34-111 3H5-00	BS34-111 3J6-00
Main jet No.		
Cylinders No. 1 and 4	115	110
Cylinders No. 2 and 3	120	120
Needle jet No.	X-2	X-2
Starter jet No.	25	25
Pilot jet No.	42.5	42.5
Air jet—main	140	140
Air jet—pilot	185	185
Jet needle	51 Z7	5 GL 16
Float needle height*	0.906 ± 0.20 in. (23.0 ± 0.5 mm)	0.906 ± 0.20 in. (23.0 ± 0.5 mm)
Idle mixture screw**	Pre-set	Pre-set
Fuel valve seat	0.079 in. (2.0 mm)	0.079 in. (2.0 mm)
Throttle valve No.	135	135
Engine idle speed	1,100 rpm	1,100 rpm

  *Above gasket surface.
**Pre-set at factory — do not reset

	XS1100H	XS1100SH, LH
Manufacturer	Mikuni	Mikuni
Model No.	BS34-111 3H5-01	BS34-111 3J6-00
Main jet No.		
Cylinders No. 1 and 4	115	110
Cylinders No. 2 and 3	120	120
Needle jet No.	X-2	X-2
Starter jet No.	25	25
Pilot jet No.	42.5	42.5
Air jet—main	140	140
Air jet—pilot	185	185
Jet needle	51 Z7	5 GL 16
Float level*	0.12 ± 0.04 in. (3 ± 1 mm)	0.12 ± 0.04 in. 3 ± 1 mm)
Idle mixture screw**	Pre-set	Pre-set
Fuel valve seat	0.079 in. (2.0 mm)	0.079 in. (2.0 mm)
Throttle valve No.	135	135
Engine idle speed	1,100 rpm	1,100 rpm

  *Below top surface of the float bowl
**Pre-set at factory — do not reset

12

Use either the Yamaha special level gauge or a piece of clear vinyl tubing with an inside diameter of 0.24 in. (6 mm). The length of the tubing should be long enough to reach from one side of the carburetor assembly to the other, approximately 24 in. (600 mm) long.

NOTE

WARNING

Before starting any procedure involving gasoline have a class B fire extinguisher rated for gasoline or chemical fires within reach. Do not smoke, allow anyone to smoke or work where there are any open flames. The work area must be well-ventilated.

1. Turn both fuel shutoff valves to the ON or RESERVE position.
2. Start with the No. 1 carburetor (left-hand side). Place a small container under the carburetor to catch any fuel that may drip from the float bowl.
3. Connect the tube to the float bowl nozzle.
4. Hold the loose end of the tube up above the float bowl level and loosen the drain screw. Fuel will flow into the tube. Be sure to hold the loose end up or the fuel will flow out of the tube.
5. Start the engine and let it run for 2-3 minutes. This is necessary to make sure the fuel level is at normal operating level in the float bowl.
6. Hold the loose end of the tube up against the No. 1 carburetor body (**Figure 12**). Check the fuel level in the tube and mark it with a grease pencil or a piece of masking tape.
7. Insert a golf tee into the open end of the tube so fuel will not drain out when moving the tube from side to side.
8. Move the tube to the other side of the bike and remove the golf tee. Repeat Step 6, holding the tube up against the No. 4 (right-hand) carburetor body. The dimension should be the same; if not the bike and carburetor assembly are not level.

NOTE
Always insert the golf tee in the tube whenever moving the tube with gasoline in it.

9. Readjust the shims under the centerstand or adjust the jack until exactly level—*this is*

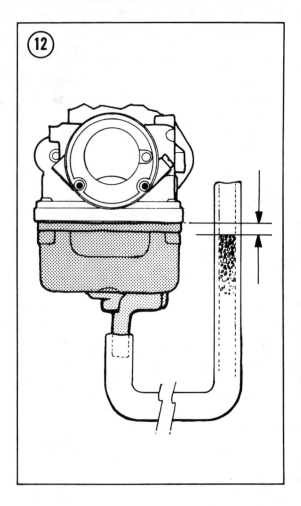

necessary to obtain correct measurements. Repeat Steps 6-8 until the bike is level.

10. After the carburetor assembly is level hold the loose end of the tube up against the No. 1 carburetor body. Check the fuel level in the tube. It should be 0.12 +/- 0.04 in. (3 +/- 1 mm) below the top surface of the float bowl (**Figure 12**).
11. Tighten the drain screw and hold both ends of the tube at the same height so fuel will not drain out. Remove the tube from the carburetor float bowl nozzle. Immediately wipe up any spilled fuel on the engine.

WARNING
Do not let any fuel spill on the exhaust system as it is warm.

12. Repeat Steps 2-6, 10 and 11 for the No. 2, 3 and 4 carburetors. Record the measurements of all 4 carburetors.

13. If the fuel level is incorrect on any of the carburetors, remove the carburetor assembly and adjust the float as described under *Float Adjustment* in Chapter Six in the main body of the book. Do not use the float level specification listed in Step 5; it is for pre-1980 models.

14. Adjust the float tang on affected carburetor(s). If the fuel level on one or more of the carburetors is correct, use that as a guide for correct float height.

15. Bend the float tang upward very slightly to lower the fuel level; bend the float tang downward to raise the fuel level.

16. Install the carburetor assembly and repeat this procedure until all fuel levels are correct.

CAUTION
The floats on all 4 carburetors must be adjusted to exactly the same position to maintain the same fuel/air mixture to all 4 cylinders.

CHAPTER SEVEN

ELECTRICAL SYSTEM

LIGHTING SYSTEM

Refer to **Table 5** for replacement bulbs.

License Plate Light (Special Models)

Remove the 2 nuts and lockwashers securing the chrome cover and lens and remove it. Wash out the inside of the lens with a mild detergent. Replace the bulb(s) and install the lens and cover.

EMERGENCY FLASHER SYSTEM

The emergency flasher system operates all 4 directional signals simultaneously when the switch is turned on. The switch is located on the lower left-hand side of the handlebar switch assembly and the flasher is located under the seat, on the left-hand side, above the leading edge of the rear fender.

The flasher system will work with the ignition switch in any position (ON, OFF or P).

12

Table 5   REPLACEMENT BULBS

Item	Wattage	Candlepower
Headlight		
Model H, G	55/65 (quartz)	—
Model SG, SH, LG, LH	55/60 (quartz)	—
Tail/brakelight (2)	8/27	3/32
Directional lights (4)	27	32
License plate light (2)*	3.8	—
Indicator lights (7)	3.4	1
Meter light	3.4	1
Parking light	8	4
*Special models only (SG, SH, LG, LH)		

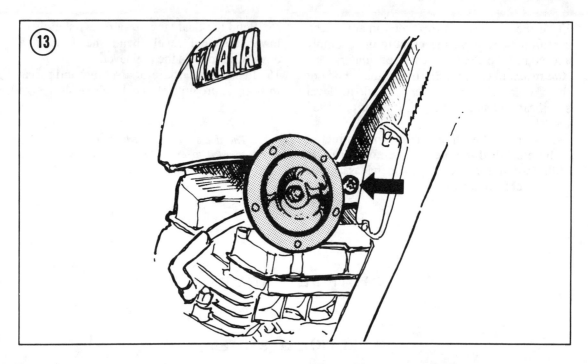

Flasher Replacement

1. Remove the seat and disconnect the battery negative lead from the battery.
2. Disconnect the electrical wires to the flasher and pull it out of the rubber mounting on the frame.
3. Transfer wires to the new relay and install the relay in the rubber mount.
4. Connect the battery negative lead and install the seat.

HORN

Removal/Installation

1. Disconnect the horn connector from the electrical harness.
2. Remove the bolt securing the horn to the frame bracket (**Figure 13**).
3. Repeat for the other horn if necessary.

FUSES

There are 5 fuses used on the XS1100 since 1980. Four are located in the fuse panel located under the right-hand side panel (**Figure 14**).

In the 4-fuse panel, the taillight fuse (10A) is located on the left-hand side of the panel; continuing from left to right are the headlight (10A), turn signal (20A) and ignition (10A).

The main fuse (30A) is located in a holder under the left-hand side panel.

There are 2 spare fuses located within the fuse panel and one spare within the main fuse holder; always carry spares.

Whenever a fuse blows, find out the reason for the failure before replacing the fuse. Usually, the trouble is a short circuit in the wiring. This may be caused by worn-through insulation or a disconnected wire shorting to ground.

CAUTION
Never substitute aluminum foil or wire for a fuse. Never use a higher amperage fuse than specified. An overload could result in fire and complete loss of the bike.

CHAPTER EIGHT

FRONT SUSPENSION AND STEERING

FRONT WHEEL
(EXCEPT SPECIAL MODEL)

Removal

1. Place a wooden block under the crankcase to lift the front of the bike off the ground.
2. Unscrew the speedometer cable (A, **Figure 15**) and pull it out.
3. Remove the axle nut cotter pin and nut (**Figure 16**). Discard the cotter pin.

> *NOTE*
> *Never reuse a cotter pin.*

4. Remove the 2 nuts (B, **Figure 15**) securing the front axle holder and remove it.
5. Remove the 4 bolts securing the front fender and remove it.
6. Push the axle out with a drift or screwdriver and remove it.

7. Slowly lower the wheel and remove it. Rotate the front forks slightly so the brake calipers will pivot outward leaving room for the wheel to pass by. Be careful not to damage either the wheel rim or the caliper assembly.

> *CAUTION*
> *Do not set the wheel down on the disc surface as it may get scratched or warped. Place it on a couple of wood blocks (**Figure 17**).*

> *NOTE*
> *Insert a piece of wood in both calipers in place of the disc. That way, if the brake lever is inadvertently squeezed, the piston will not be forced out of the cylinder. If this does happen, the caliper might have to be disassembled to reseat the piston and the system will have to be bled. By using the wood, bleeding the brake is not necessary when installing the wheel.*

12

Inspection

Measure the lateral and vertical runout of the wheel rim with a dial indicator as shown in **Figure 18**. The maximum lateral runout is 0.04 in. (1 mm) and the maximum vertical runout is 0.08 in. (2 mm). If the runout exceeds these dimensions, check the wheel bearing condition and/or replace the wheel. The stock aluminum wheel cannot be serviced, but must be replaced.

Installation

1. When installing the wheel, carefully insert the discs into the caliper assemblies—do not damage the leading edge of the brake pads.
2. Make sure the locating slot in the speedometer gear case is aligned with the boss on the fork tube (**Figure 19**).
3. Insert the axle and install it. Then install the axle nut; do not tighten it at this time.
4. Install the axle holder, washers and self-locking nuts; do not tighten the nuts at this time. Tighten the axle nut to 76 ft.-lb. (105 N•m). Install a new cotter pin. Move the forks up and down several times. Move the left-hand fork leg back and forth sideways until the left-hand disc is centered within the caliper assembly (**Figure 20**). Tighten the front axle holder nut first and then the rear nut to 14.5 ft.-lb. (20 N•m).

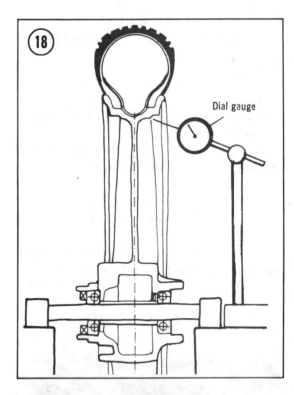

Dial gauge

> *WARNING*
> *The clamp nuts must be tightened in this manner and to this torque value. After installation is complete, there will be a slight gap (**Figure 21**) at the rear, with no gap at the front. If done incorrectly, the studs could fail, resulting in loss of control of the bike when riding. Be sure to install the axle holder with the arrow facing forward.*

> *NOTE*
> *Never reuse a cotter pin on the axle nut; always install a new one and bend the ends over completely.*

5. Install the front fender and tighten the 4 bolts securely.
6. Insert the speedometer cable.

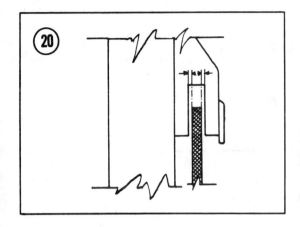

NOTE
Rotate the wheel slowly when inserting the cable so that it will engage properly.

7. After the wheel is installed, completely rotate it and apply the brake several times to make sure it rotates freely.

FRONT FORKS

The front forks on both models are now the air/oil type. Follow the same procedures as described under *Front Forks, Removal/Installation* and *Disassembly, Inspection, Assembly* in Chapter Eight in the main body of this book. Refer to **Table 6** for fork spring free length.

When assembling the fork, fill each fork tube with the correct amount of fresh fork oil. Refer to **Table 3**.

Table 6   FRONT FORK SPRING FREE LENGTH

Model	Free Length
Model G, H	20.31 in. (516 mm)
Model SG, SH, LG, LH	24.10 in. (612.2 mm)

CHAPTER NINE

REAR SUSPENSION AND FINAL DRIVE

REAR WHEEL

Removal/Installation

On model XS1100H (since 1981), in order to remove the rear wheel, the saddlebag assembly must be removed. Refer to *Saddlebag Removal/Installation* in Chapter Eleven of this supplement.

CHAPTER TEN

BRAKES

BRAKE DISC
(FRONT AND REAR)

Removal/Installation

The brake discs are slotted to aid in cooling, to remove water from the disc and to lower unsprung weight. The specifications are the same as on discs without slots.

When installing the disc onto the wheel the direction of the slots must be positioned in relation to the wheel as shown in **Figure 22**. They are marked R (right-hand side) or L (left-hand side) and must be installed on the correct side of the wheel (**Figure 23**). Torque values are the same as on previous models.

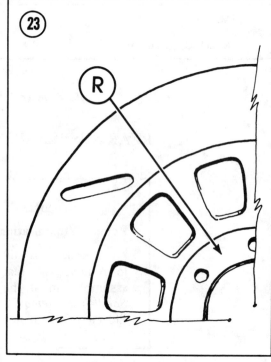

CHAPTER ELEVEN

FRAME AND REPAINTING

TOURING COMPONENTS

Since 1981 the Special has been called the Venturer 1100. It is a full-dressed touring bike complete with fairing, saddlebags and luggage rack. These items will have to be removed to gain access to some components.

Fairing Removal

1. Place the bike on the centerstand; remove the right- and left-hand side covers.
2. Remove the seat and disconnect the battery negative lead.
3. Remove the rear bolt (A, **Figure 24**) securing the rear of the fuel tank. Disconnect the fuel gauge electrical connector (B, **Figure 24**).
4. Turn both fuel shutoff valves to the ON or RES position, lift up on the rear of the tank and remove the fuel lines to the carburetors and vacuum lines to the intake manifolds (**Figure 25**).
5. Pull the tank to the rear and remove it.
6. Disconnect the electrical harness from the fairing.
7. Carefully remove the screws and washers securing both lower sections to the fairing.

NOTE
The next step requires the aid of a helper. The fairing is not that heavy but is bulky and could be damaged if you try to remove it by yourself.

8. Remove the fairing mounting bolts and remove the fairing.

12

Fairing Installation

1. Have a helper hold the fairing in position and install the fairing mounting bolts. Tighten the bolts securely.
2. Hold the lower section in place and start the special screw and washer into the inner hole, adjacent to the fork tube. Maintain an even inward pressure on the screw so that the well-nut in the fairing will not pull out. Start all screws evenly and when the screw starts to tighten, one or two full turns are required to make the rubber swell out on the inside of the fairing wall. DO NOT overtighten the screws as the well-nuts will pull out of the fairing. Install both lower sections.
3. Plug in the wiring harness; make sure the connection is tight.
4. Install the fuel tank and connect the fuel and vacuum lines.
5. Connect the battery negative cable and connect the fuel gauge connector.
6. Install the seat and side covers.

Windshield Replacement

1. Remove all fasteners, both clips and the old windshield.
2. Remove all traces of the old foam tape from the fairing where the windshield was attached. The surface must be clean to achieve a watertight seam for the new windshield.
3. On the new windshield, puncture the foam tape at each attachment bolt hole. Use one of the nylon attachment bolts for this purpose. Do not use a metal bolt as it may fracture the hole, cause a crack and damage the windshield.
4. Position the 2 clips on the windshield about 4 5/8 in. (118 mm) above the upper hole on each side of the windshield.
5. Place the windshield on the fairing and slightly bend the windshield inward so that the clip studs will align with the holes in the fairing.
6. Insert the studs of the 2 clips through the top fairing mounting holes. Install a black bushing and a 6 mm keeper nut on each stud.
7. From the outside (or front of the fairing) install a nylon bolt through the windshield and fairing. Slide a small nylon washer onto the bolt from the inside and install the nut.

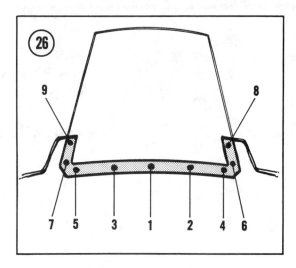

Tighten the nut only finger-tight. Repeat for all remaining bolts.
8. Tighten the bolts in the torque sequence shown in **Figure 26**.
9. Install a rubber protective tip over the exposed clip studs.

> *NOTE*
> *Always remove the windshield from the fairing when moving the bike on a trailer or open bed truck. Never use the fairing as a tie-down point when securing the bike to the trailer or truck.*

Windshield Cleaning

Be very careful cleaning the windshield as it can be easily scratched or damaged. Do not use a cleaner with an abrasive, a combination cleaner and wax or any solvent that contains ethyl or methyl alcohol. Never use gasoline or cleaning solvent. These products will either scratch or totally destroy the surface of the windshield.

To remove oil, grease or road tar use isopropyl alcohol, naptha or kerosene. Then wash the windshield with a solution of mild soap and water. Dry gently with a soft cloth or chamois—do not press hard.

> *NOTE*
> *When removing grungy road tar make sure there are no small stones or sand imbedded in it. Carefully remove any abrasive particles prior to performing any rubbing action with a cleaner. This will help minimize scratching.*

Many commercial windshield cleaners are available (such as Yamaha Windscreen Cleaner). If using a cleaner other than the one from Yamaha, make sure it is safe for use on plastic and test it on a small area first.

Saddlebag
Removal/Installation

1. Remove the seat and the rear footpegs.
2. Remove the upper shock absorber mounting nuts.
3. Remove the side plate mounting plate bolts.
4. Open up both saddlebag lids.
5. Slide the saddlebag assembly to the rear and off the bike. Both saddlebags and all mounting hardware will come off as an assembly.
6. If the saddlebag assembly is going to be left off for some length of time, reinstall the mounting nuts on the shock absorbers.
7. Install by reversing these removal steps. Tighten the shock absorber nuts to 23 ft.-lb. (32 N•m).

12

INDEX

13

WIRING DIAGRAMS

1978 XS1100E & 1979 XS1100F

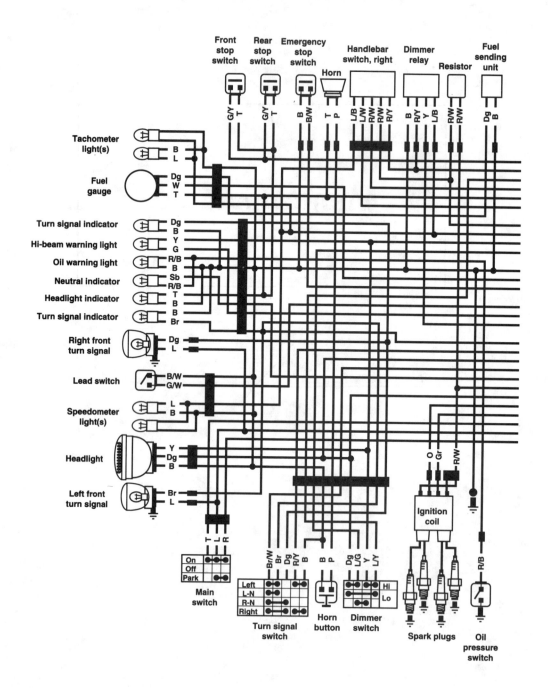

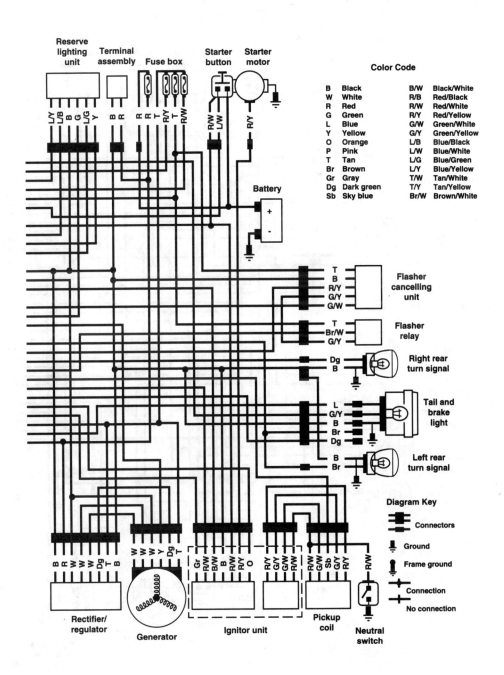

Reserve lighting unit — Terminal assembly — Fuse box — Starter button — Starter motor

Color Code

B	Black	B/W	Black/White
W	White	R/B	Red/Black
R	Red	R/W	Red/White
G	Green	R/Y	Red/Yellow
L	Blue	G/W	Green/White
Y	Yellow	G/Y	Green/Yellow
O	Orange	L/B	Blue/Black
P	Pink	L/W	Blue/White
T	Tan	L/G	Blue/Green
Br	Brown	L/Y	Blue/Yellow
Gr	Gray	T/W	Tan/White
Dg	Dark green	T/Y	Tan/Yellow
Sb	Sky blue	Br/W	Brown/White

Battery

Flasher cancelling unit

Flasher relay

Right rear turn signal

Tail and brake light

Left rear turn signal

Diagram Key

Connectors

Ground

Frame ground

Connection

No connection

Rectifier/regulator — Generator — Ignitor unit — Pickup coil — Neutral switch

14

1979 XS1100SF

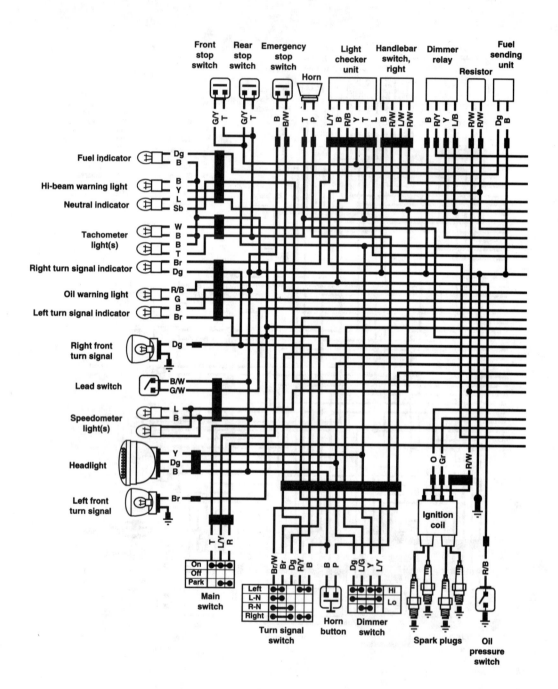